EVERYDAY SECTARIANISM IN URBAN LEBANON

PRINCETON STUDIES IN CULTURE AND TECHNOLOGY
Tom Boellstorff and Bill Maurer, series editors

PRINCETON STUDIES IN
CULTURE AND
TECHNOLOGY

This series presents innovative work that extends classic ethnographic methods and questions into areas of pressing interest in technology and economics. It explores the varied ways new technologies combine with older technologies and cultural understandings to shape novel forms of subjectivity, embodiment, knowledge, place, and community. By doing so, the series demonstrates the relevance of anthropological inquiry to emerging forms of digital culture in the broadest sense.

EVERYDAY SECTARIANISM IN URBAN LEBANON

Infrastructures, Public Services, and Power

Joanne Randa Nucho

PRINCETON UNIVERSITY PRESS

Princeton and Oxford

Library of Congress Cataloging-in-Publication Data

Names: Nucho, Joanne Randa, 1979– author.
Title: Everyday sectarianism in urban Lebanon : infrastructures, public services,
    and power / Joanne Nucho.
Description: Princeton : Princeton University Press, [2017] | Series: Princeton studies
    in culture and technology | Includes bibliographical references and index.
Identifiers: LCCN 2016005279 | ISBN 9780691168968 (hardcover : alk. paper) |
    ISBN 9780691168975 (pbk. : alk. paper)
Subjects: LCSH: Civil society—Lebanon. | Religion and civil society—Lebanon. | Municipal
    services—Political aspects—Lebanon. | Public welfare—Political aspects—Lebanon. | Public
    welfare—Religious aspects. | Infrastructure (Economics)—Lebanon. | Lebanon—Politics and
    government.
Classification: LCC JQ1828.A91 N83 2017 | DDC 306.2095692—dc23
    LC record available at https://lccn.loc.gov/2016005279

British Library Cataloging-in-Publication Data is available

This book has been composed in Janson Text LT Std

Printed on acid-free paper. ∞

Printed in the United States of America

10 9 8 7 6 5 4 3 2 1

In memory of my grandmother,
Yegsapeth Isabel Kouyoumjian

Contents

_____

Illustrations

Note on Language

Throughout this book, I have used simplified transliteration systems that would assist the reader unfamiliar with Western Armenian and the spoken Lebanese dialect of Arabic. I have eliminated most diacritical markings and have tried to use more common spellings of both the Western Armenian and Lebanese Arabic dialects. For both Western Armenian and Arabic, I have opted to transliterate all words to reflect the way they are commonly pronounced in Lebanon. To aid the reader unfamiliar with Western Armenian, I have added an *s* to indicate plurals (e.g., *shirket*s and *masnajough*s rather than *shirketner* or *masnajoughner*).

Acknowledgments

_____

This book would not have been possible without the encouragement and intellectual exchange of so many supportive interlocutors and scholars over the years. I am especially grateful to have had such wonderful mentors at the University of California, Irvine. Bill Maurer has provided ongoing support and guidance throughout the trajectory of this project and my development as a scholar. Through numerous meetings and discussions over the years, Lara Deeb has always been an important teacher and interlocutor, and I thank her for her encouragement at every phase of my research. Our conversations helped shape the outcome of this book in more ways than I can count. I am also deeply indebted to Julia Elyachar for providing intellectual and professional mentorship, and for her ongoing support and friendship. Tom Boellstorff, Susan Slyomovics, Rei Terada, the late Al Maysles, and the late George Stoney were also important teachers and mentors.

I was fortunate to have the opportunity to present my research at Columbia University in 2013. I am grateful to everyone in attendance, particularly Lila Abu-Lughod, Brian Larkin, Elizabeth Povinelli, and Rosalind Morris for their suggestions, comments, and questions. Their insights had a significant impact on the writing of this book as well as the ongoing development of my filmmaking practice.

I am grateful to my friends and family in Lebanon for making my time there so memorable. Conversations we had during days at the beach, car rides around the country, and lavish home-cooked meals, aside from being great fun, also affected the writing of this book in significant ways. My cousin Salpie Djounderian and her wonderful family were always generous and welcoming; I am forever grateful to them for giving me a "home away from home" in Lebanon. I am also grateful to Azadouhie Kaladjian and the late Bebo Simonian for sharing with me their memories and welcoming me as a member of the family. During my time in Lebanon, I was very fortunate to have had the great company and friendship of Jared McCormick, George Awde, Bonnie, Christopher, Joseph Coubat and the entire Coubat family, Dali and Maissam Nimer, Nizar Haraké, Kristine Khoury, Belal Hibri, Omer

Shah, Jowe Harfouche, Eyad Houssami, Wael Lazkani, Ramzi Mezher, Garine
Aivazian, Haig Papazian, Antoine Atallah, Tania El Alam, Mazen Khaled, and
Nizar Kinge. I am grateful to Mona Fawaz and Mona Harb at the American
University of Beirut who provided excellent guidance and feedback during
my fieldwork in Beirut. I thank the librarians at Haigazian University, the
American University of Beirut, and the Institut français du Proche-Orient
for welcoming me as a researcher. I especially thank Rosy Kuftedjian for
her friendship and for helping me see Bourj Hammoud through her eyes,
the lens of her camera, and her paintbrush.

I thank my colleagues at UC Irvine who created a supportive environment for the mutual exchange of ideas and of course friendship. I especially
thank Alexandra Lippman, Adonia Lugo, Cristina Bejarano, Elsa Fan, Seo
Young Park, Nalika Gajaweera, Khaldun Bshara, Ameeth Vijay, Marisa
Menna, Kyriaki Papageorgiou, Sheena Nahm, and Michelle Cho. Alexandra Seggerman and Claire Panetta were wonderful classmates at the CASA
program in Cairo in 2008, and conversations with them continue to shape
and influence my research.

At New York University, I have been incredibly lucky to find a sup-
portive community of scholars in the writing of this book. Through many
conversations and discussions, I have learned much from my new colleagues
Helga Tawil-Souri, Begum Adalet, Arang Keshavarzian, Zachary Lockman,
Asli Igsiz, Linda Sayed, Faye Ginsburg, Tejaswini Ganti, Bruce Grant, Ali
Mirsepassi, Nader Uthman, Michael Gilsenan and Zvi Ben-Dor Benite.
Anny Bakalian, Paul Kockelman, Benoit Challand, Tsolin Nalbantian,
Aseel Sawalha, Madeline Reeves, Munira Khayat, and Christa Salamandra
provided important comments at various points of writing and presenting
the research leading up to this book project. I thank Suad Joseph at the
University of California, Davis, for her valuable insights and support. I am
incredibly grateful to Greta Scharnweber, Arthur Starr, Simone Rutkowitz,
Anna Reumert, Mone Makkawi, Sara Dima, Abi Saab, and Adnan Moussa at
the Kevorkian Center. I also thank Fred Appel at Princeton University Press,
who has been tremendously supportive and engaged with this project, copy
editor Anita O'Brien, and production editor Deborah Tegarden.

My partner Jeff Ono has always encouraged me throughout the long
process of ethnographic fieldwork and writing. Through his imagination,
resourcefulness, creativity, and commitment to the *process* of making/doing/
creating, he has shown me that the journey is just as important as the outcome. Our son, Shant, cheered me on with his joyful laughter and gave me
a new reason to hope and maintain hope as a guiding force in everything I
do. We would all be wise to be attentive to the wonder in the everyday, as
he always reminds me.

My late grandmother, Yegsapeth Isabel Kouyoumjian, or "Medzmama,"
inspired me in my desire to write about Armenians in Lebanon. Her

encouragement, love, guidance, and unfailing support were crucial in shaping the outcome of this book. Her brilliant stories as well as her own tenacity in the face of many adversities have had the profoundest impact on me. My grandmother and my mother, Shenorhig, are not here today to see me complete this long journey back to their home, but I know they would have always encouraged me to keep going, no matter how difficult the road.

Kelly Kawar and the entire Kawar family, Jade Gordon, Jennifer Quinly, Lara Schnitger and Matt Monahan, Suzy Halajian, Lisa Mark and Channing Hansen, Daniel Rafinejad (and Dariush and Shanaz), Jed Lackritz, Jessie Ward, Susan Morrell, Dan Fetherston, Renee Valenzuela, Molly Schnick, Katharina Steiner, and Laura Jaramillo are also important friends and mentors in this journey. I also thank my sisters Natalie and Eileen.

Many others remain anonymous here as I write these words, but they are there whenever I think about the hustle and bustle of Bourj Hammoud and all the people I spoke with every day as I walked through the city. There are so many moments that go unmentioned in creating the impressions that inspired this project. The people of Bourj Hammoud and their collective achievements in producing the city power this book and propel me forward, and I hope to do them justice with my words.

Generous funding for this project came from the Wenner-Gren Foundation and a Fulbright-Hays award. At the University of California, Irvine, funding was provided by the School of Social Sciences, the Department of Anthropology, the Center for Unconventional Security, the Institute for Money, Technology and Financial Inclusion, a Chancellor's Club Fellowship, the Center for Citizen Peacebuilding, and the Center for Global Peace and Conflict Studies. I also thank the Center for Humanities at New York University for its support.

EVERYDAY SECTARIANISM IN URBAN LEBANON

INTRODUCTION

One late August afternoon, in the thick humidity of the Beirut summer, I was on one of the many private buses moving at a snail's pace across the traffic-clogged streets between the west of the city, where I was visiting the library at Haigazian University, and Bourj Hammoud, just east of Beirut's municipal boundary. Since the 1930s most of Bourj Hammoud's social and political infrastructure and educational institutions have been dominated by the Armenian population that was settled in Lebanon in the wake of the genocide in former Ottoman lands (present-day Turkey). Haigazian University was one of the few Armenian cultural institutions in the western part of the city after the end of the 1975–90 Lebanese civil war, in which violence and ethnic cleansing had transformed many Beirut neighborhoods.

We were barely moving. At this rate, it would take over an hour to reach my destination. The bus stopped at the large intersection in the middle of the city where it routinely does—either to change drivers or for the driver to have a short break. The driver jumped out and walked across the street to urinate against a wall. A woman sitting a few rows behind grew impatient with the wait and burst out: "Wayn al dawleh? Shufu hayda Lubnan!" (Where is the state? Look, this is Lebanon!).

I had heard this phrase before often—during rolling electricity cuts or intense traffic jams—but not to scold someone for inappropriate behavior. Friends explained to me later that such use of *wayn al dawleh* was not unusual. In Beirut in 2011 it had come to express anger or humor or a hopeless appeal for efficient service provision or for accountability when that service was nowhere to be found. *Wayn al dawleh* is not the only phrase deployed in everyday life through which Lebanese express the longing for dependable infrastructure and anger at a government that seems unable, or unwilling, to provide it. In quite a different context, for example, the seven-year-old son of a friend of mine jumped up after hearing the familiar switch-off of the hum of the private electricity generator and said, "Ijit al dawleh!" (The state is here!), meaning that the national electricity grid was providing power again. That moment shaped the temporality of household life in neighborhoods like Bourj Hammoud, where government electricity was on for only eight to fifteen hours a day. Washing machines begin their work, air conditioners groan to life, and elevators resume their way up and down the heights of residential buildings. In each apartment of each building on each street in neighborhoods like Bourj Hammoud, people negotiate these multiple flows of electricity on a daily basis. State agencies like Electricité du Liban are but one player in this flow of services providing the infrastructure of daily life in the household. For many people in such neighborhoods, this means paying for a subscription to a generator owned by a local patron who provides electricity for that particular block. While generator owners have a reputation for comprising an unscrupulous and ruthless "mafia" that monopolizes electricity provision in much of the country, in some contexts, generator owners have described having to pay local patrons linked to sectarian political parties for permission to operate ("Lights" 2015; Mohsen 2012). These systems pump power through wires as equal players with state utilities and kick in when the national grid supply cuts out.

As much as each household has successfully patched together platforms for the provision of essential infrastructure for family life, the frustration with the lack of "someone" in charge of it all and the failure of the state to provide these services as public goods is expressed through the utterances of daily life. Another often-repeated query in Lebanon, "Meen al-mas'oul?" (Who is in charge/responsible?), is used to locate whomever is "supposed" to be in charge in a particular context to manage resources or maintain infrastructures. In its literal translation, it is a call to locate power or responsibility, a frustration that, in 2015, was expressed as a revolt against inefficient garbage collection but quickly spread to a broader critique of state infrastructures.[1] The unfortunate case of the driver lacking a proper place to take a restroom break raised the ire of the passenger who thought that this was yet another example of a wayward public and moral order of behavior in Lebanon and the inability to locate anyone or any governing body to "take responsibility" for the broken infrastructure and perception of disorder.[2] "Who is in charge" is a constant refrain. Where does power reside, and in which actors—a "failed" state, a sectarian political party, a distant nation, or another state linked to a Lebanese sectarian political faction? What is organizing the flows of people, money, and things through urban streets, mediated at different levels of accountability with the family, sectarian institutions, and the state?

The notion of the "failed state" is pervasive. It is often held to be accountable for the lack of security and for crumbling infrastructure. The common explanation is that this failed state, moreover, is entwined in the patronage networks of more powerful states, such as Syria, Saudi Arabia, France, the United States, and Iran. In the context of Lebanon, however, the very notion of state sovereignty can be understood only in the regional political context of networks of external patrons "because this patronage provided the strongest guarantee for the [Lebanese] elites to maintain their positions of power" (Picard 2002, 180). External patronage provides the support for Lebanese political actors to remain in power, and thus state sovereignty can be understood only within context of these relationships (Picard 2002, 179). International discourses about the benefits of a powerful, centralized sovereign state have led to projects "aimed at reinforcing Lebanon's 'weak' domestic sovereignty against 'extremist elements'" (Fregonese 2012, 655). Many European and American organizations involved in the reconstruction effort after the 2006 war in Lebanon, for example, tend to favor "good governance" programs alongside traditional infrastructure-building or relief work. At least in the immediate postconflict state, "rebuilding and reforming the state was regarded as a cure-all intervention." (Hamieh and Mac Ginty 2010, 112) In Lebanon, however, many nonstate or parastate actors are involved at every level of governance as well as in the provision of public services, infrastructures, and urban planning projects, and the line between political parties and militias is especially thin in times of violence as "both state actors and nonstate militias performed sovereignty practices increasingly resembling each other, and coconstituting each other through Beirut's physical environment" (Fregonese 2012, 655).[3]

The concept of jurisdiction, literally the speaking of the law but in this case the ability to enact authority, is helpful in thinking about the entangled practices of state and nonstate actors, organizations, and institutions. The overlap of actors, of the jurisdictions they activate and legitimate through the cultivation of powerful networks of patronage, is not only spatial or territorial but also temporal, based very much on timing and context (Valverde 2009). The activation of jurisdiction is a continuous unfolding that is much more contingent than it is often imagined to be and, in the case of urban planning in Lebanon, involves processes as complex and diverse as transnational charities, European municipalities, neighborhood political clubs, and diasporic remittances and return migrations. These negotiations and contestations produce the built urban environment—both its material infrastructures and its sectarian geographies.[4] While the case of Lebanon appears exceptional, it actually allows us to shed light on the multiple forces at play in most places in the world today in ways that go beyond the dichotomies of "state" and "nongovernmental organizations" (Elyachar 2003). I approach the study of these forces, institutions, and actors through an analysis of the provision of infrastructure, a public good of the nation-state in the postcolonial context, and of the creation and reproduction of sectarian geographies in Beirut and its environs. The popular Lebanese saying "Where is the state?" both points to what Paul Kockelman (2010) identifies as agency, in terms of which of these forces can be held accountable for action and for failure, while at the same time accurately captures the multiplicity of forces at play. When one asks, "Who is in charge?," the answer of who or what maintains infrastructure or order is not always obvious. I reorient the latter into the question that guides my analysis: what are the ways in which overlapping jurisdictions negotiated between various actors produce what we have come to understand as sectarian spaces and publics?

SECTARIANISM AS DYNAMIC PROCESS

This book is a reexamination of sectarianism as a process, as opposed to an essentialized or primordial identity, through a focus on the urban infrastructures and services provided and managed, in part, by institutions affiliated with sectarian parties and religious organizations, as well as municipalities and transnational organizations. I build on the careful work of scholars who situate the production of sectarianism in Lebanon as a modern social and political phenomenon that is dynamic and processual (Joseph 2008; U. Makdisi 2000; Weiss 2010). Part of the difficulty of thinking through sectarianism as a concept in Lebanon is that the same term refers to multiple things. Sectarianism can, for example, refer to Lebanon's institutionalized confessional governance system in which the sect is posited as the key register of citizenship and includes a quota system of parliamentary representation based on sect, as well as fifteen personal status courts corresponding to its eighteen officially recognized religious sects. Sectarianism is also "a way of being in the world that depends upon a set of cultural markers and social practices" (Weiss 2010, 13) that have shifted and changed over time.[5] While sectarian identity is an important means of differentiation in Lebanon, it cannot be collapsed onto religion or theology (Joseph 2008). In fact, understandings of sectarian community and sectarian identity are linked in critical ways to gender, class, and geography (Deeb and Harb 2013). But sectarianism in Lebanon is not an ancient system bubbling up to disrupt modernity imposed on a reluctant Middle East. Rather, the logic of sectarianism is a form of modernization. It is the legacy of a nineteenth-century modernization project in Mt. Lebanon that "privileged the religious community rather than elite status as the basis for any project of modernization, citizenship and civilization" (U. Makdisi 2000, 7). Sectarianism, the meaning of sect, and the sectarian community, both in terms of the modern institutions of governance and in everyday geographies of the city, are all concepts that have shifted over time, particularly since the civil war era of 1975–90.

Sectarianism as a mode of political power and social organization emerges alongside many different sets of infrastructural and institutional investments. However, infrastructure is not a representation, a static diagram of the underlying logics of sectarianism. Rather, infrastructures are the channels through which the activity or process of sectarianism is produced in specific instances as opposed to other modes of differentiation (Elyachar 2010; Larkin 2008; Maurer 2013). Infrastructure is not only what makes things move through space; rather, it is what creates and recreates the spaces through which circulation happens (Larkin 2013; Povinelli 2011). The infrastructures I discuss here do not merely represent the action of sectarian belonging but create and shape the subjects who can circulate through them.[6] Who or what gets to count as part of the sectarian community? We know that sectarian identity is not essential—that is, it is not an inborn quality of the person in question. Rather, membership in the sectarian community is relational: it is a node in a relational field. Here it can be helpful to draw on recent theorizations of "channel" and "infrastructure" (Elyachar 2010; Kockelman 2010). Specifically, what gets to count as an exteriority to a channel, a person excluded from the community, is a matter of position or perspective. Because channels and infrastructures, things like electricity cables or telephone wires, are designed against noise and interruption, the channel is also, in a sense, "defined by its capacity to fail," leaving it open to change and recalibration (Kockelman 2010, 409) Just as channels and infrastructures serve to create spaces of connection and conjoined action, they also serve to differentiate, subtract, or reroute people and things.[7]

Infrastructure is a policy imperative in much of the world, both in "advanced" countries facing crumbling infrastructures and in the global South as a symbol of failures of the postcolonial era. It has become an important topic among scholars in the past twenty years. For my interlocutors in Lebanon, infrastructure and service provision were topics of daily debate and concern and were directly interwoven with an apparently totally different topic, the notion of a sectarian community. I conducted much of my research in the municipality of Bourj Hammoud to the east of Beirut. There I explored the production and reproduction of "sectarian community" both through the proliferation of sectarian organizations that provide infrastructures and services like medical care and education as well as through urban-planning strategies and urban infrastructure projects at the municipality. One of my aims in writing an ethnography of infrastructures and services that connect and disconnect people is to contribute to the critique of sectarian identity as ancient and unchanging (Abu Rish 2015b; Joseph 1975, 2008; U. Makdisi 2000). As the notion of sectarianism is often used as explanation for conflict throughout the region, it is critical to think about the construction of sectarianism in Lebanon as it relates to other contexts, such as Syria and even Iraq.[8] By approaching the networks of sectarianism as something made and remade in the built environment and through people's daily interactions, producing sectarian community becomes an ongoing, changing process rather than a timeless category.[9]

Sectarian belonging, I show through my fieldwork in Bourj Hammoud, is constructed and recalibrated on a daily basis. Sectarianism and sectarian community only appear to be primordial and immutable. They are actually nothing of the kind, which we can see best when we study sectarianism together with—rather than apart from—the materiality of urban infrastructures, things like electricity generators and parking lots, and the channels produced through institutions and essential services. Begoña Aretxaga (1997, 24), writing about Belfast in Northern Ireland, compellingly argues that "place . . . is both the product of relations of power and the material through which such relations are culturally articulated, challenged and reproduced." Likewise, in Lebanon, the relationship between infrastructures in urban spaces and sectarianism is dialogic—many urban infrastructures and services are produced by sectarian political and religious organizations at the same time that they are the channels through which sectarian belonging and exclusion are experienced, produced, and recalibrated. Indeed, it is the very networks of infrastructures, institutions, and services that reproduce particular notions of sectarian belonging and community, as seen in my own ethnographic research as well as in the work of Suad Joseph (1975, 1983, 1994a, 1994b, 1996, 1999), Judith Harik (1993), Elizabeth Picard (2000, 2002), Nizar Hamzeh (2001), Mona Harb (2007, 2010), Catherine Le Thomas (2010), Bruno Lefort (2011), Paul Kingston (2013), Isabelle Rivoal (2014), and Melanie Cammett (2014).

In her prescient study of Bourj Hammoud at the cusp of the Lebanese civil war, Suad Joseph (1975) showed how sectarian institutions served as mediators of state resources. This politicized sectarian identity: individuals mobilized ethnoreligious sectarian affiliations in order to obtain resources and services from political parties and religious institutions in the early 1970s. People came to feel more and more part of a sect whose institutions cultivate sectarian identity.[10] Nearly forty years after Joseph's seminal research, similar kinds of sectarian organizations in Bourj Hammoud, and many other sect-affiliated institutions in Lebanon, are firmly integrated into a system of service provision in which sectarian political parties and religious institutions maintain affiliated clinics, schools, and charities. During the Lebanese civil war of 1975–90, the city was divided into zones dominated by oppositional factions. In the context of the breakdown of the state, sect-affiliated parties and militias were more active in the maintenance of basic services and infrastructures, including things like garbage collection (Davie 1991) but also telephone, postal, and electricity services (Migliorino 2008).[11] After the war, many sectarian militias and parties that had assumed responsibility for these services created formalized social welfare institutions (Cammett 2014). While many see the provision of services through social welfare institutions in the context of Lebanon as something specifically Islamic, this is certainly not the case. Organizations affiliated with sectarian religious institutions and political parties have long served as important distribution hubs for state resources (Joseph 1975). Today, international organizations also work with these same sectarian religious institutions and political parties.[12] The irony is that the same international organizations that are trying to combat the so-called weak state and increase good governance integrate into a fragmented order of service and infrastructure provision that is sectarian in nature.[13] While much of this happens through an ideology of localism or "the community," in the context of Lebanon "community" is translated as "sect."

Sectarian community is, most obviously, produced through the mobilization of ethnoreligious identities. But those identities do not exist in the abstract or in isolation. They are linked to class, gender, and geography. Even sets of documentation like informal property *rukhsa*s, or permits, and the pressures of real estate speculation in greater Beirut that always affect the everyday-ness of sectarian identity are factors that shape individuals' access to services and profoundly influence the built environment while rendering sectarian community irreducible to ethnoreligious identity alone.[14] While people do often intentionally mobilize sectarian identities to create connections and to access services, they also come to feel and understand themselves as part of a community through the pathways and channels created by these services as well as the materiality of urban space.

Everyday sectarianism is about the ways that identity shapes interactions in everyday life, but it is a dynamic identity that itself is necessarily shaped by the political-sectarian structures, discourses, and practices of Lebanese state institutions and local municipal governments. Sectarianism, however, is also about the discourses and practices of nongovernmental sect-affiliated organizations in Lebanon, such as charities, schools, and religious institutions, that have developed and changed over time. Notions of sectarian community are produced not only through engaging with sectarian institutions but also through the day-to-day exercise of "being" within the material landscape those institutions produce, even within neighborhoods that are demographi-cally diverse. The process is deeply dialogic—the very materiality of the city, its urban infrastructures and spaces, clinics and schools, also produce and reproduce sectarian publics through processes that are not limited to the actions of political parties or the Lebanese confessional state alone but are worked out through various negotiations, some of them transnational in scale. This book explores this dialogical loop between the production of infrastructures by a wide range of sectarian political parties, state institu-tions, and transnational actors and the ways in which the materiality of these infrastructures and services—things like bridges and roads, clinic waiting rooms, informal housing, and the networks and neighborhood spaces they create and divide—profoundly shape changing notions of what sectarian "community" means and how one comes to belong to it or be excluded from it.

Lebanon makes visible a broader pattern in which access to infrastructures is part of the way people begin to imagine themselves as part of a public. The public I describe is bound together through everyday practices of procuring housing, electricity, medical services and favors, such that infrastructures are "learned as part of membership" (Star 1999, 381). Sometimes these forms of membership are understood in terms of belonging to a sectarian community. The Lebanese political system has institutionalized the sect as a dominant category of citizenship and "imagined community" (Anderson 1983). Sect is also formed through the navigation of services and urban infrastructures stretching across overlapping jurisdictions inside Lebanon and across national boundaries. These quotidian processes involve sociotechnical arrangements of people and things that are inseparable from what some might call society (Latour 1993). Those infrastructures often fail; failure, in turn, is significant, meaningful, and constitutive of fragmented publics. Electricity does not flow evenly through one set of cables. Rather, low-wattage and thus un-reliable electricity is pushed through cables from sources both formal and informal. Bridges and roads shape and divide spaces into zones familiar or unknown—and thus dangerous.[15] Also powering the circulation of people are things as vastly different as credit, electricity, and medical care in Bourj Hammoud are people—or rather communicative channels formed as an outcome of their social practices through ongoing favors, gossip, and visits (Elyachar 2010). Through the negotiation of these networks, urban dwell-ers form contingent relationships that create affective bonds between them, rather than a distant-seeming nation-state (Simone 2004). These networks, even when mobilized without any direct reference to politics, are political (Singerman 1995) because they contain within them a latent potential for direct mobilization (Elyachar 2014).

If tangled wires of electrical power from multiple sources through dis-tinct channels depend on the unseen phatic labor of electricity's users, those channels are wired into apparently far away and antisectarian international organizations and technocratic organizations for reconstruction (Elyachar 2010). If, as I have argued, infrastructure helps create and reproduce sect, it emanates from no one institution or force—be it a party, religion, or cultural proclivity. It becomes clear, then, that sectarianism does not emanate from either the state or parastate organizations or political parties. It is problematic to take these scales of governance or institutions for granted as distinct, or one as somehow more powerful than another, particularly since there is so much entanglement between political actors who operate simultaneously in multiple scales and institutional spaces. I find that jurisdiction is a helpful analytic language with which to talk about the various entangled powers that engineer urban landscapes, property regimes, and social and physical infrastructures that help reproduce sectarian publics.[16] I focus on the materiality of infrastructure and the provision of services like medical care and education to ground my analysis in the ways that sectarianism and the making of sectarian community involve multiple overlapping jurisdictions that connect and disconnect people and things.[17]

Infrastructure and sectarian communities are reproduced in the present. Yet without a historical perspective none of this makes sense. For this, we need institutional and infrastructural histories. And here we need to turn most directly back to the aftermath of the 1915 Armenian genocide in former Ottoman lands, to the time when French Mandate officials eventually resettled many Armenian refugees in Lebanon. That is also when a number of Armenian-affiliated social service institutions in Lebanon were founded as relief organizations, many by Europeans and Americans but also wealthy Armenian Americans. It is also when Bourj Hammoud began its transformation from a sparsely populated agricultural periphery of Beirut to a densely populated residential and workshop area, built through the negotiations of French Mandate officials, Armenian town associations, and Lebanese elites to house the displaced Ottoman Armenians. It is important to emphasize how these organizations as well as the transnational Armenian political parties and religious institutions fit into the unfolding political dynamics in Lebanon at the time. For one thing, this meant adapting to, and helping to coconstitute, the emerging confessional system of the Lebanese government (Nalbantian 2013). Such a process of adaptation is organizational, bureaucratic, and material. It is not merely a mode of representation overlaid upon a preexisting confessional "community," or "sect." Armenian refugees were, in a sense, reconfigured as members of "sects" in order to be legible within emerging juridico-legal categories in the Lebanese political sectarian system. Recent scholarship has emphasized the institutional, infrastructural, and spatial aspects of the Armenian process of becoming part of the sectarian system in Lebanon (Migliorino 2008; Nalbantian 2011, 2013). These same scholars help us situate the processes through which the "Armenian community" as it is understood today was produced through the negotiations of various actors, not somehow transported intact from former Ottoman lands to Lebanon.

Just as producing the sect is a process negotiated through various actors, the institutionalization of the political sectarian system in Lebanon was worked out through various encounters between British, French, and Ottoman officials as well as Lebanese elites and nonelites (U. Makdisi 2000; Thompson 2000). Brian Larkin (2008, 6) writes that "at any one point urban space is made up of the historical layering of networks connected by infrastructures." In Bourj Hammoud, these infrastructural layers are deeply

connected to the negotiations of French and Ottoman officials in the twi-
light of the Ottoman Empire, as well as the mass displacements of refugees
throughout the twentieth century and beyond. As a concept worked on and
through various moments of crisis and entanglement from the neighborhood
block to the Sublime Porte, the concept of sectarianism itself has a history,
and it is to this history that I turn first.

INSTITUTIONALIZING SECTARIANISM, ENGINEERING THE URBAN

The Roots of "Sectarianism" from the Ottoman Empire to the French Mandate

Discourses about sectarianism and ethnic conflict as inevitable are nothing
new in Lebanon. They go back much further than the conflicts of the last
several decades. Historian Ussama Makdisi (1996, 26) argues that while
sectarianism in Lebanon is often posited as a violent trace of a premodern
past, it is "a nationalist creation that dates no further back than the beginnings of the modern era." In *The Culture of Sectarianism* (2000), Makdisi
contextualizes the discourses about the inevitability of sectarian conflict
in Lebanon by focusing on what many historians consider to be the first
large-scale sectarian conflict between Maronite Christians and Druze in
Mt. Lebanon, in 1860, during a time of somewhat detached Ottoman rule.
Before 1860 the region was dominated by crosscutting alliances between
leading quasi-feudal families of different sects. Makdisi argues, however,
that this was not an idyllic time without violence. Rather, "violence existed
in pre-1860 Ottoman Lebanese society, but it consisted primarily of elite
violence deployed to reaffirm a rigid, status-based social order defined as
the rule of knowledge over ignorance," and status was not stratified according to religious identity (29). Historian Leila Fawaz (1995, 17) also writes
that the Mt. Lebanon region was characterized by "a network of alliances
among its leading Druze and Maronite [Christian] families based on a chain
of clan loyalties that cut across sectarian lines and took precedence over
loyalty to village, district, or church." A number of factors were involved in
severing the ties between Druze and Christian notables and families who
traditionally ruled the Mt. Lebanon area jointly, rather than as representatives of their religious "communities" (U. Makdisi 1996; L. Fawaz 1995).
First, alignments and patron-client relationships were radically altered by
Egyptian occupation (under Muhammad Ali), European intervention, and
subsequent defeat by the Ottomans. Second, changing policies within the
Ottoman Empire, as well as pressures from European (in Lebanon, mainly

French but also British) missionaries, military actors, and merchants, created conditions where sectarian identity emerged as an important category of rule and a way in which to appeal for rights. Finally, the favored status of Maronite Christians, who reaped the profits of French investment in the silk industry in the early part of the nineteenth century, increased tensions in the lead-up to 1860 (L. Fawaz 1995).

Ussama Makdisi (2000) demonstrates how Ottoman and French officials actively constructed an interpretation of the events as an inevitable outburst of primordial ethnic hatred and ongoing violence between Christians and Druze. Both Ottoman and French officials used the idea of sectarian animosity as innate to Mt. Lebanon as justification for political and spatial governance reforms over the latter half of the nineteenth century and the early twentieth century. One of the results of the violence leading up to the events of 1860 was the production of "sectarian geographies" in Mt. Lebanon; Maronites and Druze no longer felt that their security and safety in so-called mixed areas of Mt. Lebanon were guaranteed. This moment of insecurity was not only seized on by the French seeking to intervene but also echoed in certain Lebanese sectarian discourses later on in the twentieth century.

The violence led to structural reforms as well. Ottoman, French, and British military personnel and consular officials pushed the Sublime Porte to adopt a new form of governance for the Mt. Lebanon area in the wake of the massacres (U. Makdisi 2000). In June 1861 the Ottoman government, along with France, Britain, Russia, Austria, and Prussia, adopted the Règlement Organique, which granted the Mt. Lebanon area semiautonomous status and established the mutasarrifiyya to replace the previously existing Kaymakamates, which had divided Mt. Lebanon into two parts, governed by two "mayors." The mutasarrifiyya would be ruled by a Christian mutasarrif (a kind of regional governor) appointed by the Sublime Porte (L. Fawaz 1995; Kanaan 2005; U. Makdisi 2000). At the same time, it is a notable moment in that it created a "'Lebanese' identity" with a "legal definition and was associated with a 'modern' system of administration" for the first time (Kanaan 2005, 77).

Emerging social and class divisions were reinforced through urban infrastructures as the Ottomans and the French competed in their attempts to cultivate influence over Beirut.[18] The construction of the port, tramway, and rail infrastructure created new divisions in space, rerouting people away "from their customary work and place in the city," and consolidated the power of ruling elites of different sects (Hanssen 2005, 266). By 1903 urban riots in Beirut broke out, which, as they were managed and contained by patron-client relationships, "often turned sectarian through the very act of crisis management" through these channels (Hanssen 2005, 266). Meanwhile, French infrastructural projects were changing the everyday lives of Beirut dwellers. As France's investment in the urban center came to rival the Ottomans', these projects can also be interpreted as a contest for influence. Despite these increased French infrastructural investments, Hanssen argues that Beirut's upgraded status as a provincial capital city in 1888 lies in the attempt to keep an increasingly contested region under Ottoman sovereignty. With a semiautonomous and unruly Mt. Lebanon nearby, the granting of the previously marginal town of Beirut the status of a provincial capital within the empire was regarded as an effective mode of governance, both to pacify sectarian violence and to maintain sovereignty over Beirut and Mt. Lebanon.

The next important formal transformation of the status of Lebanon occurred after World War I, with the dissolution of the Ottoman Empire. In 1918, as part of the overall Mandate arrangement, the League of Nations divided the region between French and British Mandates. Lebanon was allocated, along with the rest of "Greater Syria," to the French. The goal of the Mandate was to move along territories that were not fully "backward" like colonies and yet not civilized enough for independence into conditions of civilizational development appropriate for independence.[19] By 1920 France took another step toward the creation of Lebanon as a state when it established the borders of the État du Grand Liban, or Greater Lebanon, as a distinct territory with autonomy from the much larger "Greater Syria," though both remained under French Mandate (Longrigg 1958; Salibi 1965). It was not until 1943 that Lebanon became an independent state.

Along with Lebanese elites, French Mandate administrators created the civil and political institutions of governance that produced the modern Lebanese confessional system (Thompson 2000). The political system produced during this era, and underscored by the National Pact of 1943,[20] justifies its allocation of proportional representation using data from the 1932 census (the last one conducted in Lebanon), which shows Maronite Christians as the majority sect, with Sunni Muslims, Shi'a Muslims, and Druze as second, third, and fourth most populous sects (Picard 2002).[21] While there are eighteen other officially recognized sects (Greek Orthodox, for example), the convention follows that a Maronite Christian must be president, a Sunni Muslim must be prime minister, and a Shi'a Muslim must be Speaker of Parliament.[22] The political sectarian system was in many ways a product of the aforementioned post-1860 French, British, and Ottoman understandings of Mt. Lebanon, whereby sectarian alliances were posited as primordial and essential to the functioning of Lebanese society (U. Makdisi 2000). During and immediately after the French Mandate period, the number of officially incorporated municipalities (Arabic, *baladiyes*; French, *municipalités*) in Lebanon began to grow as French urban designs, particularly for highway infrastructure, continued to be implemented as late as the 1960s.

In addition to enacting a sectarian quota system for political representation in government offices, Lebanon's confessional system requires that laws of personal status are decided through fifteen religious courts corresponding to the eighteen recognized sects in Lebanon.[23] All marriages performed in Lebanon, for example, must be registered with one of the religious courts. The only option for a mixed-sect couple where neither one wants to convert to another religion is to perform a "civil marriage" in another country, usually nearby Cyprus. Couples married under the auspices of one of the recognized religious courts can seek a legal divorce only through the same court, barring religious conversion.[24] The rules and laws vary between courts.

Many of my Lebanese interlocutors attribute the emergence of sectarian tension in Lebanon to "foreign meddling" and "elite corruption" starting with the influence of the French in the nineteenth and twentieth centuries. Historical accounts, however, muddle this easy dichotomy between "foreign" influence and local actors. The shaping of Lebanese politics during the Mandate period and immediately after was also not a uniquely elite endeavor but rather a process worked out through a number of quotidian institutions and practices (Thompson 2000). Critical to understanding the development of Lebanese politics and juridical system are issues related to gender hierarchies, shifting patron-client relationships, and transnational migration and return migration, increasing the circulation of remittances and different notions of modernity (Khater 2001; Thompson 2000). In Lebanon, citizenship is inherited only through a male relative—one's father or one's husband. A woman can give citizenship neither to a child born to a non-Lebanese father nor to her non-Lebanese husband. Historian Elizabeth Thompson (2000) traces how such laws were drafted in negotiations between elites and French Mandate officials in transition to Lebanese independence. She argues that patriarchal elites essentially sacrificed women's demands for equal political participation and citizenship in the new nation-state; these compromises were justified in terms of sacrificing women's full rights of citizenship for alliances with religious authorities and patriarchal elites and ruling families.[25]

The making of sectarianism, and the imagining of sectarian communities, was and is a process worked out through the institutions of the Lebanese state, as well as the numerous social, juridical, religious, and cultural institutions of particular sects (Weiss 2010). It is a process that is ongoing and dynamic. In Lebanon, both governmental and sectarian institutions are entangled and coconstitutive of the Lebanese nation-state in ways that offset questions of sovereignty to one of jurisdiction. From the start of the modern Lebanese state, "sect" was coconstituted with modern state institutions. To be more specific, the powers of sectarian political factions are entangled with state institutions, particularly in terms of the urban governance of Beirut and other municipalities.[26] This last point is particularly critical when thinking about a municipality like Bourj Hammoud, which was transformed from an agricultural periphery into a densely populated suburb with the assistance of French Mandate officials in order to permanently resettle Armenian refugees from the genocide in former Ottoman lands. Armenian sects in Lebanon did not spontaneously emerge from the Armenian refugee community. Nor are those sects merely another node in the transnational Armenian diaspora, which is by no means monolithic. Rather, I argue, the Armenian sects were coproduced by French Mandate officials, Armenian political parties and town associations, and the newly formed confessional state, as well as the nexus of space, urban infrastructure building, and networks of social service organizations, schools, and churches within the municipal district of Bourj Hammoud.

A NEW ARMENIA IN LEBANON: BUILDING BOURJ HAMMOUD

Most Armenians came to Lebanon as refugees. They were displaced from Ottoman territories during the systematic massacres and deportations of 1915–19 known as the Armenian genocide.[27] Lebanese Armenian sects were created from a group of refugees from different towns and villages, of different religious backgrounds, who spoke different languages ranging from Turkish to specific local or village dialects like *hajineren*, the local dialect of the town of Hadjin, to Western Armenian. As such, the creation of Lebanese Armenian sectarian identity (as both an administrative legal category and a felt identity) is quite specific to Lebanon and its confessional system.[28] Before the arrival of the Ottoman Armenian refugees, today's Bourj Hammoud consisted of agricultural fields. Its urbanization was a direct outcome of the displacement of the surviving Ottoman Armenians. The urban form and networks of Bourj Hammoud are a direct legacy of the genocide—likewise its networks of aid, mainly from European and American missionaries, who founded the social educational and medical service institutions that still exist in the neighborhood and elsewhere in Lebanon today. Bourj Hammoud soon became the center of the new Lebanese Armenian social and cultural world.[29] It was full of theaters, publishing houses, churches, and schools, all established by refugees and their supporting NGOs, churches, and diasporic organizations. The Bourj Hammoud municipality has long been dominated by Armenian sectarian political organizations (Joseph 1975; Nalbantian 2011). We cannot understand how this is so if we ignore the extent to which the Lebanese Armenian sect and the urbanization of Bourj Hammoud were coproduced in the aftermath of genocide.

While under Ottoman rule, Armenians in what is now modern-day Turkey lived as a minority in the *millet* system that governed non-Muslim communities, though, as historian Nicola Migliorino (2008) argues, the system evolved through a long and ongoing process in which the meaning of these categories changed over time. Under this system, the patriarchs of the Apostolic Church (like their Greek Orthodox and non-Muslim counterparts) were also the main political representatives of all Armenians, regardless of their religion, in Istanbul. Though the vast majority of Armenians in Anatolia and Cilicia were subsistence farmers, shepherds, and peasants, those from the larger and well-developed towns like Adana could also be merchants, teachers, doctors, and a myriad of other professions (Miller and Miller 1993).

During the genocide of 1915–19, Armenians were sent on death marches into the deserts of Syria and Iraq (Akçam 2007, 2012; Kevorkian 2011; Suny 2015).[30] Survivors eventually settled in a number of countries in the Middle East, including Lebanon, but many ended up migrating to Europe or North America. Many Armenians in Lebanon are from Cilicia, a region in southwestern Turkey. Those that survived deportation found themselves in refugee camps, mainly in Syria, without permanent quarters and hoping to return to their villages and towns. In 1919, in an attempt to bolster their territorial interests in the Middle East, the French repatriated Armenians to Cilicia in order to create an autonomous region sympathetic to Europe and also to thwart the Kemalist nationalist aspirations to create a Turkish state out of the remnants of the Ottoman Empire (Tachjian 2004). After more than a year of military resistance from Turkish forces in Cilicia, however, France took a more conciliatory approach. In October 1921 the Treaty of Ankara assured France's withdrawal from Cilicia in exchange for Turkey's acceptance of French control over Greater Syria.

By 1922 French administrators withdrawing from Cilicia evacuated Armenian refugees who had been resettled there. Estimates vary, but between sixty thousand and eighty thousand Armenians were made refugees for a second time (Mandel 2003; Migliorino 2008; Sanjian 2001). Many of them were brought to Lebanon and found themselves on the shores of Karantina, a patch of land near the port in East Beirut that was designated as a quarantine area (Fawaz and Peillen 2003). In Karantina, the refugees lived in makeshift shacks (Meymarian and Gomidas Institute 2004). With the help of the French Mandate government, many Armenian refugees were able to leave the camp and settle in East Beirut or Bourj Hammoud within a few years.[31] For Armenians, becoming Lebanese citizens meant more than just legal rights to own property and work. They are officially recognized within the framework of sects with full political rights of participation in government (Migliorino 2008). By the 1930s much of the then-agricultural district of Bourj Hammoud had been purchased by Armenian town associations that collected resources and regrouped Armenian residents of former Ottoman towns in Lebanon (Migliorino 2008; Fawaz and Peillen 2003). These town associations subdivided plots for sale to individual association members and their families, effectively creating distinct neighborhoods that bore the name of the town of origin (Migliorino 2008; Schahgaldian 1979).[32] Both

Armenians and non-Armenians still refer to their neighborhoods by these names. Marash or Nor Marash (New Marash) in the northwestern corner of Bourj Hammoud was the first neighborhood to be built by what is still the largest and most powerful of the Armenian town associations, Marash. As Keith Watenpaugh (2015, 619) argues, the building of new neighborhoods for Armenians in Aleppo and Beirut was part of a project of "moving the refugees into modern urban society as members of what French policy makers identified as the respectable lower-middle class." The relationship between notions of modernity, class, and religious identity in a burgeoning Lebanese confessional governance system as well as French interests in the region came together in urban development projects like Bourj Hammoud. The Armenian presence in Lebanon is a critical aspect of the relationship between urban infrastructure and the development of sectarian geographies under the French Mandate and beyond.

Town associations, also known as compatriotic unions, played a crucial role in marshaling resources and establishing the Armenian community in Lebanon in those early years.[33] Among the early obstacles for Armenian genocide survivors in Beirut was the great degree of linguistic, cultural, and religious diversity in their communities. Many Armenians spoke Turkish or a number of village dialects, not Western Armenian, which is the standardized modern dialect taught in Armenian schools in Lebanon today.[34] There were also differences of background in terms of rural versus urban populations, as well as religion. The three Armenian religious groups in Lebanon are the Armenian Evangelical Church, an outgrowth of European and American Protestant missionary activities in the former Ottoman Empire, the Armenian Catholic Church, and the Armenian Apostolic Church. The Apostolic Church is the most powerful and represents the majority "sect" within the Armenian community.[35] Thus, despite attempts to consolidate an Armenian national consciousness and to promote an ethnic rather than local identity, many in Lebanon continued to organize themselves according to village and regional ties.[36] None of the Armenian political parties nor the church apparatus was able to consolidate a unified Armenian bloc during the first elections in 1934, and many of the refugees remained apathetic about participation in Lebanese politics (Migliorino 2008). This, however, would change in ways that are intertwined with the production of Armenian social and political geographies in Beirut and Bourj Hammoud, which I will explain in the following section.

The project of "Armenianization," teaching Western Armenian (not Turkish or other village dialects) to the new generation of children born in Beirut while self-consciously constructing space according to village and town associations that hoped to keep their residents in close proximity, became critical in a unique way in Lebanon. Under the Lebanese confessional system, every sect must have a corresponding politico-religious apparatus for issues of personal status as well as to elect representatives to serve in the Lebanese Parliament, where seats are based on confessional demographics. In the case of the Armenians, there is a complicated overlay of the remnants of the *millet* system to the Lebanese sectarian system that makes it appear much more seamless than it is. Recent scholarship critiques the notion that Armenians represent a kind of exception or are somehow peripheral to the Lebanese confessional system by showing how their institutions and apparatuses co-emerged with the Lebanese independent state in the 1940s and 1950s (Nalbantian 2013). As Max Weiss (2010, 25) writes, "Each sectarian community in Lebanon has become sectarian in its own particular way as a result of specific sets of discursive, institutional and material transformations." The making of the Lebanese Armenian sect from a group of displaced people from elsewhere in the Ottoman Empire in the 1920s and 1930s can tell us something about the production of sectarianism in Lebanon as a political, spatial, and urban project.

Though the cultivation of Armenian national identity was a deliberate project, community leaders at the time portrayed the development of Bourj Hammoud as a reconstruction effort whereby the Armenian community was simply resurrected in a new location (Migliorino 2008). This discourse has continued into the present day. While Western Armenian is the language of daily life among Armenians in Bourj Hammoud, most people under sixty are also fluent in Arabic, as they seek work outside of the neighborhood, learn to read and write Arabic in Armenian schools, and watch Arabic-language television programs. Still, the density of Armenian institutions, the sound of the Armenian language being spoken, Armenian music echoing through the narrow streets, and the presence of Armenian script on signs and posters helps to create the special sense of Bourj Hammoud as an Armenian space, unique in the greater Beirut area. It is precisely this proximity and density of Armenian institutions that helps create the sense of an Armenian public sphere among my interlocutors.

Bourj Hammoud: The Making of an Armenian "Public Sphere"

Located just east of the Beirut River, which marks the boundary of the municipality of Beirut, Bourj Hammoud is a densely populated, mixed residential, commercial, and workshop district that is one of the oldest popular neighborhoods in the eastern part of greater Beirut. An estimated ninety thousand people live in the municipal district that comprises about 2.4 square kilometers (0.9 square mile).[37] Unlike many of the neighborhoods across the river in Beirut, Bourj Hammoud has a bustling shopping district for inexpensive goods, as well as workshops that produce shoes, jewelry, and clothing. It also has historically had some of the lowest rents for a neighborhood so close to

Figure I.1. Rooftop view of Bourj Hammoud. Photo by Rosy Kuftedjian.

Figure I.2. The Beirut River dividing Bourj Hammoud from the municipality of Beirut. Photo by author.

the Beirut districts of Ashrafiyeh and downtown. For many in Beirut, Bourj Hammoud is known as the "Armenian quarter." For some of my Armenian interlocutors, it is a special place in Lebanon where one can feel enmeshed in a world not quite like that outside the neighborhood. Hratch, a young Armenian man in his twenties, told me: "As a child growing up there, I used to think I was living in Armenia, not Lebanon . . . everything around me referenced 'Armenian' culture rather than a 'Lebanese' culture, from street signs to shop names, everything was in Armenian." Suzy, an Armenian woman in her thirties who grew up across the river in nearby Beirut, expressed how it was a place where she felt a deep sense of belonging: "It is very special to me, every time I walk there on the streets I feel secure. It's weird, but it's true. I feel familiar. As if I'm in my house."

Indeed, the space of the city is dense with Armenian schools, clinics, and businesses, and many signs are written in Armenian script. The flags of the Republic of Armenia and the Armenian Tashnag political party hang over many streets, and anti-Turkish graffiti is omnipresent on its walls. However, the stereotype of Bourj Hammoud as a monolithic Armenian district is misleading, as the city is quite demographically diverse. It is not uncommon to find flags for the Lebanese Forces (a right-wing political party affiliated with the Maronite Christian sect) as well as flags for Amal (a political party affiliated with the Shi'a Muslim sect) on certain streets in the municipality. In the early years after its initial urbanization in the 1920s and 1930s, Bourj Hammoud's population was mainly Armenian, Greek Orthodox, and Maronite. During the 1940s, however, many Armenians in Lebanon "repatriated" to Soviet Armenia, a process known in Armenian as *Nerkakht* (Nalbantian 2013).[38] Still, Bourj Hammoud remained the center of Armenian life in Lebanon, with its theaters, newspapers, cinemas, as well as workshops and artisanal ateliers. It was and still is known for its abundance of shoe and clothing manufacturers, automobile garages, locksmiths, and hardware stores. French refugee policy during the Mandate period in what would later become Syria and Lebanon focused on providing Armenians with skilled apprenticeships, sources of credit for private enterprises, and property in order to settle them permanently while maintaining "their linkage with the French state" (Watenpaugh 2004, 619). Many skills and trades are passed down from family members and through apprenticeship systems that are still functioning, particularly for trades like jewelry making. On many occasions during my research, I met second- and third-generation shoemakers, jewelers, and tailors.

During the 1950s Lebanese migrants from rural areas, mainly Shi'a Muslims, moved to Bourj Hammoud. The district was attractive because it had the advantage of affordable housing and proximity to jobs in nearby industrial zones and service work in Beirut. Throughout the 1960s and early 1970s, further waves of migrants, mainly Shi'a and Palestinians, fleeing violence

Figure I.3. A mixed residential and business area in Bourj Hammoud. Photo by Rosy Kuftedjian.

in the South also moved to Bourj Hammoud. It became one of the most diverse neighborhoods in the metropolitan Beirut area but also gained the reputation of being part of the so-called poverty belt that ringed Beirut as migrants fleeing violence and seeking better economic conditions moved to the city (Fawaz and Peillen 2003; Traboulsi 2007). The southern part of Bourj Hammoud, Naba'a (which means "spring" and was named for a water source that was once there), became the most densely populated area as new, taller apartment buildings were constructed to accommodate the influx of new residents.

Despite the diversity of residents, the Armenian Tashnag Party dominates the Bourj Hammoud municipality through its formal and informal institutions of governance, infrastructure provision, and security (Joseph 1975). Tashnag (short for Hay Heghapokhagan Tashnagtsutian, or the Armenian Revolutionary Federation), Hnchag (Sotsial Temograd Hnchagian Goosagtsootiun, or the Social Democrat Hnchagian Party), and Ramgavar (Ramgavar Azadagan Goosagtsootiun, or the Armenian Democratic Liberal Party), the three primary transnational Armenian political parties active in Lebanon today, were all founded in the nineteenth century and were, in different ways, committed to Armenian nationalism and independence from the Ottoman Empire.[39] After a protracted political battle that exploded, at

Figure I.4. The Naba'a neighborhood of Bourj Hammoud. Photo by author.

times, into assassinations and street clashes that reached their zenith when the parties were on opposing sides of the Lebanese civil conflict in 1958, Tashnag emerged as the dominant Armenian political party in Lebanon, specifically within the Armenian Apostolic Church institutions, schools, and the municipality of Bourj Hammoud (Migliorino 2008; Nalbantian 2011; Suny 1993).[40] While it is also a transnational Armenian cultural organization that organizes sporting events and scouting clubs for youths, in Lebanon it remains the most powerful Armenian political party. The Tashnag Party has led most of the schools, businesses, NGOs and municipality governance in Bourj Hammoud since the 1970s (Joseph 1975). While residents of other sects or ethnicities always populated the area, and intersectarian marriages were not uncommon, one of the impacts of Tashnag control was that Armenians received preferential access to social services and even municipality projects, such as public housing (Joseph 1975).[41] By 1976 many of the Shi'a and Palestinian residents of the area would be either "ethnically cleansed" or forced to leave the area by right-wing Christian militias using violent tactics (Sankari 2005). Some Shi'as in Bourj Hammoud were able to reclaim property after the war. While there is a Shi'a community in Bourj Hammoud today, it is a much smaller population than was there in the 1970s.

Today Tashnag maintains a strong presence in Bourj Hammoud, not only because it dominates the municipality leadership and the Armenian Apostolic Church's religious, educational, and legal apparatuses but also through a number of Tashnag-affiliated *agoumps* or "political clubs." Each neighborhood in Bourj Hammoud has its own corresponding agoump, which acts as a meeting place for various Tashnag activities, including the women's charitable auxiliary, young adult clubs, and men's committees. The agoump can also serve as an information hub, informal police station, and security office, maintaining order and taking care of neighborhood disputes. The agoumps are kept open throughout the night, with men taking shifts keeping watch, a legacy of the civil war years. The securitization of the city and the block-by-block fighting and domination of space during the civil war of 1975–90 left an enduring impact on Bourj Hammoud and much of the greater Beirut area.

THE CIVIL WAR OF 1975–90 AND AFTER: MILITARIZING THE NEIGHBORHOOD

Just as the conflicts of 1860 were oversimplified through interpretation as sectarian conflict staged between "Christian" and "Muslim" factions, the conflicts leading to the civil war were much more complex and irreducible to forms of primordial ethnic hatred or "irrational" religious conflicts. Various scholars have suggested different theories as to why the civil war, starting in 1975, stretched on through various foreign invasions and inversions of loyalties until 1990. Some have noted the divisive power of "increasingly fundamental divisions of class, wealth, political ideology, and patterns of consumption—divisions which all manifested themselves locally" (Gilsenan 1996, xv). Others have cited that the primary conflict was between differing ideas of nationalism and national identity—one faction favoring a pan-Arabist identity for Lebanon[42] and the other favoring a primarily Maronite Christian-endorsed Lebanese exceptionalism that had ultimately evolved into right-wing groups like the Kataib (Salibi 1988).[43] Still others have emphasized the conflict over Palestinian presence in Lebanon as a major factor leading to the war (Hudson 1977; Khalidi 1983), while some posit that the conflict needs to be contextualized within class-based revolts against decades of political disenfranchisement and the diversion of all capital and resources to Beirut at the expense of most of the rural population (Diab 1999; Traboulsi 2007). Finally, some have pointed to the role of clientelism through the institutions of *zu'ama*, or village and regional notables (Hourani 1981).

During the war, various factions fought in urban streets, drawing boundaries, ethnically cleansing neighborhoods, and setting up checkpoints to limit mobility and movement (Hanf 1994; Fisk 2002; J. Makdisi 1990). Many of my interlocutors in Lebanon have stories about themselves or someone they know panicking when they reached an unexpected checkpoint manned by a militia belonging to the "other" side. At the time, Lebanese ID cards listed sect as well as name and other identifiers. Militias would use the cards to identify and kidnap, torture, or kill members of "enemy" sects who were caught in the wrong place at the wrong time. All urban mobility was under the control of various factions, with losses and gains of territory the primary means with which to measure power. The war did not merely take place within the space of Beirut. Rather, it was a conflict over space itself. While the Lebanese state was technically still in existence throughout the war, it no longer managed the territories under the domination of different warring political groups within the disintegrating city of Beirut (Sarkis 1993). For the most part citizens were left to negotiate with the militias in control of various parts of the country. Access to services and a relative degree of safety were provided by an array of armed factions that had different degrees of organization and competence to provide these services and maintain basic infrastructure (Davie 1991; Khalaf and Khoury 1993).

Mobility was often restricted during the war. Even when people *could* physically travel to other parts of the city, they often were unable to owing to fears for their own security. Familiar spaces of the city soon became strange and alienating. Separate spheres of residences and consumption were developed (Khalaf 1993). For example, Jounieh, a neighboring town northeast of Beirut, became the center of consumption and leisure activities for middle- and upper-class Christians living on the east side of the city. After the war, some displaced people returned to neighborhoods like Bourj Hammoud. For the most part, however, the war's segregation had a lasting impact on spatial divisions in the city.

The demographic makeup of Bourj Hammoud was radically altered during the early years of the war. After the ethnic cleansing of Naba'a by the right-wing Christian Phalange militia, properties abandoned by displaced Shi'a and some Palestinians were squatted in by Maronite refugees from other parts of Lebanon but also some Armenians. One interlocutor described Bourj Hammoud at the time as a city "surrounded by people fighting each other," with left-wing and pro-Palestinian militias on one side and right-wing Christian militias on the other. Armenian men, and some women, guarded the parameters of the neighborhood with guns.

While state services and infrastructures began to break down, the various Armenian political and religious organizations, NGOs, social service centers, and medical clinics formed a committee called the Azkayin Khorhourt, or National Council, to organize utilities and services as well as provide aid to Armenian residents of Bourj Hammoud (Migliorino 2008). By the 1980s many Armenian organizations located outside of Bourj Hammoud had relocated there. The *arachnortaran*, or prelacy, of the Armenian Apostolic Church relocated to Bourj Hammoud from the historic grounds in the formerly elite Ottoman-era neighborhood of Zokak el-Blatt, and currently maintains both spaces (Papovka 2014). Many of downtown Beirut's Armenian-owned jewelry stores and workshops also eventually relocated to Bourj Hammoud. The arachnortaran's move to Bourj Hammoud further consolidated the spatial nexus of Armenian organizations. Because of the limits to mobility during the war and the growing sectarian divisions of space, Bourj Hammoud went from an Armenian public sphere to a kind of fortress. The Armenian concentration gave Armenian residents a sense of safety, and the highly organized coordination of services across various organizations, whether Tashnag-affiliated, Apostolic, Catholic, or Protestant, provided a vital network for survival.

After the war, many of Bourj Hammoud's displaced residents, mainly Shi'a, were able to regain ownership of their buildings.[44] While many of them did not personally return, they provided a means of migration for non-Armenian renters from their villages, towns, or kinship networks. Thus some Shi'a Muslims have returned to Bourj Hammoud. Many of the apartments in Naba'a are rented to foreign migrant workers, mostly Kurdish and Syrians, and, increasingly, refugees fleeing conflict in Syria.[45] Bourj Hammoud remains a highly diverse district but also one with its own spatial divisions and boundaries. Sectarian political actors throughout Lebanon regard such divisions in space as sites of potential flashpoints and attempt to engineer space in order to maximize security or prepare for the next war (Bou Akar 2012; Fawaz, Harb, and Gharbieh 2012). In this book I argue that these spatial divisions are not wholly fixed, not clearly demarcated, and shaped through the networks of services and materiality of infrastructures that people navigate in their everyday lives. The categories of insider/outsider are much more fluid than they appear when approaching Beirut from the static image of a map.

BEYOND THE MAP: BELONGING IN/AND THE CITY

The vast majority of Beirut's streets have no names and its buildings no addresses. Navigating through new and unknown neighborhoods is a profoundly social experience, drawing on the help of passersby on the street, actively looking around for buildings or streets resembling the directions that someone verbally related. It is rarely a solitary endeavor, as one cannot simply use a street atlas to find anything. Most people navigate using landmarks like churches, banks, or schools. Sometimes buildings are known by a particular name, and one must constantly ask people in the general vicinity of the building where it is.

Early in my fieldwork I tried to use the *Zawarib* street atlas to find a school in Bourj Hammoud.[46] I showed the atlas to one of my interlocutors who grew up in Bourj Hammoud and had spent her entire life navigating its streets. Still, she could not pinpoint where we were on the map I showed her. She tried for a moment to do so and then told me it was a waste of time to use a map; she could just explain how to get there. She proceeded to give me complicated directions involving where to turn left or right using the color and size of particular buildings and the presence of shops and schools to guide me. Through this incident I began to understand why an unfamiliar residential area would be particularly intimidating to navigate for the uninitiated. Walking through Bourj Hammoud and knowing its streets was a deeply embodied, social experience for those who grew up there and was definitely part of the shaping of their social identities.[47]

Many of my interlocutors had a sense of belonging to a neighborhood and an intimate familiarity with one part of the greater Beirut area streets that was linked to a sense of belonging and identity that did not always map neatly onto sectarian identity alone.[48] For example, while Bourj Hammoud was an important hub for Armenian political, social, medical, cultural, and educational organizations and institutions, its residents were mainly working-class artisans, shoemakers, tailors, or mechanics. Wealthier, professional Armenians tend to reside in more upscale suburbs to the northeast, even if they do work in Bourj Hammoud. These differences will be explored further in later chapters, but I mention them here to make the case that space and place matter, and that there are important differences between the Armenians who identify as being from Bourj Hammoud and those who seek to distance themselves from its reputation as a "low-class," insular Armenian "ghetto." These differences, in turn, have ramifications in terms of access to Armenian-run services, recourse to legal rights to property, as well as radically different experiences of navigating urban infrastructures in general. Belonging to a sectarian community is not a priori to other differences of access in terms of class, notions of gender propriety, and normative sexuality.

Urban planners and municipality actors in Bourj Hammoud are certainly aware of the power of the density of Armenian organizations and institutions that create and reproduce a sense of an Armenian public sphere. The "city" has long been viewed as a particular kind of spatial-temporal nexus, connected to notions of modernity, processes of capitalist production, and the instantiation of the power of the nation-state (Harvey 1985; Lefebvre 1991; Mumford 1968; Park and Burgess 1925), as well as a material to be manipulated and engineered in order to achieve a hygienic, ordered, and modern society (Holston 1989; Le Corbusier 1929; Rabinow 1989). The desire to maintain the Armenian dominance of Bourj Hammoud is important to understanding what informs municipality actors in their infrastructure improvement projects.

Popular discourses promote the idea that sects must have separate social networks in order to maintain "security" because they are assumed to be in conflict with one another from the beginning. However, it is important to be attentive to the fact that these networks can rapidly generate identifications if not identities, and they might be more contingent than people think.

A closer look at the human/material networks that form the infrastructures that power Bourj Hammoud helps to unravel the notion that sectarian space and identity are rigid and unchanging. The city is "an ordering of uncertainty and as a political arena full of potentialities" (Amin and Thrift 2002, 5). It is with this spirit that I argue that the possibility for all kinds of alliances and collaborations exists, even as many of them are threatened with foreclosure by certain sectarian political institutions.

METHODOLOGIES AND VISUAL COLLABORATIONS

Infrastructures are not a static diagram of relations between individuals or sectarian political formations, nor are they merely conduits through which sectarianism flows. Rather, the materiality of what these infrastructures are and what they mean to the subjects who navigate and experience them in everyday life are critical to the project of producing sectarian community. Just as a child excitedly shouts "Ijit al dawleh!" (The state is here!) when electricity from the national grid starts to flow, the breakdown of infrastructures is that which "makes them more visible, calling into being governments' failed promises to their people as specters that haunt contemporary collapse" (Larkin 2008, 245). In Lebanon, the perception of breakdown and failure as well as "success" hinges on the apprehension of infrastructures and the attribution of their function to a state, a political party, or a sectarian community, with much overlap between the three. Infrastructures are "conceptually unruly" because of their duality as objects that serve the purpose of circulating other things, or "matter that enable the movement of other matter" (Larkin 2013, 329). The visibility of infrastructures themselves, their histories and the ways in which they are made visible or invisible at particular times, not merely an analysis of the resources that circulate within them, is critical to unpacking the histories that make and remake the ongoing process of producing sectarian community.

It is this attention to visibility and sensorial experience of the city that informed my approach to fieldwork. I spent months videotaping Bourj Hammoud with the help of several of my interlocutors. While I had initially approached my filmmaking practice as observational, filming became a much more dynamic process.[49] My camera served as an important site of collaboration, a staging ground for eliciting memories and rethinking the mundane infrastructures of everyday life together.[50] One particular example illustrative of this collaborative process occurred early on in my fieldwork. I was filming in Nor Marash, a neighborhood within Bourj Hammoud where I conducted much of my research. As I focused my lens on the tangled wires hanging from the walls, a woman in her seventies whom I had spoken with on a few occasions peeked her head out of a doorway and asked

me, amusedly, why I was filming a wall. When I told her I was filming the
electricity cables, we eventually started talking about *ishtirak*, the system
through which individuals can purchase electricity from private generator
owners. She then recalled the days before ishtirak existed, before the civil
war of 1975–90. This was a conversation I rarely had, as the decades of war
and its aftermath had completely normalized the presence of two or more
sources of electricity for most people in Lebanon—the national grid, the
ishtirak, and, for some who lacked the resources for their own subscriptions
and could elude getting cited for doing so, the sharing of electricity between
two apartments. In this and many other incidents, the camera was a catalyst
for conversations about the material and tacit infrastructures of the city, evok-
ing memories and helping to make visible that which had become mundane
in my interlocutors' attempts to familiarize me with the neighborhood. My
interlocutor's memories about the days before one had to navigate multiple
sources of electricity helped me visualize the most elusive questions about
power, networks of patronage and flows of knowledge, and how all these are
inseparable from the materiality of the built environment and the processes
through which urban infrastructures are produced.

Aside from extensive filming in the streets and alleys of Bourj Hammoud
with the help of several of my interlocutors, I conducted more traditional
participant observation and interviews. I refer to my interlocutors using

Figure I.5. A tangle of electricity cables, a common sight in Bourj Hammoud
and in many urban areas in Lebanon. Photo by Rosy Kuftedjian.

pseudonyms, and I have altered incidental details of interlocutors' lives to maintain their anonymity. Most of the fieldwork leading to this book was conducted between 2008 and 2011. I conducted participant observation and interviews in and nearby Bourj Hammoud in nonprofit organizations and NGOs that are affiliated with Armenian religious or diasporic groups, agoumps, the arachnortaran, the offices of the municipality, the regional property deed office, three low-income housing projects, the informal Armenian areas of Sanjak and Arakadz, workshops, retail stores, homes and apartments, as well as Armenian newspapers, printing presses, and organizations outside of Bourj Hammoud proper. I also conducted research at the libraries of Haigazian University, the American University of Beirut, and the Institut français du Proche-Orient. Some of my most important insights, however, came from informal conversations and observations from friends who spent all their lives in Bourj Hammoud and from introductions to their wider network of friends and kin. Through the electricity cuts and the water shortages, I learned how people manage to piece together the fragmented infrastructures through the activation of human relationships, producing the dynamic network of Bourj Hammoud.

MAP OF THE BOOK

This book navigates the human and material infrastructures and services that produce a sense of belonging, sometimes sectarian, in and through the urban district of Bourj Hammoud. To unpack popular discourses about sectarianism and conflict in the wake of the past ten years of significant geopolitical regional shifts, I begin in chapter 1 with a closer examination of a new "sectarian conflict" emerging along the fault lines in space in Bourj Hammoud. This conflict led to the mass eviction of Syrian Kurds from certain parts of the municipal district. In the chapter, I trace how violence is often interpreted as a reemerging sectarian conflict that is both entrenched and inevitable immediately after it begins.

The next three chapters focus on various municipal technologies, nonprofits, and lending institutions to show that the sectarian "community" is not a naturalized social category that is simply represented by these institutions. Rather, it is a networked system with differential access to those claiming "Armenianness" through various means not narrowly limited to religious-ethnic identity. In chapter 2, I focus on the permanently temporary housing regimes of two Armenian refugee camps in order to examine the various technologies that municipality and political actors use to mobilize notions of belonging to the "community" through informal property. These processes are deeply related to specific urban histories and class associations with particular neighborhoods as well as sets of documentation and other legal technologies. Chapter 3 focuses on the role of notions of gendered propriety in differentiating access to Armenian women's organizations in Bourj Hammoud, which has important ramifications in accessing services and resources as well as understandings of belonging to the Armenian community. Chapter 4 compares an officially licensed credit facility to informal women's rotating credit associations. How might official credit institutions foreclose the possibility of crosscutting patterns of lending outside of sect-affiliated channels?

Chapter 5 jumps beyond the neighborhood scale to a city-to-city collaboration between Bourj Hammoud and a foreign municipality as a means of challenging Lebanese state infrastructure projects. I analyze the ways in which the overlapping jurisdictions of power go far beyond the fragmented infrastructures of the neighborhood block to transnational circulations of expertise and resources. In doing so, I demonstrate how the popular notion that Lebanon's infrastructural *and* conflict-oriented problems could be solved through a strong centralized state *or* through the ideology of decentralization completely ignores the way that municipal governance works through overlapping jurisdictions. While Lebanese centralized state-sponsored infrastructure projects have had a destructive impact on environmental and social conditions in Bourj Hammoud, municipality-endorsed initiatives have often been equally destructive. Chapter 5 navigates the delicate balancing act made by one urban planning expert as she tries to draw in outside experts through city-to-city collaborations to block some of the more damaging projects.

As I learned throughout my fieldwork, unexpected consequences are often just as important to the unfolding of these various projects as the intentions of their architects. The Syrian conflict, which was just beginning during the course of my fieldwork, has now escalated into a full-scale war, displacing at least one million Syrians to Lebanon. In my conclusion, I describe the ways in which many displaced Syrians in Lebanon have had to navigate the existing networks of services and aid in order to receive vital relief. As major international organizations use sect-affiliated clinics and social service centers as distribution hubs for various forms of aid and assistance for refugees, it is even more critical to think about the ways in which these institutions function within the political space of Lebanon. As the term "sectarian conflict" is presented by way of explanation for conflicts in Syria and Iraq, it is important to think about how that concept is produced, how it circulates, and what it means in different contexts. At a certain point, approaching something as always already sectarian and creating the infrastructures, institutions, and channels to accommodate it are part of the way in which it gets produced as inevitable in the first place. It is my hope that with more careful scholarship, we can demonstrate that even the most entrenched-seeming identity categories are constructed through far more contingent networks than we realize.

Chapter 1

ALL THAT ENDURES FROM PAST TO PRESENT

Temporality, Sectarianism, and a "Return" to Wartime in Lebanon

It was an excruciatingly hot August afternoon, and Araxi, an Armenian architect in her forties, suggested we go out to the balcony of her apartment in a wealthy, mainly Christian suburb north of Beirut. I was intrigued by Araxi's perspective as one of the returned expatriates who had spent many years abroad. Given her general optimism, and her decision to move back to Lebanon in 1995, I was surprised to hear her say: "I know it could happen again at any moment. At any second, it could all fall apart again." Araxi's observation that "it could happen again" underscores the insights of many of my interlocutors about the inevitability of a return to war and violence in Lebanon.[1] While some might attribute the return of violence to unresolved sectarian tensions, the open-endedness of her remark, "*it* can happen again," leaves some room to ask: what exactly is it that "returns" when violence erupts once again? Why are various conflicts perceived as repetitions even when the conditions, stakes, and positions of actors involved are novel and emergent?

I argue that it is essential to delink the notion of sectarianism from rigid and immutable forms of identity and instead focus on the ways in which various municipal technologies, nonprofits, and lending institutions help to produce notions of sectarian community or exclusion. In this chapter, however, I take a closer look at the way in which political actors and popular discourses mobilize sectarianism as an explanation for conflict as well as justification for actions taken in the aftermath of violence, creating a sectarian narrative that appears rigid, intractable, and deeply historical. Moreover, the sectarian explanation appears to give it a sense of unending repetition.

The aftermaths of three violent incidents that took place in Beirut in recent years shape my analysis: a 2009 fatal shooting in a Beirut neighborhood that was quickly forgotten, a larger street clash in Beirut in 2010 that was perceived as a harbinger of political instability, and a fight in 2011 in Bourj Hammoud that launched a large-scale eviction of Kurdish and Syrian migrant workers. This final example, the one I explore in most ethnographic detail, reveals just how a wholly new kind of "sectarian conflict" (between Armenians and Syrian-Kurds) emerges as an explanation in the aftermath of a violent incident. This sectarian explanation incorporates some traces of the past, as though causality for violence can be found in an immutable, repeating history. The explanation is a retrospective one that is novel and emergent, though it immediately appears as evidence of a generations-long animosity.

Through the unfolding of a violent incident, government officials, the military, sectarian political factions, and ordinary people take up the traces of various pasts into the folds of projects in the present. Such an incident, when refigured in familiar sectarian language, is instrumental in creating a dangerously bounded sense of community with clearly defined "outsiders." Of course that very act of exclusion is highly productive, not only in terms of producing boundaries about who and what constitutes "community" but also about the boundaries in and of urban space and notions of the "neigh- borhood" as the (sometimes violent) expression of that sense of community belonging. While there are other forms of belonging at play, all are made secondary to the discourse of awakened sectarian conflict. Nevertheless, the traces of the past that are used to create a solid sense of community in times of perceived crisis cannot be interpreted as the remnants of an ever-repeating primordial past. While violence in Bourj Hammoud, and Lebanon in general, may look cyclical, it is nonetheless also a new and emergent occurrence. In the incidents I will describe later in the chapter, enduring pasts like the Armenian genocide and the ethnic cleansing of the Lebanese civil war are evoked in order to shape action toward the future. Even when a past as solid and real as these catastrophic incidents appears to serve as evidence against which the present can be understood and evaluated, it is always read through the lens of the present and an intentionality to shape the future and is thus full of its own layers of representations. This is not to suggest or downplay the very real affective response to the evocation of this past, nor does it take away from the reality of the still present and enduring traumas of genocide and war. Rather, it is to suggest that the affective responses are part of the way in which people actively understand and shape their present actions and imagine the future. Memory is not a singular, unitary force acting from a fixed point in the past to manipulate people in the present.

Even beyond Lebanon, ethnic or sectarian conflict is often cited as a go-to explanation after violence breaks out.[2] In the aftermath of violence, agents, observers, and analysts revive a set of scripts to explain what is underway. That said, once activated, discursive formations of ethnic hatred or vengeance are not just reenacted. Rather, actors evoke various pasts in different ways to justify certain kinds of responses to violence in the present, as well as to mobilize particular visions for the future. Recurrent violence between sectarian political factions does not express fixed, unchanging relations between the past, present, and future (Bergson 1929, 1984; Mead 2002). Recurrent conflict is neither repetitive nor predictable—even if it draws on established scripts—because it is not the manifestation of eternal, primordial sectarian hatred or vengeance rooted in a distant unchanging past. Henri Bergson's notion of duration (*durée*) can help us here.[3] Popular collective narratives of past events endure and serve to justify particular notions of the present and to set in motion particular futures. Indeed, Bergson's notion of duration helps us rethink the cause-and-effect relations given by prevalent discourses about sectarianism, in which an ancient, violent past creates the inevitable conditions for the present. It is particularly useful when considering the relationship between the multiple histories of the past and individual memories of violence in the construction of identity in the context of Lebanon. Focusing on the subjective experience of time and memory is an important aspect of understanding processes of violence, particularly those that are portrayed as repetitive (Kleinman, Das, and Lock 1997). As George Herbert Mead shows us, the past is always interpreted through multiple layers of other "pasts." The past, in other words, can be experienced only through representational layers that build over time and accrue other significances. Every emerging present creates new pasts, and there is always a reconstructive element to understanding the past in relation to the present. This is not to deny the past's "irrevocability." Rather, it unsettles the permanence of particular interpretations of the past, the state of "what it was" that can change in relation to the emergent present (Mead 2002).

Perhaps because of the lack of an official state history of the civil war, the politics of memory are an intense focus of debate in Lebanon.[4] Memory work and memorialization function in a way that makes history or "histories" available and real again, though the ways in which they can be resurrected are, in some sense, contingent. What looks like a pattern of sectarian violence, a cycle of endless evictions, displacements, ethnic cleansing, and genocide, is called into vision, seemingly out of thin air, from a repository of violence. While maintaining this concept of repetition, it is still possible to imagine violence emerging, repeatedly, in the same place, even potentially involving the same actors, without it being the *same* violence. What looks like a pattern, like a "return" to war, is more likely a return to "wartime," a kind of temporality with productive capacities to rework, dissolve, or intensify different kinds of relations or realize certain futures. This familiar temporality may look like the same, endlessly repeated loop of retribution or vengeance doled out in cycles, what some call "sectarian violence," an explanation that seems to emerge from the past and is always used to describe conflict in Lebanon.

HISTORIES OF SECTARIANISM, TRACES OF CONFLICT

Like most places in Lebanon, Bourj Hammoud bears the scars of violent conflict. Bullet holes pockmark the sides of buildings, and splatter-shaped masses of brick plug up the holes left by shells, rockets, and mortar fire. During the first few months of my fieldwork, I found it was easier to notice these scars on buildings and walls. Whenever I would look at a cluster of bullet holes, I would imagine the sounds and sights of the moment they were made. What kind of battle was taking place when the person holding the machine gun fired on this mass of lifeless concrete? Even when I couldn't imagine a complete kind of scenario, I would think about the time that these battle scars point toward. On the one hand, bullet holes in Bourj Hammoud are signifiers whose interpretation depends on context, on who is seeing them, on who is seeing past them or ignoring them as part of the normalized landscape. On the other hand, however, as indices of the bullets that made them, they maintain their signification—they always point back to the moment of their making by an instrument of death or war. Charles Peirce (1902, 2.304) uses the bullet hole as an example of an index, which is "a sign which would, at once, lose the character which makes it a sign if its object were removed, but would not lose that character if there were no interpretant." While the bullet holes indicated that *something* violent had transpired, the context of that incident and the sign of the bullet hole could refer to a number of different objects depending on the viewer's knowledge, position, and sense of cause-and-effect relations.[5] For example, the bullet hole could serve as a sign of the breakdown of a state, the presence of a particular political faction or militia, a Russian-made Kalashnikov or an American M16, and all the broader connotations of these competing technologies of war in the Middle East in the context of the 1970s and 1980s. The sense I had of trying to piece together the moment when those bullet holes were made was facilitated not only through a careful reading of visual "evidence." Photographs, anecdotal stories, films, and my imagination filled in the gaps of experience and my understanding of cause-and-effect relations—what sort of object produced this sign? Whatever past was there, it was immediately compounded with a number of other representations.

I stopped noticing the bullet holes and other war damage after a time, like most people who live or work in Beirut. I did not willfully ignore them; they simply receded to the background along with all the other sights and sounds of the everyday. When things started to become mundane, it wasn't that these traces became invisible to me. Rather, I didn't make an attempt to see them. They were always visible, though they just didn't seem as relevant as other sights, sounds, and smells in my immediate vicinity. They didn't prompt me to imagine what had transpired to create that scar; I simply didn't try to access that imaginary. The traces, in a sense, seemed to lose

Figure 1.1. A building bearing the scars left by bullets. Photo by Rosy Kuftedjian.

their urgency through daily viewing. Noticing the bullet holes again would require some kind of event or effect that would draw my attention back to their probable causes.

Sometimes the evidence of war is made visible again through the mundane structures of daily life. The physical infrastructure of Bourj Hammoud, which never fully recovered after the war, is one such example. It is impossible to walk through the district without noticing the abundance of electricity cables, low-hanging wires crisscrossing above narrow intersections, snaking along the sides of buildings and coalescing dramatically into boxes where one can access ishtirak, a subscription to a privately owned generator. The enormous garbage mountain directly adjacent to the fisherman's port, where garbage was hastily piled up during the war, is another highly visible (and smelly), example. Both the proliferation of ishtirak electricity cables and the ongoing presence of the garbage mountain are not only a result of the Lebanese wars but also perpetuated through forms of bureaucratic theft that continue to compromise systems like electricity distribution. Decades after the start of the war in the 1970s, constant electricity and water shortages and pollution of the seafront and the air have become mundane realities. The electricity cables, and their relationship to wartime, are *made invisible* through routine and habit. At key moments, however, municipal officials can again make things like the garbage mountain visible by drawing attention to them to do certain kinds of work, such as attracting funding or expertise from transnational bodies like the EU, the World Bank, or Euromed for environmental improvement projects.

Most traces are not hidden from view, their histories or underlying relationships obscured from an unknowing public. I suggest that we can think about Beirutis' or Bourj Hammoud residents' relationship to those traces not as a direct visual clue but as part of a broader "field of consciousness" (Mead 2002). Their relationship to such traces includes an excess of associations to different pasts evoked by memories of personal experiences, stories told by others, as well as photographs and films. For Mead, there is no stable *past* of which to speak. Rather, "this past extends indefinitely, there being nothing to stop it, since any moment of it, being represented, has its past, and so on" (6). Thus, even when these traces are made visible at particular moments, and can appear to serve as evidence of the repetition of sectarian conflict, it is not a stable past repeated but a past with its own excesses and layered histories of representations.

The ability to see, to not see, or to ignore the traces of conflict is based on different sorts of lived experiences of being in the right (or wrong) place at the right time—a time in the past, a time in the continuously emerging present, a time in the imagined future. A trace might be patched up and made invisible to others, but more often, things could be made explicit through a story, a memory recounted to another, which would make the trace visible. One longtime Bourj Hammoud resident pointed out the corner of a now repaired ceiling where a shell had broken through the wall, destroying half of his apartment. After he pointed it out, I could see where the wall had been patched, a thin crack remaining as the only evidence of the great violence that had brought down that wall. It then became impossible to *not* see it, even if it did not always have the same effect on me; it was no longer invisible. In other instances, the invisibility of war's traces did not depend on a trompe l'oeil of plaster and paint. A friend of mine could not cross the old bridge connecting Bourj Hammoud with Beirut without recalling how his father, a taxi driver who risked his life to collect the large sums garnered by a fare across this once deadly bridge, was killed by a sniper's bullet. Visibility, in this instance, depended on having been present at a certain place and time.

The traces of conflict are always there, densely multiplied and layered, accessible, not locked into a distant past but not always brought together or all simultaneously made visible. It takes a certain kind of moment, a particular sort of trigger, to awaken these various temporalities and make them coalesce, if only for a short time, to make things visible and suddenly all too clear.[6] Moments of cohesion are marked by times when actors share a sense of casual processes, of what caused the bullet holes in the first place, though even these explanations can and do shift and change. Clarity, however, can sometimes be more destructive than murk, particularly when it makes visible and material the histories of displacement and ethnic cleansing so abundant in Bourj Hammoud and makes them available and real again. Some argue that the lack of an official accounting of Lebanese history disables the possibility of any real and lasting peace between various groups who participated in the war. However, the nature of the recent conflicts has shifted away from the configuration of the civil war era. While some of the same leaders of militias who fought against each other during the war have returned to lead sectarian political parties, the factions and their political alignments have changed considerably. It is unlikely that a state-sanctioned, official attempt at civil war reconciliation would be able to assuage these factional shifts between different sectarian political parties.

Still, despite these major shifts, many recent eruptions of violence are still interpreted as outbursts of sectarian animosity, though in ways that were very different from those of the civil war years. Rather than reading into these events a kind of repetition, it is also possible to see how actors actively reach back into the past, or in this case a historical explanation mobilized in the past, for the resources to explain the present and shape the future. Bergson's concept of duration helps to position the past as part of a continuum, neither cyclical nor linear, which contains the conditions of possibility not only for the present as it is currently lived and experienced but also for a number of other possible presents and futures (Bergson 1929, 1984). This *virtual* past, in Bergson's terms, contains the resources or potential for the likewise virtual future. Bergson stresses the open-endedness of becoming against the interpretation that would look to a virtual past for validation of the present as inevitable. This backward-looking reconstruction of the potentiality of the past is something done after the fact, to give the effect of a dominant potential in the past that determines the present. The past is not a deterministic line pushing out inevitabilities that are identified as such only later on.[7] For this reason, various shifts in the context of the past ten years of Lebanese politics, while appearing continuous with older rifts, must be read within the relatively recent geopolitical context of the region.

TEMPORALIZING VIOLENCE: FLASHPOINTS AND INTERPRETATION

In popular media and Lebanese popular discourse, much of the political stalemate in Lebanon in the past decade has been attributed to the conflict between the two main opposing political factions: "March 14," a coalition of parties in alignment with the Future Party, affiliated with the Sunni sect and led by the son of the assassinated former prime minister Rafic Hariri, and

"March 8," a coalition of opposition parties, including Hizbullah (affiliated with the Shi'a sect) and Tashnag.[8] While there are Christian parties in both coalitions, the split is perceived in Lebanon and elsewhere as Sunni-Shi'a. On one level it is a conflict between Sunni-Shi'i political parties in Lebanon, but the conflict cannot be reduced to differences related to those identities. Even when my interlocutors acknowledged the conflict, they did not attribute it to long-standing animosities between the two sects. The conflict in Lebanon is about very particular conditions, and it happens, for the first time in Lebanon's history, to have played out along Sunni-Shi'i lines partially because those are the lines of division in relation to other geopolitical and local economic and political issues in this particular historical moment. The Sunni-Shi'i conflict needs to be understood within the context of Saudi ascendency in regional politics as well as the polarity between Saudi Arabia and Iran, and the ways in which the March 14 and March 8 factions were split between their support of (and backing from) Saudi Arabia, Syria, and Iran.[9] With few exceptions, my interlocutors identified the conflict as a very recent one, having to do with geopolitical shifts or "meddling outside forces" such as the United States and Iran.

In May 2008 the most extensive fighting since the civil war era erupted on the streets of Beirut between March 8 and March 14 forces after a nearly two-year buildup of animosity over several issues, including the right to veto power in Parliament as well as the handling of the tribunal investigating the assassination of former prime minister Hariri. This incident, which is sometimes referred to as Hizbullah's "takeover" of Beirut, shocked and surprised many who until that point had not imagined that Beirut's airport and streets would again be shut down by internal fighting. While an agreement was reached on May 21 that officially ended the conflict, there have been sporadic clashes since then. Though I do not attribute all neighborhood disputes to this divide, at times relations between members loyal to March 14 and March 8 factions have been tense. Occasionally this tension has erupted into full-scale street battles. The uprisings in Syria have only intensified these tensions, as the March 8 and March 14 factions have expressed support for different sides of the conflict, with March 8 supporting the governmental forces of Bashar al-Assad and March 14 supporting the opposition. With the emergence of groups like the Islamic State, or ISIS, the "pro-Western" Future Party has made efforts to publicly distance itself from some of these radical Islamist groups, though it still officially takes an anti-Assad stance. Hizbullah, on the other hand, has taken an active role in supporting government forces within Syria.

I recount these examples with much caution, as there is a tendency to overattribute any dispute in neighborhoods with a large population of both Sunnis and Shi'a to a political rift dividing Sunni and Shi'a residents. This is a slightly different yet related problem in dealing with the Sunni-Shi'a conflict as it is perceived and represented in Lebanon, whereas elsewhere the assumption is that people are fighting over religious ideas. Sometimes, however, attributing a clash to this split is simply inaccurate, as was the case in my first ethnographic example of the aftermath of a violent incident that occurred in a Beirut neighborhood called Aisha Bakkar in 2009. In the Heathrow airport en route to Beirut in June 2009, I was sitting beside a visibly agitated woman who turned to me at one point and said: "Did you hear what happened?" This woman lived in an area adjacent to Aisha Bakkar and was worried that a repeat of the 2008 clashes would flare up in her neighborhood. When I told her that it appeared to be an isolated incident, she responded: "That's how it always starts, with a shooting, and then it spreads."

Despite the fears of my fellow passenger, we flew to Beirut and disembarked without incident. The airport seemed to be functioning as usual, my taxi driver said nothing of the incident, and there were no additional checkpoints or anything remarkable on the streets. A day later the local news reported that the shooting was part of a "family dispute," and the only fatality was a woman caught in the crossfire who was also the sister-in-law of the gunman. No further explanation was given, and the whole incident, which had emblazoned the headlines of international news a mere day before, disappeared into obscurity. For every dispute that ends up being interpreted as a flashpoint for a conflict between the two major political factions, there are perhaps dozens of disputes that are quickly forgotten because they cannot as easily be mapped onto such a discourse of sectarian or ethnic violence. It is no wonder that the incident above, glossed as domestic violence, was safely condemned to the "private" sphere of the family, distinguished from the "real" politics of the state, and relegated to the backwater of history.[10] The incident was interpreted as a "family" dispute and safely filed away as a "nonsectarian," and thus less dangerous, conflict.

For both journalistic accounts of conflict and Lebanese popular discourses, a violent incident would have to be glossed as "sectarian" to serve as a flashpoint plunging Lebanon into war. Of course a "flashpoint" event can be recognized only in retrospect. Whatever doesn't fit into that narrative, or cannot be neatly classified as "sectarian," has not been woven into popular understandings of the past, or an official history. Lebanese will probably not memorialize the aforementioned event in popular discourse as the determining precursor to the present moment, or as the necessary precondition for the present. Identifying a moment as a flashpoint involves the retrospective reconstruction of a virtual past, in the Bergsonian sense, literally a reaching back rather than a mundane march forward.

The way in which my fellow passenger had initially imagined the Aisha Bakkar incident as a flashpoint incident that would spread violence across the city reminded me of the often-cited incident that "sparked" the civil war of the 1970s and 1980s: the shooting of a bus of mainly Palestinian civilians by

the right-wing Phalange militia in 1975. In the Lebanese popular imagination, this incident is remembered as a breaking point beyond which Lebanon
was plunged into a decade and a half of darkness and violence. Lebanese
filmmaker Ziad Doueiri depicted the bus massacre at the beginning of the
film *West Beirut* (1997). The scene is framed by the point of view of the main
character, a teenage boy just thrown out of his classroom for a pun that the
teacher interpreted as insolent toward the French language and, more important, the French "civilization." After he is thrown out of class, he walks
out onto the open-air hallway and looks down at the street to see gunmen
in balaclavas surround a bus and kill the men, women, and children inside.
The young man's loss of innocence coincides with this horrific moment that
seems to plunge Lebanon into an irreversible path to war while connecting
it concretely to Lebanon's French Mandate past. The notion that such a
moment can usher in a return to violence is one that has some purchase in
the popular media, both in Lebanon and abroad.

The second of the violent incidents that occurred during the course of my
fieldwork was interpreted in quite a different way. In August 2010 a minor
clash broke out between members of rival factions in Bourj Abi Haidar, a
neighborhood where the majority of residents are Sunni and Shi'a. According
to rumor and Lebanese news reports at the time, what started as a dispute
over a parking space quickly escalated into an armed battle, much larger
than the dispute in Aisha Bakkar mentioned above. An air of tension spread,
as the sound of rocket-propelled grenades and gunfire echoed over the city.
Some were particularly alarmed because the fighters involved were members
of a smaller Sunni group not directly affiliated with the Future Party and
the Shi'a party Hizbullah. The Lebanese Army was deployed to assuage the
situation, but apparently it was the leadership of the two groups in conflict
that ended the dispute. Within a few hours everything was quiet, and the
two parties issued a joint statement that the clashes were not sectarian or
political in nature. Still, despite the statement, many of my interlocutors
saw the Bourj Abi Haidar incident as a potentially destabilizing one, or an
ominous sign of things to come, because it had involved members of Sunni
and Shi'a parties. Rumors, conjecture, and theories of all kinds continued to
circulate for weeks. By contrast, the Aisha Bakkar incident, as it was related to
a "domestic" dispute, was filed away as "nonpolitical" and quietly forgotten.

Such flare-ups, then, are not entirely uncommon in Beirut. Some incidents are sparked by rising tensions between members of opposing political factions. But there are many other motivations that could incite a local
dispute—disputes between friends or neighbors, or even feuds between large,
"important" families. Any number of things could create the conditions
for violence. But even when many of my interlocutors in Bourj Hammoud
tended to attribute a clash to sectarian tension, most agreed that sectarian
political affiliations are always shifting. Most framed the dispute between

March 8 and March 14 within the same discourse of outside "meddling"—interference by the United States, France, Russia, Iran, or any number of powerful nation-states they imagined were manipulating their local clients to wage proxy wars. This explanation has long been used to explain the atrocities of the civil war era. Tracing the ever-shifting alliances does not require a long memory because most political parties in Lebanon have rapidly changed affiliations, usually more than once. The disputes between parties are rarely organized along the same factional lines. In fact, the factional alliances appear and disappear, rearranging the political landscape and remaking factional relationships and political imaginaries. Many of the parties today were not even in existence a few decades ago. Though these disputes are often between members of different religious sects, they are not motivated by religion or ancient animosities. In fact, the tension apparent in mixed Sunni-Shi'a neighborhoods in Beirut is relatively recent, having little to do with any kind of innate animosity between the sects. Rather this tension can be understood only within the past decade of Lebanese politics in a context where a U.S.-Saudi versus Iranian-Syrian polarization has become a key register through which politics in the region plays out.

LOOKING TO THE PAST TO SHAPE THE FUTURE

To challenge the ways in which the Shi'a–Sunni "split" has been used recently as a deterministic explanation for violence, it is crucial to take a closer look at the histories that get picked up in making the dispute seem not only ancient and unending but also directly attributable to sectarian violence today, across a number of very different contexts (Iraq, Lebanon, Bahrain).[11] It is essential to look at the ways in which certain notions of Shi'a pasts are mobilized in specific contexts at particular times.[12] In Lebanon, Shi'a associated with the politics of resistance to Israeli occupation during the 1980s and 1990s, particularly those sympathetic to Hizbullah, take up the commemoration of the seventh-century battle of Karbala, a foundational moment for Shi'i Islam, in ways that both are novel and sometimes contain echoes of Iranian deployments of this history. The initial split between what were later known as Sunni and Shi'a Islam started after the death of the Prophet Muhammad when there was a divide between the followers of Umar Ibn Al Khuttab, a companion of Muhammad, who became the leader of the community that would be known as Sunni, and followers of Muhammad's son-in-law Ali, who became the leader of the group that would develop into the Shi'a. In 680 CE a political battle took place at Karbala between Caliph Yazid and Husayn, the grandson of Prophet Muhammad and son of Ali, that hastened the distinctions between Ali's followers and the larger Sunni community. It was not until the eighth century, however, with the formation of Shiʻa Islamic jurisprudence that the Shiʻa could be spoken of as a distinct theological and political entity.[13] Husayn was martyred in the battle, an event Shiʻa commemorate on the tenth day of the month of Muharram, which in Lebanon is called Ashura. The battle of Karbala is taken up by Hizbullah in Lebanon in particular ways, in a very specific context that highlights resistance and struggle against the Israeli occupation of South Lebanon in the 1980s and 1990s (Deeb 2006).

Hizbullah and Shiʻa political activists invoke the commemoration of Karbala, through the highly organized "authenticated" Muharram events, not to stoke animosity toward Sunnis but for a number of other aims, ranging from mobilization against occupation to discourses of self-improvement and progress toward "civilization" within what Lara Deeb (2006) calls an "enchanted modern." This enchanted modern, a rethinking of Weberian notions of disenchantment as a precondition of modernity, helps articulate the ways in which continuity and duration are ongoing projects of this particular kind of political Shiʻa thought that is not framed within a discourse of return to a traditional, nonmodern past but is oriented toward a better, more progressive future. For pious Shiʻas in Lebanon crafting a modern political project of resistance, the commemoration of the battle of Karbala becomes a reaching back to the virtual past to find the resources for a still-unfolding future. The crafting of continuity between past, present, and future takes place in the present as part of a distinctly political project. The memory of the battle is not an ancient, primordial call for vengeance against Sunnis. Deeb writes that within the Lebanese context many Shiʻas rely on the battle of Karbala neither to return to the past nor to imagine a definite future. Rather, Karbala is part of the way her Shiʻa interlocutors envision a "non-new future" in the context of a "continuity and constancy of a battle between good and evil that is consistently foreshadowed and re-instantiated in different eras. This was often articulated . . . as the idea that 'there is a Yazid and a Husayn in every time, in every nation, in every era'" (2009: 247).

Likewise, Maren Milligan's (2012, 2014) work on Sunni political identity mobilization in Tripoli is helpful in detangling the deterministic "ancient" sectarian feud explanation for violence into its more complicated political and social causes. In the context of explosive violence in Tripoli, a city in the north of Lebanon that is a major beacon of Sunni political identity mobilization, Milligan (2012) argues that "contending narratives of pain underneath the increasingly sharp tenor of sectarian hate speech" from much more recent histories must be taken into account. In 1986, during Lebanon's civil war, fifteen Syrian soldiers were killed by what the military believed were Sunni Islamists. In reprisal, the Syrian military surrounded the mainly Sunni neighborhood of Bab al-Tabbana and massacred between two hundred and eight hundred people; many Sunnis believe that the ʻAlawi

ADP militia was responsible for carrying out the massacres, though some have disputed this. 'Alawis, too, recount narratives of suffering rooted in the political conflicts of the 1970s and 1980s and recall having to flee Tripoli and 'Akkar to Syria in 1976 (Milligan 2012). Still, the deterministic frame of Sunni versus 'Alawi or Sunni versus Shi'a has been repeated more recently in the context of the Syrian conflict without adequate understanding of how these frames developed within particular networks of political patronage especially during times of conflict, such as the Lebanese civil war. Today the charge that the 'Alawi ADP is working with the Syrian regime against rebels along with a broad coalition that includes Hizbullah only exacerbates the discourse of sectarian rifts as the driving force of conflict. However, it is important to think about how and when sectarian discourse is mobilized in shifting political contexts. Again, it would be incorrect to assign an "ancient" status to these discourses.

For my Armenian interlocutors in Bourj Hammoud, the memory of the Armenian genocide has at times played a similar role in constructing a political identity, a sense of continuity with a past and a different way of constructing a "non-new future," to borrow Deeb's phrasing. The linkages between the Lebanese Shi'a political imaginary and the Lebanese Armenian one are not merely coincidental but spring from a historiography that illuminates marginalization, struggle, and overcoming in the Lebanese political context. For the Armenian political imaginary in Lebanon, it is the genocide that gives Armenian political organizations like the Tashnag Party their images of martyrdom, sacrifice, and struggle. While stories of massacres, starvation, and deprivation abound, there are also many stories of heroic resistance. The doomed defense of Hadjin, a town in Adana province where outnumbered Armenian *fedayee* attempted to fight off Turkish forces in 1922, is one such story.[14] The date that Hadjin fell to Turkish forces is commemorated annually everywhere that Armenians who claim descent from this town reside, from Beirut to Buenos Aires, Baghdad to Pasadena. Narratives like the one about Hadjin are meant to galvanize the possibility of resistance against the odds. Even within the space of the commemoration ceremonies, however, there is a constant slippage between the genocide memories related by the children of survivors (now in their seventies and eighties) and their own personal memories of war and displacement in Lebanon. Many genocide stories conjure up a kind of temporality of struggle, of risking personal safety for the survival of the Armenians. This temporality has been evoked in different contexts, from Tashnag members' narratives of defending Bourj Hammoud during the Lebanese wars of the 1970s and 1980s to the context of the Armenian war with Azerbaijan in Nagorno-Karabakh in the 1990s.[15]

The specters of displacement and the not-so-distant past of the Armenian genocide are ever-present in the Lebanese Armenian political, social, and spatial milieu. Nowhere is this more concentrated than in Bourj Hammoud.

In Armenian schools, churches, official commemoration ceremonies, and everyday language, the history of the genocide is transmitted through talk, text, and the legacy of institutional arrangements, relief organizations, and property regimes of the "camp" and the "temporary" settlement.[16] However, the genocide histories are not experienced as a pure past, unchanged and unadulterated, shot through time and space untransformed. Rather, the past of the genocide is bundled up, in crucial ways, with many other pasts that have to do with their embeddedness in Lebanese political institutions and processes, as well as the creation of an Armenian transnational identity in the diaspora (Schahgaldian 1979; Suny 1993). Even in the attempt to create a standardized history of genocide commemoration, the memory of displacement and the suffering brought about through death, violence, and destruction is always mingling with the Lebanese events of 1958 (in which the two major Armenian political parties, Tashnag and Hnchag launched all-out war against each other and purged each other's members from their respective "territories") and the civil war of 1975–90. The layering of these pasts is built into the institutions and structures of Bourj Hammoud, quite literally in the short buildings erected by Armenian refugees in the 1920s and the bullet holes from the 1970s, but also the Armenian refugee camp Sanjak and the cinderblock buildings that hark back to a different time, another overlapping duration. The duration that began with the genocide never really ended; it mingles with and melds into the other durations of Lebanese conflicts in both affective and material or institutional ways.

For many Armenians involved in political or social organizations in Bourj Hammoud, the affective work of the genocide, which perpetuates memories of suffering, displacement, and death, is often mobilized in very different contexts. The material traces of the war or displacement create a repository of experiences and images from which to interpret the present and shape the future. An Armenian NGO in Lebanon typifies a kind of institutional trace, enduring or unfolding into different forms while still containing its own past. This particular NGO started as an American relief organization that provided health care and sustenance to Armenian refugee children and subsequent generations of Armenian children born in Lebanon, then became an emergency dispensary during the civil war. Today, in addition to pediatric services, it has taken on a model of "self-reliance" and offers vocational training to Armenian women and teenage girls in Bourj Hammoud as a reinterpretation of its initial mission—ensuring the welfare of the "next generation" of Armenians through an intervention with women who will be "future mothers." Now this same NGO also turns its attention to helping Syrian Armenians who have fled the war in Syria.

During perceived moments of "crisis," these traces and their temporalities and intertwined relationships are made more visible, more legible, to those who might otherwise allow them to fade into the background of daily life.

The logics of wartime, of insecurity, of ethnic cleansing (Ottoman, Turkish, and Lebanese) are not awakened from slumber only to return, intact, to haunt the present. Rather, they are activated, actualized from a virtual past in order to make possible a certain kind of future and to retroactively justify a present as inevitable. I turn my attention now to the third ethnographic example of this activation as it played out in the aftermath of a violent incident that occurred during my fieldwork.

A FAMILIAR TEMPORALITY (RE)EMERGES

One night in the fall of 2011 I received an alarming text message from a friend who had heard that a fight between two young men in Bourj Hammoud had escalated. Apparently the fight between the two men—a Kurdish worker and an Armenian—had grown to the extent that the Lebanese Army had to intervene, closing off several nearby streets and effectively trapping residents indoors for the duration of the conflict. My friend was worried that the fight might escalate into a street clash.

It was unusual for the army to be called in to break up a fight in the Nor Marash area of Bourj Hammoud. Sometimes the army might intervene in the Naba'a area, home to many migrant workers, perhaps to settle a dispute between two men with knives rather than rocket-propelled grenade launchers. In these instances the army would act as a kind of riot police, controlling the gathering crowd. No shots would be fired, though quite often non-Lebanese migrant workers would be arrested, as the army and police in general are much more likely to lay the blame on Syrian workers than on Lebanese.[17] In Nor Marash, Arax, or any of the districts adjacent to the main shopping areas of Bourj Hammoud, the Tashnag Party exerts a strong security presence in the form of agoumps, the Tashnag political clubs that serve both as meeting places for a variety of social events as well as an informal police station in each neighborhood. There had been little tension between residents in this part of Bourj Hammoud in the past several decades, and popular discourses do not portray it as a flashpoint area for violence as in other parts of Beirut. It is rare that a full-scale battle would erupt on the streets, perhaps due in part to the fact that Bourj Hammoud is not an area in which the March 8/March 14 split has played out in an obvious way.

Because of the usual stability and also the fact that Tashnag maintains such a strong presence in the area, the Lebanese Army would not normally be called in to intervene in what they would consider a dispute in "Armenian territory," and therefore the responsibility of Tashnag. A Bourj Hammoud *mukhtar*, or locally elected official, once told me that the *darak*, a kind of armed police unit, always defers to the Armenian agoump whenever it handles a dispute involving an Armenian in Bourj Hammoud. The logic that "Armenian" affairs are the responsibility of Tashnag is a very strong current in Lebanon, and not just among my Armenian interlocutors. It is echoed in racist discourses about Armenians as somehow "unassimilated" into Lebanon and autonomous from the state. The fact that the army was called in to break up the fight in Nor Marash was a clear indication that this was no ordinary dispute. Even if the Tashnag Party did not intend to involve the Lebanese state in the aftermath of the fight, in retrospect I realized that the military presence heralded a different sort of reaction.[18]

The next morning, while the fight was over, it was clear that something had changed in Bourj Hammoud. There were no traces of the violence of the night before, but it seemed that everyone I spoke with that day, from the doorman of a social service center where I conducted participant observation to the man selling coffee in the municipality square, was talking about it. There were few details about the nature of the dispute, but the young Armenian man was in the hospital; he was injured but expected to recover. Rumor had it that after the Lebanese Army had shown up to quiet the scene, several Kurdish men were arrested, though no Armenians were implicated in any crime. At the same time, several of my Armenian interlocutors were talking about the "threat" of Kurdish workers. I constantly heard the same refrain about how the area had become unsafe owing to the encroachment of *odar*s (non-Armenians, literally "foreigners" or "others") who had started to leave "their" area of Naba'a and move into the formerly "safe" area of Bourj Hammoud proper.

After the fight there was a major shift in the focus of my Armenian interlocutors' fear of migrant workers. Many of them emphasized the particular threat of Kurds and not Syrians or any other migrant worker community. There was a kind of exceptionalism by which Kurds were perceived as especially dangerous and distinct from Arab Syrian workers. While both groups were citizens of Syria, traveled with similar papers, and occupied similar positions in the Lebanese labor market, Armenian interlocutors tended to single out Kurds as particularly threatening. Most people I spoke with after the fight never mentioned a single Kurdish "man" who was responsible for the violence but rather the threat posed by "the Kurds" as a group that had trespassed over an important social and spatial border.

Non-Armenian Lebanese interlocutors tended not to emphasize the *Kurdishness* of the workers or distinguish them from Syrians as a distinct threat to the safety of their neighborhoods, even those of my interlocutors who live in Naba'a and are surely aware of the fact that most of the migrant workers who live there are Kurds who speak Arabic with a strong Kurdish accent. Rather, non-Armenian residents tended not to distinguish Syrian Kurds and Arab Syrian workers. If non-Armenian interlocutors did regard them as threatening, it was mainly because they viewed single male migrant workers living outside of the normative family context or familiar kinship network as suspicious. Still, in popular Lebanese discourse the term "Kurd" is often used as shorthand for itinerant people with an inflection that might be closer to a derogatory term like "gypsy." While many of my Shi'a and Maronite Christian interlocutors in areas adjacent to or within Naba'a referred to the migrants only as "Syrians," the derogatory connotation of the term "Kurd" would have been familiar to most of them. For many of my Armenian interlocutors, the term "Kurd" could evoke different associations related to the genocide, specifically that Kurds were instrumental in carrying out the Ottoman-era massacres of Armenians as well as assisting in the perpetration of the Armenian genocide on the ground.[19] Despite the fact that most Armenians in Bourj Hammoud are aware of this history, this did not previously translate to open hostility toward Kurds living in the district. Immediately after the fight, however, the involvement of Kurds in the Armenian genocide was invoked as a trace from another time to explain the present and to make a certain kind of future possible.

The gossip about the fight did not simply die down as I expected it would. In the following days and weeks, a number of Kurdish and Syrian workers were evicted from their apartments. At first it was unclear whether these were evictions carried out by the municipality or individual landlords. People told stories about how *all* the Kurds were going back to Syria, that the municipality or the agoump (the shorthand term for the Tashnag Party) had outlawed them from renting apartments in much of Bourj Hammoud (though not Naba'a), and that many had observed workers walking toward Charles Helou, Beirut's main bus station for connections to Syrian cities, carrying suitcases and bags. The details were vague, and there was much conflicting information surrounding what had happened. One interlocutor said that *all* foreign migrant workers without proper documentation of rental leases were being evicted, and that no one with their documents in order would be targeted. However, the activities seemed clearly focused on Syrian workers (particularly Kurds) living in areas that were mainly Armenian in terms of businesses and residents.

The Lebanese media quickly picked up on the story, sensationalizing it further, and attributing the waves of evictions to the Tashnag Party's alignment with the March 8 alliance and the embattled Syrian regime that had much to gain from the eviction or deportation of Kurds back to Syria. A few articles even claimed that the Syrian regime had ordered the Tashnag Party to displace Kurds from Bourj Hammoud and, preferably, to deport them from Lebanon so that the regime could keep better track of its Kurdish subjects back in Syria and prevent them from organizing antiregime activities in Lebanon. An opinion piece in a Lebanese news source suggested that Tashnag had specifically targeted Syrians who had participated in antiregime demonstrations at the Syrian embassy (Jazzini 2011). By connecting the evictions to the burgeoning uprising in Syria, the news outlet effectively scaled up the events, taking them out of the realm of the local and particular into the scale of the Syrian state and its relation to Lebanese political parties like Tashnag. Lebanese and Armenian imaginaries about the power of Syrian surveillance and control would support such a hypothesis. One Armenian interlocutor from Syria once told me: "If Syria wants you, they could find you even in your mother's womb!"

At the time of the fight, the troubles in Syria had gone on for just long enough to convince people that antiregime activists might be organizing in Lebanon. Some people I interviewed—both Bourj Hammoud residents and other Lebanese who were following the developments via news reports—believed that the evictions might have something to do with Syria. Others, however, insisted that the evictions were purely a "local" reaction to the perceived threat posed by Kurdish and Syrian workers moving into the neighborhood. The official party line espoused by Tashnag MPs suggested that what was happening in Bourj Hammoud was merely an enforcement of immigration laws, and Tashnag was by no means targeting Kurds who were protesting in Beirut against the Syrian regime.

I spoke with a Kurdish worker named Agir who was living a block away from where the fight had taken place. This area, very Armenian in composition, was an unusual place for Agir to rent an apartment. While Syrian workers had taken up residence in other parts of Bourj Hammoud, it was still far more common for Kurdish workers to live in Naba'a. While he was not the only worker living on the street at the time, he was the only one who was living with his family. Agir was probably willing to pay much higher rent to live in this part of Bourj Hammoud because it was much less dense in population than Naba'a and closer to services and amenities like the small medical dispensary next door. He and his son, a toddler at the time, would often socialize on the street with the Armenian doorman of the dispensary. His wife had taken her son in to the clinic for vaccinations, and the family was a ubiquitous part of social life on the narrow street.

After learning that a group of five Syrian migrant workers were evicted from a nearby apartment, I was surprised to hear that Agir and his family had also been asked to leave their apartment. There was some confusion at first as to whether Agir had actually been evicted, as he was still living in his apartment several days after the other workers had left. The doorman of the dispensary and I started chatting with a Syrian employee of the workshop downstairs from Agir's apartment, a sewing shop where various articles of clothing were assembled for sale in the local market. When Agir returned from work, he reluctantly confirmed what had happened. Apparently the landlord had given him a sudden notice to leave the building. Agir made plans to leave as quickly as possible. Suddenly this neighbor had been transformed into a stranger to be evicted. Given the history of ethnic cleansing in Bourj

Hammoud's Naba'a area, with Shi'a and Palestinians forcefully evicted by the right-wing Christian Phalange militia in the mid-1970s, the discourse of "others" awakened by the eviction of Kurds from Bourj Hammoud had ominous undertones.

Like most political parties in Lebanon, the Tashnag Party maintained an armed presence during the war (Tölölyan 2000). Many of my Armenian interlocutors beamed with pride at relating how Tashnag members kept Bourj Hammoud safe during the long Lebanese civil war of 1975–90, standing guard under sniper fire at the perimeters of Armenian neighborhoods. Many insisted that sectarian relationships are the only recourse at times of crisis or emergency and justified the evictions as a reasonable measure toward safeguarding one's own sectarian community. It seemed that the othering of Kurds, in this instance, had created the conditions of possibility for elaborating what sectarian relationships mean, or perhaps reevaluating what they *should* or *could* mean in the future.

The evictions took on a particular urgency because of the context of ongoing insecurity in the present that many perceived as a direct line from a traumatic past. Many who were in favor of Kurds being evicted started to contextualize their feelings within older histories of the genocide. I lost count of how many times I heard people say that Kurds were the ones who carried out the genocide and acted as mercenaries; it was they who killed us. Histories of the genocide started blurring into narratives about the Lebanese wars and then again into accounts of violent crimes in Naba'a, directly attributed by my interlocutors to the rise of Kurdish migration into the area. While narrating the many reasons why Kurds should not live in certain areas of Bourj Hammoud, my interlocutors slipped between pasts, weaving them into a new thread, a new temporality that made visible and clear the border separating who and what areas were part of the community and that which was outside. These various traces of different pasts from different contexts were activated in order to frame the present situation not only as a "crisis" but also as a repeated crisis that has "returned" or reemerged as a threat from a distant and not so distant past.

Still, other histories about Kurdish leaders who assisted Armenians during the genocide have reemerged in recent years, particularly in the context of Armenian and Kurdish collaboration in genocide recognition. Revisiting these pasts has meant reevaluating moments of collaboration or affinity between Armenians and Kurds in order to make a particular kind of present or future possible. In 2015 the Gomidas Institute, an Armenian research organization, organized an event in Diyarbakir, Turkey, to commemorate the centenary of the Armenian genocide. One of the activities was to visit the grave of Mihemede Miste, the Kurdish tribal leader who opposed the genocide and assisted Armenians.[20] In 1927 members of the Tashnag Party had signed a pact in Beirut with the newly founded Kurdish Hoybun (Independence) nationalist movement (Tachjian 2004). In the 1920s this collaboration was "vigorously supported" by the Tashnag Party in the diaspora (Baibourtian 2013, 346). Even though Turkish Kemalist forces brutally suppressed the subsequent Kurdish revolts in 1930, the narratives and images of this period served to galvanize a new generation of Kurdish political activism in Turkey by the 1970s (Tachjian 2004).[21]

The conditions of possibility for certain kinds of affinities or political solidarities between Armenians and Kurds are not limited to the afore-mentioned events of the 1920s or 1930s. Just one year before the fight that appeared to irreparably damage relations between Armenians and Kurds in Bourj Hammoud, both joined together to protest Turkish prime minister Recep Tayyip Erdogan's official visit to Lebanon in 2010. On the day of Erdogan's visit, a large group of people walked west from Bourj Hammoud to gather in protest at Martyrs Square, a monument to the men hanged for plotting against Ottoman rule in 1916. In a sea of Armenian and Lebanese flags, Armenian political leaders gave speeches linking their opposition to Turkish denial of the genocide to memories of the hanged martyrs of 1916. A large contingent of Kurds had walked along with the Armenians from Bourj Hammoud carrying Kurdish political flags and banners with images of Kurdish leaders and martyrs. In the spirit of a Bergsonian notion of duration, possibly in some yet-unimagined future, such an affinity might be forged again, particularly if we understand time as plural and nonprogressive. If Lebanon's past is a resource of imagining the future, it contains not only stories of violence and displacement but also unintended consequences. It is with this in mind that we can perhaps read some hope into the openness of the future yet unformed.

UNCERTAIN FUTURES

While some in the Lebanese press speculated that the Bourj Hammoud evictions of Kurdish workers was somehow a veiled attempt to deport potential dissidents who could be organizing against the regime in Lebanon back to Syria, it would be difficult to verify this claim. Of course, this incident was interpreted in the context of a growing conflict in Syria that created much unease and fears about the impact on Lebanon in those early days before it seemed a point of no return had been reached. In 2011 there were very few Syrians displaced to Lebanon due to the conflict, but the situation still cast a shadow on Lebanese fears about what could happen if Syria was consumed by violence. Even if the incident was not related in the way that the Lebanese press speculated, it was still connected to the growing atmosphere of foreboding and fear. At the time of writing, there are over one million officially registered Syrian refugees in Lebanon according to the United Nations High Commissioner for Refugees (UNHCR), though the number

of displaced is likely much higher.[22] The fears of instability threatening
Lebanon as a result of the conflict as well as ongoing racialized and othering discourses about Syrians might only exacerbate their precariousness.[23]
In January 2015 Lebanon issued new restrictions on Syrians' entry to the
country that could curtail most Syrians' ability to enter and stay for more
than a short period of time.[24]

In the aftermath of a fight between two people on the streets of Bourj
Hammoud, the meaning of a particular dispute was expanded beyond an
altercation between two individuals because the traces of various pasts that
endured in Bourj Hammoud (affective, institutional, material) became visible and available again. The specters of genocide, violent displacement, and
ethnic cleansing that are ever present in the everyday life of Bourj Hammoud
residents made it possible to interpret this event as a trigger, indicating that
Kurds pose a danger to the entire Armenian community. In this context,
actors reconsider the past in order to make a particular present outcome
inevitable as well as weave various temporalities into enduring forms that are
renewed and created anew through novel combinations in order to do work
in the present and create the conditions of possibility for particular futures.
Wartime is not only a time of destruction but also a productive moment
that forges new relations between the past and the future. I ask, however, is
it not also possible that a particular reading of the events surrounding the
evictions of 2011 could be accessed in some unknown future in ways that
we are unable to anticipate? The temporality of displacement or wartime
along with its familiar sharp boundaries of who is an acceptable neighbor
and who is included or excluded in one's own "community" was activated
in unexpected ways, through part of an ongoing duration of past evictions,
displacements, and violence. Both continuous and emergent, the temporalities of different forms of eviction and displacement endure.

While traces of various pasts are invoked to make sense of the present,
institutions themselves can also function as traces whose meanings transform
in time. Informal property regimes, for example, are often constructed and
maintained within temporalities of the "permanently temporary," particularly
in the context of Lebanon's histories of displacement and migration. The
precarious temporality of the camp, however, is integral to the maintenance
of political influence in municipal districts and the consolidation of power by
sectarian political parties. In this context, maintaining ownership of property
depends on the ability to make claims of belonging, not only through recourse
to past tenure or ethnoreligious identity alone. The eviction of Kurds and
more specifically their vilification serves to create and reformulate definitions of "community" and relationships between people that might, in other
contexts, be excluded as well. I now turn to the temporalities of belonging
and exclusion that are invoked through the temporary property regimes of
eighty-year-old refugee camps in Bourj Hammoud.

Chapter 2

PERMANENTLY TEMPORARY

Constructing "Armenianness" through Informal Property Regimes

In the summer of 2009 the municipality of Bourj Hammoud launched an outdoor summer photo exhibition, music, and film festival focusing on Armenian cultural production. The festival was held in a former factory's outdoor yard and drew a crowd of nightly visitors in a city with little public space and few free cultural events. The factory yard, with its open space and unpaved gravel surfaces, was a unique setting for an event catering to Bourj Hammoud's Armenian residents. Many large Armenian cultural events were held in the Hamazkayin building, Der Melkonian theater, or one of Bourj Hammoud's many social centers affiliated with either the Tashnag Party or one of the three religious institutions (Protestant, Catholic, or Apostolic), with considerable overlap.

Another major distinction apparent in the cultural event was the content of the photographs on display. Absent were the usual images of Bourj Hammoud's many workshops and jewelry makers that correspond to notions of Armenians as expert craftspeople within Lebanese popular discourse.[1] In fact, municipality actors often engage in these same discourses about Bourj Hammoud in order to position it as a site of Armenian authenticity in other contexts.[2] In this particular exhibition, however, many of the photos depicted were portraits of people who lived in Sanjak camp, the last remaining Armenian refugee camp in Bourj Hammoud, which has been slated for destruction and redevelopment. Unlike the usual photographs highlighting entrepreneurial shoemakers and jewelers, the images of Sanjak camp functioned as a public appeal to the plight of Sanjak residents.[3] Images of elderly people standing in front of semidestroyed homes in a camp that was slowly being demolished by the municipality were interspersed with photographs of children playing in the narrow alleyways between the few cinder block

houses that remained. The night after the opening, one of the subjects of
these photographs approached an interlocutor affiliated with the event to
ask him why his photo was exhibited in the context of a photo essay about
Sanjak. My interlocutor had reassured him that "it was dignified, that he
had dignity in that photo."

Just a few months later, Tamar, a psychologist who worked at an Armenian
social service center in Bourj Hammoud, showed me a photograph of her
grandparents in front of the home they were building in the 1930s in Arakadz.
Named for a mountain in Armenia, Arakadz was another informal settlement
in Bourj Hammoud built by Armenian refugees. Both of her grandparents,
dressed in black, stood in front of a pile of dirt and cinder blocks with serious
expressions. It was with great warmth and pride that she related their story,
how they built the home, which is still standing, and how much time she
spent in their home as a child. In stark contrast to representations of Sanjak
as a place of destitution and hopelessness, images of Arakadz proliferate in
social media and are framed with nostalgia. One popular YouTube video
about Arakadz combines watercolor paintings of the neighborhood with old
photographs as well as contemporary images, including the interior of the
filmmaker's grandmother's abandoned home, set to music. Comments both
from within Lebanon and from Lebanese Armenians who emigrated abroad
expressed gratitude to the filmmaker for sharing these images with them
and reminding them of their own memories of parents and grandparents.

While both Sanjak and Arakadz are informal settlements constructed
during a time when Armenian refugees were still urbanizing what later
became the municipality of Bourj Hammoud, there are stark differences in
the ways they are understood as places of destitution or places of nostalgia.[4]
To examine the dialogic process between the built environment and notions
of community, the owning of one's home and the mobilization of notions
of authenticity and belonging, I focus in this chapter on these two "permanently temporary" Armenian informal settlements. While Sanjak is slated
for destruction, and more than half of it has already been demolished, there
has been little public outcry or discussion in Bourj Hammoud. Arakadz,
on the other hand, while not necessarily protected from the possibility of
eventual destruction, circulates as an image of nostalgia, an important locus
of collective memory for Lebanese Armenians. Both Sanjak and Arakadz are
informal neighborhoods where the municipality has granted Armenians only
temporary property rights, but what accounts for this difference? How do
some people and neighborhoods get excluded and others included through
the mobilization of notions of authenticity, community, and belonging and
the temporary regimes of informal property? While the discourses explaining and justifying violence and eviction in chapter 1 appear to draw lines
around a community in a way that seems entrenched and naturalized, the
very appearance of an Armenian sect as an intact "community" can come

into view only at a moment when there is such a clearly defined "outside." Here the frictions that intersect what appears as a coherent "community" in chapter 1 are foregrounded, as are the exclusions underlying its formation.

During the immediate postwar era, the politics of displacement and resettlement came to the fore amid the rampant redevelopment and rebuilding of downtown Beirut in the 1990s, a moment that anthropologist Aseel Sawalha (2010) captures ethnographically. Sawalha notes that successful bids for resettlement compensation from the Ministry of the Displaced for people displaced during the war tended to work through appeals to sectarian political patrons who occupied positions within state institutions or were connected to state actors, developers, or investors. In the context of intensified real estate speculation in Beirut today, ongoing security of residency in informal settlements, even as it has survived decades of insecurity and violence, is profoundly challenged, making all kind of claims to belonging ever more heightened and critical (Krijnen and Fawaz 2010; M. Fawaz 2009a).

My aim in this chapter is to analyze the various technologies that municipal and political actors use to produce notions of belonging to and exclusion from sectarian community through the mobilization of informal property relations and contracts. As Ananya Roy (2003, 18) writes, forms of informality like squatting can sometimes function as a "mechanism of dominance" rather than a form of resistance. The relationship between property, kinship and belonging is dialogic, and so while sectarian political actors mobilize these technologies in an attempt to draw boundaries, these informal property regimes and the neighborhoods produced by them are also agential in creating a sense of belonging or exclusion from sectarian community as well as other forms of belonging (Maurer 1997). The process of producing normative subjects who belong, and are properly Armenian, is connected to various other discourses about progress and modernity that are reproduced through municipal actors' attitudes toward these "temporary" spaces. Residents' ability to make claims on their properties depend on making claims to belonging to the Armenian community as well as their ability to make claims about their neighborhood's authenticity and historical importance. Armenianness, then, is about more than simply belonging to an ethnoreligious sect. Notions of class, proper domesticity, and gendered propriety underlie the construction of what is normative and who gets to count in the equation where the "greater good" is calculated. Thus a closer look at the way that community is constructed and how the built environment is used to enforce these notions of belonging is vital to understanding how the dialogic process of sectarianizing identities and space works.[5] My interlocutors imagine community not only as something linked to memory and feeling, though constructed through rank, gender, sect, and class, but also as something that can be engineered through space and proven through sets of documentation. Belonging can be perpetuated (or destroyed) through neighborly relationships forged through proximity and time.

The jurisdictional technologies of the municipality, such as the cadastral map and the title deed, are but two instruments at play in the definition of who properly owns what.[6] This is not a story about community forms of ownership that are usurped by municipality maneuverings. Rather, municipal technologies are precisely what enable Sanjak and Arakadz residents to own property, but these same technologies are what could eventually undermine their status as property owners.[7] Furthermore, because Sanjak and Arakadz have different social meanings and occupy different roles in popular histories of the neighborhood, residents of the two camps can make very different sorts of claims of ownership and belonging to varying degrees of effectiveness. The disputes within the municipality and various community leaders as to whether Sanjak camp and Arakadz were sites that needed to be "saved" or "erased" shed light on the processes by which sectarian belonging was constructed, and what kind of community they sought to construct through urban planning techniques and shifting temporary property arrangements.[8] All this takes place within a temporality of the temporary, the not-yet-settled space of the refugee camp.

CAMP SANJAK

Taline walked ahead of me confidently, weaving through the narrow alleyways of Sanjak camp, nimbly stepping over puddles in high-heeled boots. "The worst days of my life were spent in this place," she said loudly, barely audible over the sound of rain hitting the corrugated metal roofs of the shacks, "I haven't stepped foot in here for years." It was a cold and wet December day, and Taline's wide umbrella barely protected us from the sheets of water that seemed to be literally pouring out of the sky. I had visited Sanjak before but never when it was raining. Though the rain had just begun, poor drainage meant that the narrow alleys were already flooding.

Sanjak camp was built in the 1930s by the last wave of Armenian refugees fleeing the sanjak (or administrative district) of Alexandretta in what is now Turkey. By the early 2000s it was the last remaining Armenian refugee camp in Lebanon. Many structures built during the 1930s were still standing, some rebuilt after various waves of shelling in the 1980s but maintaining the same basic structure of cinder block walls and a corrugated metal roof. Starting in 2007 the municipality of Bourj Hammoud had begun tearing down parts of the camp. Sanjak residents told me that owners of each house were offered compensation between $3,000 and $5,000 at the time. Original owners renting the houses to others were forced to accept the fee, and the renters were

Figure 2.1. Sanjak camp. Photo by Rosy Kuftedjian.

evicted without any compensation. The camp had become a focal point of the changes in Bourj Hammoud but also in the greater metropolitan Beirut area. In the context of rampant real estate speculation, land values anywhere near Beirut had sharply risen.[9] By 2008 land values in Bourj Hammoud, particularly those in close proximity to the highway, were up to $2,000 per square meter (Asmar 2008). The camp's proximity to the highway made it an especially attractive location for businesses. The municipality unveiled its plans for the camp early on in the process: a mixed-use residential and shopping center called Saint Jacques, an obvious play on the Sanjak name.

Over strong cups of coffee in the outdoor café in Bourj Hammoud's main square a few weeks before we planned to visit the camp together, Taline told me the story of how she came to live in Sanjak. A mother of two in her midthirties and originally from Aleppo, Syria, she had spent her first several years in Lebanon living in the camp. She was nineteen years old when her parents decided to move to Beirut in search of greater economic opportunity in the mid-1990s. Many Aleppine Armenians had done the same, using the well-established network of relatives, neighbors, and friends in Bourj Hammoud to find employment and housing. Her parents went ahead of her, taking her younger brother, then only ten, and leaving her behind in Aleppo for a few months until they became better established. After about six months they sent for Taline, explaining that they had found a *villa*, a real stand-alone house, in Bourj Hammoud. Taline could hardly believe what her parents were telling her. How could they possibly have found a detached house in Lebanon when they could only afford an apartment in Aleppo? When she arrived in Bourj Hammoud and saw the Sanjak camp that would be her home, she was filled with dread. "It was not a villa," she said, "and looking at the shack made of cinder block and corrugated metal, I did not know how I would survive there." Still, despite the hardship she faced in those early years in Sanjak, she related fond memories of the close relationships she formed while living there. One particularly moving incident happened shortly after she arrived: "The neighbors had heard, somehow, that my grandfather had passed away. He wasn't even living with us at the time, but my family wore black and went into mourning. Neighbors started arriving in groups with food and comforting words. They came and checked on us for several days."

Taline marveled that despite the fact that she and her family were new-comers to the camp, they were immediately welcomed with great warmth. However, while Taline still admired the neighborly care and close connections among the people in Sanjak, she said that with it came a complete lack of privacy. She recounted with laughter that shortly after she married Hagop, her neighbor in Sanjak, and they moved into their own house in the camp, she would often come home to find his relatives sitting in her living room, drinking coffee. They had simply let themselves in and helped themselves to her kitchen. Taline insisted it would be futile to complain about such things in Sanjak. There was simply a different way of living in the camp, one that differed from anywhere else in Bourj Hammoud. She could see that now that she was living in an apartment on Arax, the main shopping street in Bourj Hammoud, where neighbors and friends did not simply let themselves in when you weren't home. Despite some nostalgia for the close relationships she had in the camp, the rules and habits of Arax were much more to Taline's liking. She much preferred the greater sense of privacy from her neighbors, even if that meant that her relationships with them were relatively impersonal in comparison to her friendships in Sanjak. "Still," she said, "when I see the children playing in the alleys in Sanjak, I know there is no place like it. It's in the city but it feels like a little village."

Vrejouhie, another longtime resident, echoed Taline's sentiments about life in Sanjak. Vrejouhie lived with her adult son (age twenty-one) and daughter (eighteen) in a one-bedroom house. She had purchased the home for $5,000 in the early 2000s. Ownership gave her a sense of security that she would not have been able to have had she been renting an apartment somewhere else. By 2010 rents in Bourj Hammoud for a comparable apartment ranged anywhere from $300 to $500 a month. Wages in Bourj Hammoud were low, but the cost of food and other amenities had risen dramatically in the past five years, and with it the rents. Making ends meet in a rental apartment would have been quite difficult for Vrejouhie and her family. Despite the shortcomings of her modest dwellings, Vrejouhie viewed the ability to own her home outright as an advantage over renting.

Another obvious advantage of living in Sanjak was the fact that Vrejouhie did not have to pay for ishtirak, or subscription to a privately owned generator. Despite its informal appearance, Sanjak was formally connected to the government grid of electricity and water. While Sanjak is technically a camp, a piece of land privately owned and leased to the municipality on a temporary basis, the municipality had historically eased its Armenian residents into permanent settlement there, helping connect residents to national water and electricity. While all of Bourj Hammoud suffered electricity shortages for several hours a day, different parts of the city were cut at different times of day. Sanjak camp happens to be divided between two different areas that run on two different schedules. To have access to electricity continuously, Vrejouhie and a neighbor on the other side of the camp connected their electricity lines together, so that each one can access electricity when their respective side is cut. The municipality had installed electricity meters several years before, so they were billed for their usage. However, this system of sharing government-provided electricity within the Sanjak camp still worked out to be cheaper and gave users access to more ampage than any kind of ishtirak system would have. Normally, when running on ishtirak power, one has much less electricity than with the government grid, and only one or two small appliances can be left on. With Vrejouhie's system of sharing, she could always keep her refrigerator running, unless in the unlikely event that both adjacent grids were cut, which is rare even in Bourj Hammoud.[10]

As we walked through the camp, Taline noted how much it had changed in the years since she had last visited. Most people had moved, half of the camp had been torn down, and the remaining hundred people were crowded into a small corner. Those whose homes were bulldozed during the first stage of the municipality's plan were forced to take homes vacated by owners who had taken the municipality's settlement and moved elsewhere. Only owners remained; renters had to leave when the evictions began. Those who remained in the camp were holding out until the municipality or the Armenian nonprofit diasporic network provided them with housing alternatives, as had occurred in the past with previous camp residents whose homes had been destroyed. In the 1970s Armenian charity organizations in collaboration with the Armenian Apostolic Church had worked to construct low-income housing projects to resettle people who were living in camps. Without other housing options, many residents have stayed in their homes because the money offered by the municipality (a maximum of $5,000 as of 2010) is not nearly enough to secure new property. In the current rental market, $5,000 would barely fund a year or two of rent. Not many people in Sanjak wanted to give up property ownership for an uncertain and highly inflated rental market that they could not afford.

Figure 2.2. A destroyed house in Sanjak camp. Photo by Rosy Kuftedjian.

Most of the houses in Sanjak have one or two rooms, and while single families individually occupy most, occasionally there would be a second level attached that belonged to someone else, as a separate apartment. One such split-level house belonged to Azad and Vahram, a married couple in their fifties with a twenty-year-old daughter and a ten-year-old son. They welcomed us inside just as the rain was getting heavier. The living room doubled as a bedroom for the two children, and there was a tiny, closet-sized room where Azad and Vahram slept. Even compared to the typically compact Bourj Hammoud apartments, the Sanjak dwellings were very small. Azad and Vahram's place was relatively large, in that it had a separate kitchen and bedroom space. Most kitchens in Sanjak were equipped with only a burner and a small sink, but every house I went into had running water and electricity.

As Azad disappeared into the kitchen to make a small pot of coffee, we suddenly heard a loud thud outside. We looked outside the open door of the living room to see that a medium-sized tree, somehow growing out of the thin layer of concrete that covered the narrow alleyways outside, had snapped in half owing to the force of the wind and toppled over. Luckily no electricity wires were taken down with the tree, and my hosts simply laughed it off and said they would deal with it later. "This is nothing. You should see when it floods!" Vahram said. Taline explained that the camp residents had a system in place to deal with the floods that would periodically engulf the camp during the rainy winter season. If water began to collect in nearby Dawra, which sits at a higher elevation in the east of Bourj Hammoud, someone would notify the camp that it was time to prepare for the coming flood. Taline told me later that her husband has a photograph of himself in a small inflatable raft during one of the Sanjak floods. It was clear that the rainy season was a constant challenge to residents.

From within Azad and Vahram's house, the sound of the rain wasn't as loud as it was in other people's homes because they were on the first floor of a two-level apartment. Vahram had built the second level himself years before. In other homes where people lived directly under a corrugated metal roof, the sound of the rain was deafening. Because the municipality regards the houses in Sanjak as temporary, residents reported that municipal codes forbid owners from replacing corrugated metal roofs with other, more permanent materials. While the municipality prohibited certain renovations in order to keep the houses in a kind of temporary state, residents were able to buy and sell property and even register property ownership at the municipality without obtaining official deeds. For example, Vahram had sold the upstairs room to the current resident for $4,500, the average cost of the houses in the 1990s. I asked him how he was able to sell the room, if they registered the transaction somewhere, and if he held a title deed to the property. Vahram explained that all transactions of sale are registered at the municipality, but that the documents held by property owners are not really *tapu*, the Turkish word used by many Armenians meaning "title deeds." Rather, each owner held a *rukhsa*, a kind of permit indicating ownership of the house but not the land underneath it. The municipality recognized the rukhsa as proof of ownership of the house while maintaining that this ownership was still somehow temporary, as the land belonged to a private owner. By the time I began conducting initial fieldwork in 2008, the municipality was forcing most people who rented in Sanjak to leave, including those who ran small businesses out of rented shacks by the highway. By 2011 the only families who remained were those who possessed a rukhsa.

The rukhsa, held by the owner, is also registered with the municipality. It is treated as a legally binding agreement declaring the name of the person who owns the *takhshibeh*, or "shack," built on the plot registered on the cadastral map, which belongs to a private owner whose name is mentioned on the permit. The "shack" itself is also given a number, and the document verifies that the structure was constructed before 1960 and is therefore a legally constructed building that conforms to pre-1960 codes. While the rukhsa gives the owner the right to own the building, it denies the owner any claim to the land. Sometime in the mid-2000s the municipality may have purchased the land from the private owner mentioned (ostensibly the last legal owners of the land), though details about the transaction are vague and difficult to verify. While the land in Bourj Hammoud near the highway was worth up to $2,000 per square meter in 2008 (Asmar 2008), the private owner would not have been able to sell it because it was a legally sanctioned camp since the 1930s. Only the municipality would have had the power to expropriate land from Sanjak residents, and it would have been able to do so at a much cheaper rate because it had to compensate them only for their homes, not for the value of the land.

As a document of ownership, the rukhsa allowed Sanjak residents to sell their homes and have the transactions recorded, something that does not happen with all sales transactions of "informal" property in Lebanon. Often such transactions will be registered with a notary public. While the documents might look official and are treated as such by those involved in the transaction, the regional property registry does not recognize them. The rukhsas issued through the municipality are not registered at the regional property registry; the registry includes only owners of the plots of land on the cadastral map. When these are legally subdivided and sold, the owners' names and transactions appear on the regional property registry documents. However, the municipality of Bourj Hammoud issued rukhsas only as "shack" permits, which did not correspond to landownership. The land would still be registered as belonging to the private owner in the regional property registry for that particular district. This allowed the municipality

Figure 2.3. The autostrade (highway) side of Sanjak camp. Photo by Rosy Kuftedjian.

to maintain a great degree of control over informal property ownership. For example, sales to non-Armenians were forbidden: while Syrian migrant workers rented property in Sanjak in the past, they could never buy a house.

Through the localization of the registration of rukhsa permits to the municipality, Armenian municipal actors managed the Sanjak camp as a permanently temporary space exclusively for Armenians. The effect of this arrangement was that the municipality and the Tashnag Party that dominates it were the exclusive guarantors of Sanjak residents' property rights. The fact that Sanjak owners were buying only the house and not the land made the properties affordable to people who could not buy elsewhere. While a certain amount of uncertainty was built in to the transaction, as the camp was always treated as "temporary," it remained a fixture in Bourj Hammoud for nearly eighty years. Most Sanjak residents, like many other Lebanese who live in the informal settlements that proliferated both before and especially during the civil war period of 1975–90, prefer the uncertainty of the camp's eventual destruction to the uncertainty of the unaffordable rental market (M. Fawaz 2009a, 2009b). Owning a home gave Sanjak residents a sense of security that even if they were unemployed or their employment brought incredibly low wages, they could still support themselves.

The Sanjak residents I spoke with never really thought that the municipality would evict them without another housing option in place. Recent shifts in policy toward informal settlements, however, have turned from a more "laissez faire" approach in Lebanon, whereby government actors simply ignore informal settlements, to a move toward actively enforcing "market-type" or "neoliberal" relations of individual property ownership by destroying informal settlements (M. Fawaz 2013, 2014). The destruction of informal settlements forces residents into the unaffordable rental market and allows developers to use seized land to construct highly speculative real estate projects (Krijnen and Fawaz 2010). In many situations, state or municipal actors are instrumental to these processes. As one architect I interviewed explained, municipalities have the power to evict residents through connections to sectarian political parties and their affiliated institutions, through all kinds of coercive means, in ways that a private owner acting alone cannot always do. It is within this context of rapidly shifting policies toward informality and high land values that Sanjak is under threat of destruction.

SANJAK'S "EMPTINESS"

Despite the pressure on informal settlements in Lebanon, many Sanjak camp residents had trusted that the Tashnag Party and the Armenian political actors who dominated it would advocate to keep them in Bourj Hammoud. Many of the owners who remained were those who were holding out for a better option. They tended to be the most vulnerable members of the community—the old, the infirm, those with children who had disabilities, or those whose job skills were no longer in demand. For years the earning capacity for people working in jewelry-making, shoe-making, or other traditional apprenticed jobs in Bourj Hammoud had been declining. Unemployment was high, and even if workers had other skills, they often lacked the connections needed to get into another industry. Low-paying service jobs could not sustain a family, even with both parents and often children working. Most of the people I interviewed in Sanjak from 2008 to 2011 were unwilling to leave, not only because they had few alternatives but also because they also valued the community they had with their neighbors and the safety they felt they enjoyed in the camp. Some liked the fact that they lived in small homes rather than apartments and that their children could play outside their doors and in the alleyways through which no cars or motorcycles could pass. In other words, many of my interlocutors appreciated their neighborhood and did not see Sanjak in the way that Taline did—as a place of misery and struggle.

Many of the Sanjak owners I interviewed feel ambivalence about the actions of the municipality and were hesitant to criticize the Tashnag Party for not advocating for them enough. Most of them are party members or at least have an affinity for the party, and quite a few are very active in agoump activities. They are confused by what they see as a contradiction—that the municipality that is dominated by their party that represents their own Armenian "community" seems to be acting against their interests. When the municipality announced the Saint Jacques plan and began to tear down Sanjak homes in 2008, the situation of who actually owned the land was still unclear to most residents. There was much confusion among most of the people I spoke with in Sanjak as to whether the municipality had acquired ownership of the plot, or if there was some absentee landlord who was still holding on to a piece of the land. This seemed to provide an explanation to the residents as to why half the camp had been torn down while the other half was left standing. The confusion and opacity surrounding the municipality's expropriation of the Sanjak plot were echoed across all my interviews with people whom I truly expected would know more about the details of the transaction, including some lower-level municipal employees. The ambiguity or opacity of the municipality's actions served to occlude any attempts to piece together what had happened, and how soon the rest of the camp was to be torn down.[11] Rumors were rapidly circulating; people received word that they were going to be resettled in other apartments only to find out later that this was unsubstantiated. Residents were confused and fearful about their uncertain futures.

Things were different during the war, Vahram insisted. During the 1980s, when Vahram's sister lived in the upstairs room, two shells destroyed it completely. An international Catholic charity that has operated in Lebanon since the 1970s gave him the money to rebuild the room. Many other Sanjak residents echoed Vahram's story about the help and resources that came into the camp in the aftermath of war-era bombings and destruction. Some residents remember an unnamed Swiss man, a member of an evangelical relief organization, spearheading these improvements. Others remembered an order of French Catholic nuns, some Armenian, some Lebanese, some French, called the *petites soeurs*, who lived in Sanjak and served as social workers and provided educational opportunities and lectures for children and mothers.

It may seem paradoxical that Vahram and many other residents look back at the war years with nostalgia as a time of plenty.[12] However, when viewed in terms of the services and opportunities available during the war and the relative lack of assistance today, my interlocutors struggle economically more now than during the 1970s and 1980s. "Things were better during the war, even under the bombs, everyone had work and money," Vahram insisted. It wasn't only the loss of resources and material stability that led to a feeling of emptiness in the camp, though.[13] Vahram went on to say: "Now there is nothing, everyone is leaving the camp and it's being torn down and people are struggling much more than they were during the war. The community is gone. The agoump used to set up guards at the corners of the camp so that no one would trespass who didn't live here. Now the agoump has become weaker and the government has become stronger."

Vahram's feelings about Sanjak's emptiness are not only based on the fact that many of his longtime neighbors and friends have been forced to leave their homes. Rather, he seemed to be mourning the fact that to be an Armenian in Sanjak, or in Bourj Hammoud more generally, *meant* something very particular during the war. It meant that you lived in an area that was safe, where you had access to things because you could claim membership in a community whose boundaries, owing to the circumstance of violent conflict, seemed very clear.[14] Each neighborhood in Bourj Hammoud had a Tashnag-affiliated agoump that acts not only as a place for the charitable women's auxiliary and men's committees to meet but also as a kind of informal security office staffed by neighborhood members who take care of local disputes. During the war especially, the agoump was very involved in providing security, and one's own neighbors were responsible for policing and maintaining order and continuity. Vahram's last statement about the agoump becoming weaker and the government becoming stronger was a way of expressing the fact that the powers that appear to be controlling the fate of Sanjak residents seem faceless, unaccountable, distant. In the context of Vahram's comments, the agoump is shorthand for both the political party as well as the political clubs of the Tashnag Party. Sanjak had an agoump, but Vahram and others commented that its influence seems to have declined in recent years. The proof of this, for Vahram and others, was that the municipality did not seem to be operating in Sanjak's best interests, something that the agoump always did.

While in the 1970s the Armenian philanthropic community's response was to build social housing projects in order to lodge those who were leaving the various camps that were slowly being destroyed in and around Bourj Hammoud, there is little practical mobilization around the Sanjak issue today. Even the Bourj Hammoud municipality, which helped construct the *masaken* or "public" housing project exclusively for Armenian residents of Bourj Hammoud in the 1970s, has not taken an active role in resettling Sanjak residents.[15] Some Armenian community leaders I spoke with who are employed in various NGOs or affiliated with one of the three Armenian churches (Catholic, Apostolic, or Protestant) identified a lack of funds as the primary reason why no one was planning a housing project for the displaced Sanjak residents. It is true that many international charities funding Armenian projects, both Armenian diaspora funded and otherwise, had started to decrease their funding to Lebanese projects in recent years. Since the independence of the Republic of Armenia, the devastating earthquake in Armenia in 1988, the subsequent war between Armenia and Azerbaijan over the Nagorno-Karabakh region, and the official end of the Lebanese civil war in the early 1990s, many diasporic resources have focused on Armenia. The global economic crisis of 2008 also affected the endowments of several charities and philanthropic organizations, and many of the NGOs that relied on them suffered huge budget cuts. More recently, diasporic Armenian organizations in the United States and Europe have focused their efforts on Syrian Armenian refugees fleeing the conflict since 2011.

Still, despite economic difficulties and shifting priorities among transnational Armenian charities and philanthropic organizations, I also detected a lack of will among Lebanese Armenian actors and institutions. Some Armenian social and political actors in Bourj Hammoud, even those who had taken part in the social housing projects of the 1970s, believed that a shift had to take place in terms of how social services are provided. These managers of social centers and clinics thought it was time for Sanjak residents to submit to the pressures of rent or mortgage payments in order to improve their own lot.[16] Many expressed doubt that such a plan would adequately "rehabilitate" the camp residents, suggesting it would be more beneficial if each of them were forced to come up with solutions individually.[17] It is within the context of what some might call the neoliberal turn, the extension of economic rationalization to more domains of life and the shift toward the self as "the primary agent of the art of governing," that municipal actors as well as many of my interlocutors in social service provision in Bourj Hammoud regard the destruction of the camp and the ejection of its residents into the rental market as rehabilitative (Elyachar 2005, 193).[18] One interlocutor who was peripherally involved in the early days of one low-income housing project in the 1970s felt that such projects simply encourage "ghettoism." "Personal progress and improvement," he said, "is leaving Bourj Hammoud to move elsewhere." In his view, Bourj Hammoud was not a place for the upwardly mobile, and Armenians who were able to move to the higher-income suburbs to the northeast should do so.

Throughout many of my interviews, I noticed a surprising consistency in portraying Sanjak residents as "backward," "low-class," and somehow arrested in their development on the road to becoming modern, economically successful, and industrious Lebanese Armenian subjects. To a lesser degree, some wealthier Armenians in the eastern suburbs of Beirut hold a similar attitude toward Bourj Hammoud Armenians. Some middle- and upper-class interlocutors, for example, reproduced popular stereotypes about the latter as not assimilated enough to Lebanon and lacking fluency in Arabic. Implicit in their statements is the notion that the camp especially represents a kind of backwardness that Armenians should have risen out of. Despite its status as the last Armenian refugee camp in Lebanon, only a handful of activists have discussed Sanjak in terms of commemoration or historic preservation.[19] My earliest questions along these lines were met with laughter and incredulity. Historical photos of camps were one thing, but a living camp today was quite another. One interlocutor said that it was an "unhygienic" space, both medically and socially, and that the proximity of the homes, the overcrowding, and the "mixing" between the renting migrant workers (who had long been evicted along with all other renters) and the Armenians there had led to "immoral" behavior.[20]

While the popular images and sentimental videos on YouTube about Arakadz circulate as images of collective memory and kinship within the context of an Armenian neighborhood, it became clear through various interviews about Sanjak that there was a definite hierarchy of what it meant to be properly "Armenian." For many of my interlocutors involved in social work, medical services, and politics, Sanjak should be uprooted entirely—as a community, it was doomed to remain a hopeless ghetto. Only individual self-help could rehabilitate the Sanjak residents. This vision of progress was incompatible with the one held by many Sanjak residents who wanted not only to remain in their homes but also to maintain their community in all senses of that word and truly valued their neighborhood. They were not simply "waiting for handouts," as detractors would often tell me. The sense of community that arose during the war—that of mutual obligations, favors, and a sense of belonging based on being an Armenian from the neighborhood—was something that many in Sanjak struggled to maintain.

The story of Arakadz might shed light on why the quality of "belonging" within an authentic vision of "Armenianness" makes the possibilities for the future somewhat different, even across two spaces whose residents have similar kinds of informal property arrangements with the municipality. While many professional and political elites regard Sanjak as a space of backwardness and part of a past they seek to forget, they see Arakadz as an authentic space that reflects the industriousness of Armenians and an important part of the popular history so many labor to remember.

ARAKADZ

Mariam and Ardashes, an Armenian couple in their late sixties, lived in a small, two-story brick and concrete building in Arakadz. Having moved to Arakadz at the age of seven, when her father built the house she currently lives in, Mariam was known throughout the neighborhood as someone knowledgeable about the history of the area. Active in the local chapter of the Tashnag Party's women's auxiliary at the agoump, Mariam also worked part time taking care of an elderly and infirm woman to cover expenses. The couple never had children but were very active in the neighborhood. Mariam noted her own role in keeping the area safe, taking up a gun to protect Arakadz from "others" during the violent street battles raging nearby in the 1970s.

Mariam told me what she remembered of her early childhood years in Arakadz and what her parents and older residents had passed on to her. Also known as Kerezmanots, or "cemetery area," Arakadz had in the early days been an Armenian cemetery. Like many parts of Bourj Hammoud, particularly the Nor Marash area, the town association of Marash had purchased the Kerezmanots land from its Lebanese owners in the 1920s. The association eventually gave the land over to the municipality to manage. The plot soon fell into disuse as a cemetery, Mariam said, because of the damp conditions of the soil, which made it impossible to properly inter the bodies. In those days the municipality granted Armenian families permission to build temporary shacks with corrugated metal roofs that looked much like the structures still standing in Sanjak. I was told that for some time the temporary houses coexisted with a few scattered graves. I once heard a story, perhaps apocryphal, about how a coffin had started to rise up through the floor of one of the houses after a particularly strong rain. The area is subject to flooding and there is an underground spring beneath this part of Bourj Hammoud, so perhaps there is some truth to the story. By the 1950s the municipality made a decision to permanently move the graves to a larger cemetery just outside of Bourj Hammoud, which is still there today. Many people I spoke with in Bourj Hammoud joked that the transfer was probably left incomplete and there were still some coffins lingering under the ground.

Figure 2.4. Arakadz. Photo by Rosy Kuftedjian.

After the graves were moved, the municipality granted some Armenian families permission to build permanent structures on the land and installed more effective drainage for the streets. Many of these families were moving from camps or camplike conditions in nearby areas. Others lacked the funds to buy property. Mariam's father built her home during this time. Like Sanjak, the municipality issued ownership documents, rukhsas, designating the name of the owner of each structure, but not the land underneath the building, after the Marash village association gave it to the municipality of Bourj Hammoud to manage. These documents were not recorded at the regional property registry either, and the municipality, which limited ownership strictly to Armenians, controlled the transactions of buying and selling property. Unlike Sanjak, the municipality owned the land underneath the buildings. Also unlike Sanjak, the land is designated on the cadastral map as a large plot marked as public domain rather than belonging to a private owner. The fact that there are buildings on the property is not designated anywhere on the cadastral map nor in the property registry documents. Like Sanjak, the municipality office maintains the only records of who holds rukhsas for these houses.

I discovered the file containing unofficial maps of the houses in Arakadz while looking up the large plot on the Bourj Hammoud cadastral map at the municipality. Many of the files documenting owners and renters of individual plots were incomplete, partially as a result of the municipality's inability to account for all the unpermitted additions and buildings added during the years of the war, and partially because many landlords do not register their renters with the municipality. This is a tactic often used by landlords who prefer to rent to male migrant workers without a proper lease. They charge each worker a certain amount and crowd as many lodgers as possible in the apartment. These men are not given a proper lease and can be evicted at any time, creating more flexibility for the landlord to charge more and more rent, and leaving workers extremely vulnerable.

The file for the large Arakadz plot also contained sketches of buildings surrounding a courtyard. There were other documents within the file that appeared to indicate the names of people registered in various buildings, as well as a sketch of the buildings as they stand today. I later learned that the sketches of the buildings around a courtyard were for a project proposed by the municipality in the 1990s. At that time the plan was to tear down the old buildings, as they were crowded together and not built up to current standards, and build new structures for the residents to live in. It was going to be the first public municipal housing project in Bourj Hammoud in twenty years. One of my interlocutors at the municipality was regretful that the plans were buried and no action was ever taken and produced another folder containing newspaper clips about Arakadz, as well as letters from people who grew up there. The outpouring of nostalgia for Arakadz was in marked contrast to the relative silence about Sanjak's destruction.

Tamar, an Armenian psychologist who volunteered at a local NGO, explained to me the nostalgic longing for Arakadz I saw and heard so frequently among my Armenian interlocutors who were familiar with Bourj Hammoud.

During the 1980s, when Tamar was in college, Haigazian College (now Haigazian University) had moved its campus temporarily from western Beirut to
eastern Beirut to avoid the worst of the violence that was raging in that part
of town. While Haigazian was open to all Lebanese students and is indeed
well attended by members of every Lebanese sect, the administration was
largely Armenian. Many Armenians and most Armenian institutions at that
time had moved to eastern Beirut or Bourj Hammoud. While her parents
lived in a suburb further away to the northeast of Beirut, Tamar continued
attending Haigazian because she was able to live with her grandmother in
Arakadz. She repeated the refrain I often heard from many people who felt
nostalgic about Arakadz: "Arakadz for me is a real neighborhood. It reminds
me of my grandmother, and of everyone's grandmother."

For many with nostalgic feelings about Arakadz, the neighborhood represented the last real bastion of a generation now lost, of those Armenians
who came to Lebanon as refugees, and who perhaps spoke Turkish better
than Armenian. However, the emphasis on grandmothers is about more than
just generational difference; it is about the image of a nurturing, authentic
past that is narrated, in part, through the gendering of space and dualisms
of private/public or, in this case, perhaps domestic/public.[21] It is precisely
this domestic space, the space of the grandmother's home, and the longing
for a connection to that past that is being cultivated. While Sanjak camp
seemed to represent misery, suffering, and a past that should have been
overcome long ago, Arakadz presented a safer history to look back on, one
in which Armenians finally lived in concrete apartments instead of cinder
block shacks. Arakadz represented the safety and permanence of a real home
in Lebanon. Even though it is designated as "temporary," it bears more re-
semblance to the buildings around it. Sanjak, on the other hand, is marked
by its appearance. It was always a camp, and it is not integrated into the
urban network of streets the way that Arakadz is. Tamar never described her
time in Arakadz as uncomfortable, the social atmosphere as stifling. Talking
about a grandmother in Arakadz does not carry the same kind of stigma that
admitting you grew up in Sanjak does.

Mariam also believed that the fate of the people in Arakadz would be
different from that of those living in Sanjak. She trusted the municipality,
citing the fact that she even paid a yearly tax on her property as proof that
officials had granted Arakadz a permanent status. She remarked: "If this
neighborhood is emptied of Armenians, there won't be any Armenians
left in this area! The head of the municipality needs to keep us here. They
are Armenian too." Ardashes said he had heard about a plan to tear down
the buildings and construct new ones for the property owners in Arakadz.
"But with every new plan, it seems that ten or fifteen years goes by with
no action!" he laughed. In Arakadz, most interlocutors did not believe
that the municipality would dream of tearing down the buildings without

constructing an alternative for the current residents. But in Beirut's rapidly shifting landscape, might Ardashes be mistaken?

RAPID CHANGES, SHIFTING SPACES

Ardashes's comment reminded me that in the current atmosphere in Beirut, where shifting government regulations and public interventions have enabled the acceleration of real estate speculation by Gulf and expatriate Lebanese investors and buyers, perhaps the future was not as secure as people thought. Through the active involvement of state institutions and public actors, Beirut has become a "permanent (re)construction site" with high-end luxury towers replacing older, smaller buildings throughout the city (Krijnen and Fawaz 2010, 245). Existing renters displaced by high-end development "are either bribed or bullied into leaving or see their neighborhood change beyond recognition" (Krijnen 2013). Popular neighborhoods in the eastern sector of Beirut where previously only vegetable sellers and small markets had set up shop were now becoming gentrified, as wine bars, art bookstores, and upscale French restaurants that were far too expensive for most Lebanese began to pop up alongside the new luxury towers that were rapidly replacing old buildings.[22] By 2014 this eastward spread of new businesses catering to the upper and middle classes of Lebanese, Lebanese expatriates, and tourists had gone further than I imagined it could, nearly up to the Beirut River dividing Bourj Hammoud from Beirut. Bourj Hammoud was one of the only remaining popular districts so close to municipal Beirut's eastern border.[23] Everything further northeast of the city was much more expensive, and luxury high-rise developments had been constructed in the municipalities around Bourj Hammoud. While the Tashnag-dominated municipality has always maintained the importance of keeping Armenian institutions as well as Armenian bodies in Bourj Hammoud, various actors within the municipality have their own particular aims that don't overlap completely. In the context of rising property values of land so close to the central Beirut district, could there be some friction in maintaining this vision?

In the context of the pressure of rising real estate costs, the municipality's differential treatment of Sanjak and Arakadz, two "temporary" camp spaces, shows how notions of belonging and authentic Armenianness are not natural or inevitable, nor are they based narrowly on belonging to an ethnoreligious sect. The construction of the sectarian community is tempered with other kinds of belonging or exclusion that have to do with notions of propriety and authenticity. Claims to property, even informal property, always involve infrastructures, legal codes or the circumnavigation of legal codes, and sets of documentation practices that are put into motion to distinguish who is a legitimate member of the Armenian community and who is not. Sanjak reflects a past that many want to forget—the Armenian refugees in Lebanon, living in flooded camps and struggling to survive. Arakadz reflects the nostalgia of the Armenians who built permanent structures on top of what was essentially a graveyard, putting down roots and "pulling themselves up" through industriousness and ingenuity. Arakadz represents those who live with the ghosts of the pasts but can overcome their adversities. Sanjak is a shameful reminder to many Armenians of the refugee state they would like to relegate to the past. Because of these differences, political and social actors and elites who used to be involved with resettling Armenians who lived in camps into more permanent housing have distanced themselves from Sanjak. Though there was little public outcry over the fate of Sanjak, it remains to be seen whether Arakadz will face a similar fate, or whether its reputation as a nostalgic and authentic Armenian space will save its residents from eviction.

In late 2011 I received word that Ardashes had passed away. Reflecting on my conversations with him, I remembered how I would see him standing outside of Arakadz, leaning against the gate that separated the small neighborhood from the main street. The gate was there to protect people in Arakadz from the perceived threat of Syrian migrant workers and other odars, or "non-Armenians." Until 2013, however, it had always been unlocked. Some speculated the gate was locked because of the feelings of insecurity prompted by the escalating conflict in Syria, the increase in the number of displaced Syrians in Bourj Hammoud, and a general sense of unease. Ardashes would wait in front of that gate, back when it was unlocked, every day for Mariam

Figure 2.5. Gate at the entrance to Arakadz. Photo by Rosy Kuftedjian.

to return from work, as he was too ill to work himself. When I heard the news of his death, I went to pay my respects to Mariam. Dressed in black, she could barely hold back her tears: "Now I am all alone." She told me she had tried to focus her energies on her volunteer work with the women's auxiliary, but it had been difficult to adjust to living without Ardashes. She had more bad news too: apparently the municipality had sent a surveyor to Arakadz. He didn't have anything to report about why the municipality was suddenly interested in measuring the area, but for Mariam it was an ominous sign of things to come. Might the more permanent Arakadz be demolished like Sanjak?

What the cases of Sanjak and Arakadz show is that belonging and the content of "Armenianness," or inclusion in sectarian community, is a process deeply entangled with notions of property ownership. In turn, proving ownership, even in informal property regimes, is a dialogic process that involves sets of documents and records as well as claims to belonging to a sectarian community. One must mobilize notions of belonging to have informal property claims upheld, but only a property claim in the right neighborhood could allow one to make such a claim to "belonging." Popular histories revered Arakadz as a neighborhood of importance and authenticity. Sanjak was reviled as a "backward" space. Thus residents of Arakadz were more likely to be part of the calculation of the "greater good" that municipal planners had to consider when making their plans. The informal settlements in Lebanon, and their uneven treatment, cannot simply be attributed to purely economic forces. Rather, the logics of sectarian belonging and community, as well as the logics of class, geographic histories, and locations of power, are deeply implicated in the process of how each claim to property is contested, upheld, or denied. Despite the long-standing claims to informal housing in Sanjak and Arakadz, the rising tide of land values coupled with shifting priorities of Armenian political patrons could still potentially undermine housing security.

A claim to belonging, however, is not necessarily limited to belonging to an ethnoreligious sect and is complicated by other factors of geography and class, and the mapping of neighborhoods and the people within them onto notions of progress or "backwardness," morality or impropriety. In the next chapter I explore the ways in which gendered propriety, notions of morality, and normativity influence claims to belonging and differentiate access to Bourj Hammoud's social and medical service centers.

Chapter 3

BUILDING THE NETWORKS

NGOs, Gender, and "Community"

It was a Friday, which was typically the lecture day for one of the three women's groups active at an Armenian medical clinic where I conducted research during the course of my fieldwork. Araxi and Lucine, two social workers, were assembling gift bags to be distributed to the women in attendance. The gift bags were full of samples of cosmetics, feminine hygiene products, and small, decorative coin purses. The samples were distributed among women's societies, dispensaries, and the like by way of transnational charities who had somehow acquired travel-sized bottles of mouthwash, toothpaste, or feminine products from large corporations eager to reach new markets. Occasionally companies would even call the center with an offer to come and present a public lecture on some topic relating to women's health, hygiene, or childrearing, providing samples of everything from powdered milk and infant formula to deodorant or even nonperishable food items.

I wandered into the kitchen to find more women hastily filling plastic cups with orange juice and putting petit fours onto large trays. There was always a huge turnout for weekly lectures for the women's groups. As soon as the sixty or so women started to arrive, the buzz of conversation and the crowding of people trying to fit into several rows of chairs crammed into the auditorium made it nearly impossible to hear the person next to you speak unless she shouted above the din. As usual, today's lecture would be something pertaining to health or medical conditions appropriate for the audience: mainly women in their thirties through sixties. The guest speaker was a doctor from an Armenian-owned medical laboratory that performed much of the lab work for the patients receiving medical care at the center. He had come to speak to the women about diabetes prevention and had prepared a number of slides to illustrate his point about diet and exercise.

Toward the end of the lecture, which was conducted entirely in Armenian, he reiterated his main points about not smoking, getting exercise, and avoiding sugary foods. "Don't drink soda or juice," he said, as I helped distribute the small plastic cups of orange juice to the women seated around us. "Only occasionally," he said, correcting himself as he received a cup. The women listened attentively, nodding in agreement and boisterously applauding when he was finished. He passed out pamphlets about diabetes prevention and the women eagerly browsed them as they shuffled out the door, collecting their gift bags as they emerged onto the street.

There are three major medical and social service centers in Bourj Hammoud that are Armenian-run but offer certain services to non-Armenians, particularly after 2011 when international aid organizations increased funding to assist Syrian refugees.[1] Still, most lectures at these centers were conducted entirely in Armenian, and the attendees were usually all women. Services at all the medical clinics I visited are open to the public, and I did often see non-Armenians in the medical sections of these clinics. It was rarer to see non-Armenians seeking help from social workers or attending the lecture series, social clubs, and professional development courses offered by the social development department of the clinics. While there were a few exceptions, it was normatively understood that to access nonessential medical services, one had to make a claim to *being* Armenian through birth or, to a lesser extent, marriage, though in practice this was much less straightforward. The assumption of a two-tiered system was firmly in place: medical care was technically open to all, but to access the full range of services one had to be able to claim a kind of membership in the community. As Melanie Cammett (2014, 8) writes, such services can "signal who is a member of a protected group," though in her case study this is not always limited to one's own religious or ethnic group.[2] In the case of Bourj Hammoud, even as there were many services open to non-Armenians at Armenian institutions, not all the attendant networks were open to everyone.

Full membership in the "community" went beyond the official services offered by the various NGOs, centers, and clubs in Bourj Hammoud and beyond. Rather, it also allowed access to the "informal" networks and special favors that come with having *wasta*, the colloquial Arabic term for connections, a process known throughout the Lebanese social, political, and economic system as the way "things get done." These networks, what Suad Joseph (1994b) called "relational rights," were not neutral flows of power.[3] Services were procured through highly gendered relationality, but there were still limits that constrained relationships in ways that weren't always predictable. Non-Armenian men, for example, even if they were married to Armenian women, would rarely become involved in the social worlds or currents of Armenian wasta. The unofficial rules regarding access to the only "public" housing project for low-income Armenian families in Bourj Hammoud are one example of this. While an Armenian man married to a non-Armenian woman could purchase or rent an apartment there, an Armenian woman married to a non-Armenian man would have a lot more difficulty doing so. While non-Armenian women married to Armenian men were much more likely to do so, particularly if they spoke Armenian, their ability to claim membership in the Armenian community and all its institutions was not always fully acknowledged in every situation.

In this chapter I examine the role of notions of gender propriety in differentiating access to Armenians women's organizations in Bourj Hammoud, and, in turn, in differentiating access to the networks of services and resources that they provide. Many of these organizations have existed for much of the twentieth century, having emerged in response to the Armenian refugee crisis and enduring into the present to deal with ongoing issues of poverty and conflict in Lebanon. In these organizations the role of women as the primary caregivers and caretakers of the Armenian home, replete with discourses of progress through hygiene and proper childrearing, is conflated with the role of women in providing "relief" to the ailing Armenian community in times of violent conflict or economic hardship.[4] The discourse in Lebanon that promotes the idea of women primarily as "mothers" during times of extreme violence and war echoes other situations where civil conflict and unrest are ongoing.[5] The education offered at many of these institutions is geared toward making women better heads of household and better mothers, and keeping their children safe, healthy, and *connected* to the Armenian community by enrolling them in Armenian schools and involving them in Armenian cultural activities for youth like traditional dance, music, or scouting clubs. The lectures aim to "improve" the Armenian community by "modernizing" women's care work through sharing of expert knowledge, as well as bringing women into the fold of the networks of these organizations.[6]

The very structure of the lecture described above, with a middle-class Armenian doctor addressing an audience of working-class Armenian women, is typical of these events that often take a paternalistic tone with poorer women. While many women's organizations used to actively recruit from the community they served, growing professionalization in the fields of social work, nursing, psychology, and even a few MBAs in organizational management have only widened the gap between the paid employees of these NGOs and the client base. This move toward greater professionalization of positions that used to be learned on the job (including among some of the nurses I encountered at various medical centers) has made it more difficult for poor women without access to higher education to move into the ranks of leadership in many of these organizations.[7] Women without formalized training are more likely to work with the women's charity auxiliary affiliated with the Tashnag Party, which is also engaged in community service-related work, although its mission is more narrowly articulated as service to the Armenian community. Many other Armenian NGOs, however, like the clinic described above, operate with limited access to members of other sects and non-Lebanese citizens. This division of labor between the work of the official Tashnag women's league and the "professionalized" NGOs that target women's health and development leads to different experiences and understandings of sectarian belonging and community (Murdock 2008). I use Donna Murdock's definition of professionalized NGOs to distinguish those organizations "staffed by well-educated women with degrees in social work, community organization, policy or development" and the important implications this has not only for those seeking services but also for those seeking to participate in the networks within which these organizations are embedded (3).[8]

The Armenian "community" is produced through these material and social networks of organizations and institutions and their affiliated infrastructures and services, which are, in turn, connected to transnational circulations of resources and knowledge that move through international organizations, charities, and even corporations seeking new markets. Sectarian community, then, is not a naturalized, a priori social category existing "out there" but rather a networked system with differential access to those claiming "Armenianness" through various means. At the same time, the very notion of what community is or which Armenian community networks one can access through these institutions is not static. In this chapter I argue that normative ideas about womanhood, gendered divisions of labor, and the proper management of the "domestic" sphere create trajectories through and to these publics via different institutional channels. Because gender becomes a key route to access to these infrastructures, it is inextricable from the ways in which people imagine themselves as part of a "public," at times a "sect" in the context of political representation in Lebanon, or as a "community" of Armenians in Lebanon, or a community in Bourj Hammoud.[9] However, normative notions of gender provide only varying degrees of access to these networks, which also rest on distinctions of class, not narrowly in terms of class as a position in an economic system but rather as a position as a node of networked infrastructures. In other words, the way I mobilize the terminology of class is not as a narrowly economic category but one that is deeply entangled within channels of services produced by sectarian political organizations, professionalized NGOs, religious groups, and specific neighborhoods. It is within this context that normative notions of gendered propriety can help provide access to valuable "communicative channels" of services, knowledge, and, importantly, connections to people who can help maintain these infrastructures.[10]

This chapter will focus on the work of two distinct types of institutions—a transnational Armenian NGO and the various women's organizations affiliated with the Armenian Tashnag Party. Through a closer look at these organizations,

I will show how gender, particularly the performance of normative notions of gender roles and gendered propriety, enables or disables access to the networks that produce the Armenian community in various forms. Access to these channels of services and their attendant resources differs based on women's abilities to mobilize gender, kinship, and family relations, particular kinds of class positions and professional training, linguistic skills, and even spatial, neighborhood connections. Gender propriety and class positioning allow women to connect social infrastructures, to network into other networks glossed as "Armenian middle class," or "Tashnag Party base."[11] I begin with an ethnographic exploration of different cases in which gendered propriety profoundly shaped outcomes for women seeking services at an Armenian social service center in Bourj Hammoud. In some cases, appeals to gendered propriety can be a powerful tool that can produce outcomes that go against patriarchal cultural and legal norms in Lebanon and in the Armenian Lebanese community.

BUILDING CHANNELS, PRODUCING ARMENIANS

Sevan, a social worker in her early forties, heaved a deep sigh as the secretary brought in a huge stack of files representing the number of "cases," as they referred to clients in the Armenian NGO where she worked, that were in to see her that afternoon. It was early September, and the waiting room of the social assistance office was full of mothers and children waiting to see Sevan. Sevan remarked that her job was more like "relief work" than "social work," and she often spoke of the disconnection between her professional experience at the center and her formal education in social work and psychology. While she longed to make an impact in her clients' lives through long-term professional development programs and even therapeutic interventions, she found that most of her experiences in Bourj Hammoud consisted of responding to one crisis after another through the entrenched bureaucracies of paternalistic networks. Often the only response she could provide was a short-term solution—a food coupon for one of two neighborhood grocery stores or a discount on a prescription drug.

September was an especially busy time for Sevan, as mothers filed in to ask for assistance in purchasing their children's schoolbooks. Most Armenian parents in Bourj Hammoud try to send their children to Armenian schools. While there are Lebanese public schools in the district, it was rare that I encountered an Armenian family that had enrolled their students in one of them. Public schools were not entirely free, as they had their own fees for books and supplies. Still, even the poorest families would make an effort to keep their children in private Armenian schools, despite the much higher costs. Not only were parents responsible for tuition, but the sheer number of schoolbooks and workbooks that the students had to purchase each year was staggering. Because Armenian schools offered instruction in three or sometimes four languages—Armenian, Arabic, and English or French, there were even more books to be purchased than if the students were sent to a non-Armenian private school, which would usually just have Arabic and either French or English instruction. All the Armenian schools were affiliated with one of the three officially recognized Armenian churches (Armenian Catholic, Armenian Evangelical, or Armenian Apostolic). While the Apostolic schools were the most numerous in Bourj Hammoud, all three denominations made an effort to operate on a sliding scale for students who could not afford full tuition. Still, parents found it difficult to keep up with the costs, and a few were compelled, in the end, to enroll at least one of their children in a public school.

One of Sevan's clients that day had come in with her two children, telling Sevan that her daughter was enrolled in an Armenian school while her son was in a public school. The mother explained that she could not afford to keep both of them in private schools, and because her son had not excelled in school as her daughter did, she made the choice to pull him out of the Armenian school. Sevan expressed reservation at the mother's decision, telling her that her son would have trouble keeping up with the Arabic language instruction at the public school. The mother insisted that the child's father, a Lebanese Maronite Christian, could help with the Arabic lessons. After the mother left, Sevan expressed doubts that the child would stay enrolled if his parents kept him in a public school. Not only were the public schools overcrowded, the facilities worn, and the quality of instruction uneven, but for an Armenian student accustomed to being around other Armenian children, the environment, Sevan felt, would be alienating. Despite the normative and legal patriarchal kinship calculus in Lebanon, in which citizenship and official registration within a religious sect are determined solely by the father's status, this mother would likely face pressure, not just from the Armenian schools but from her family members and friends, to keep her children "Armenian," speaking the Armenian language and associating mainly with Armenians by keeping them in Armenian schools. At a public school, children would be speaking Arabic and not learning anything about Armenian history. For many parents, and especially for the staff at Armenian schools and social service centers that labored to keep the students in those schools, this was like "losing" their children to a world that they did not feel they belonged to. Of course, this fear existed alongside the possibility of their children not receiving a good education at the public school.

While the NGO's pediatric clinic was full of Lebanese women of all different sects, as well as Syrian, Filipina, Sri Lankan, and Ethiopian migrant workers and their children, the social assistance office was usually visited by Armenian women only. Whenever there were Arabic-speaking women visiting the office, their presence was usually justified by their connection to an Armenian through marriage. A few clients had an Armenian parent but did not grow up speaking the language. It was far less likely for a connection to have been through a friend or through neighborhood proximity. The vast majority of regular employees at the center were Armenian as well. The first time I visited the center, I addressed in Armenian the woman who brought in tray after tray of strong Lebanese coffee throughout the day. She looked at me without missing a beat and responded in Arabic. I found out later that she was married to an Armenian man and understood a little Armenian. Her ability to gain employment at the clinic, however, was based on her ability to claim "Armenianness" as the wife of an Armenian. Even this access was conditional, however. Hierarchies of access depend on women's abilities to adhere to normative ideas about "womanhood," "morality," and sexual propriety.

One day an Arabic-speaking woman with an infant came into the center. The woman was frail, exhausted, and extremely thin. Though her six-month old son was alert and healthy, he had never seen a pediatrician, so the woman had come in to see if she could receive assistance with routine vaccinations and checkups. Her primary reason for coming into the center, however, was to seek help in procuring identity documents for her son. While the woman lived with her partner, the child's father, they were not married. In Lebanon only men can grant citizenship to their wives or children. Because the couple were not married, the child lacked any form of identity documents. While there are some provisions for identity documents for unmarried Lebanese women after the child has reached one year of age, those documents are usually more difficult to obtain. The process is not straightforward, and for many women it is particularly difficult to get institutions and actors to assist them if they are unwed mothers.[12] In the past, even when someone was able to obtain identity documents for children whose fathers are unknown or will not claim them as their own children, the ID carried the stigmatizing words *ghair shari'i*, or "illegitimate," though this practice has thankfully ceased (Joseph 1997).

While the woman was not Armenian, her partner was. Sevan explained that this was probably why she felt she could turn to the Armenian social workers for help. Because the child's father was an Armenian man, she could legitimately make a claim for assistance, at least on the child's behalf. The woman told Sevan that her partner was still married to his Armenian wife, who lived with two of their children. He and his wife were married in the Armenian Apostolic Church, which meant that divorce was possible (unlike if they had married in the Catholic Church). Still, divorce was discouraged by church authorities and not always granted to the petitioners. The man refused to file for divorce, possibly due to the social pressure he would face if he started this legal procedure. Because he did not file for divorce, the woman explained, she was not sure that he could acknowledge paternity for a child from another relationship.

Sevan was distraught, unsure where to refer the woman, doubtful that anyone would help her. All Sevan could do was send her to the Armenian Apostolic prelacy office, the arachnortaran, and tell her to ask to speak to someone who handles marriage and birth certificates. Knowing that the case was probably hopeless, Sevan gave the woman several food coupons and arranged for her to vaccinate her child for free in the clinic rather than paying the reduced fee usually charged for medical procedures. Sevan had little hope that the woman would be able to sort out her child's dilemma. Without identity documents, this child would be unable to officially register for public school or visit a public hospital. It would prove extremely difficult for a non-Armenian, unmarried woman who had transgressed normative ideas of sexual morality and propriety to compel anyone at the Apostolic prelacy to assist her, so she would require the kind of wasta that the social workers simply did not have. This case demonstrates that the ability to mobilize institutions to grant legal status, or at least indicate where such status could be obtained, is not simply a matter of paternal claim to community or even gendered notions of sexual propriety alone. Rather, we might liken getting access to wasta as the mobilization of a number of differing scales and classifications and their "attendant moral dimensions" (for example, paternal claims to community or legal identity, gendered notions of sexual propriety, *and* personal connections to powerful religious officials) that must come together in particular ways in order to make things move (Bowker and Star 1999).[13]

I contrast this with another, more straightforward case that Sevan was managing a few months later, where an Armenian woman in her early thirties was able to make a claim against her husband because she could demonstrate her own position of moral propriety. After being married for nine years, her Armenian husband had left her for another woman who was not Armenian, and she was trying to get custody of her two children through divorce proceedings filed with the Apostolic Church. She was struggling financially and was surviving partially owing to her neighbors' assistance and the Armenian NGO's monthly food coupons. Sevan arranged for her to get free clothing from the secondhand store that the clinic ran downstairs. Sevan was much more confident about this case, confirming with the woman that she had an excellent chance of being granted not only the divorce but also full custody of the children, something notoriously difficult to achieve through many family courts. Sevan trusted that the moral sanction, in this case, would be leveled against the woman's husband.

In both instances, the women's ability to claim moral propriety as *women* and *mothers* has a profound impact on outcomes, because it directly affects their ability to access assistance through Armenian social networks and institutions. Gaining access to the community network for the first woman would have been possible only if she were married to her partner. While her child can access limited services from the social workers at various Armenian medical and social centers, she is unlikely to receive the kind of assistance she needs to obtain official documents. These documentary practices rely on a set of infrastructures, even as they interdigitate with women's infrastructures and communicative pathways (Elyachar 2010, 2011). Thus the ramifications of gendered notions of propriety and morality on access are profound and sometimes contradict patriarchal kinship and legal norms in Lebanon and Lebanese Armenian institutions.

CLIENTS, CASES, AND THE PROFESSIONALIZATION OF SOCIAL WORK

For social workers like Sevan, and other professional women who worked in NGOs, clinics, schools, and social service centers in Bourj Hammoud but lived elsewhere, the gap between their daily lives and experiences and those of their clients was often vast. While Sevan grew up in a wealthier suburb of Beirut, her grandmother lived in Bourj Hammoud, and she always felt rooted in the community. Sevan dreamed of faraway travel, but her professional intervention was destined to be much closer to home. When the war in Lebanon ended in 1990, the economic desperation in Bourj Hammoud seemed only to increase. After completing a *stage*, or internship, as part of her undergraduate coursework at Haigazian University, Sevan was able to secure a social worker position at a local NGO. The stated mission of many of these organizations is to assist women in providing for their families, as well as provide educational and medical services to "improve" and "modernize" women, particularly in regard to their roles as primary caregivers. As shown through the examples above, women can access networks and services by negotiating these normative ideas about gender and by proving themselves as "good" women by abiding by common understandings about moral propriety.[14]

However, women looking for help at the NGO mentioned above are not only seeking services from that particular organization. Rather, they seek to access the networks provided by the employees and social workers as "professional" women (Murdock 2008). These channels, forged through university educations, provided them with greater access to other professionals— professionals at other NGOs, lawyers, bureaucrats at the arachnortaran, or even the Lebanese general security office. Many families undoubtedly depended on the food coupons, prescription medication discounts, and vaccines. However, it was access to the channels that the social workers represented, whether or not they could mobilize wasta effectively, that really brought the steady stream of clients in to see Sevan. In addition to their official capacities as social workers, she and the others were professional, middle-class Armenian women with wasta, or connections in the Armenian community. This wasta was much more easily mobilized for another Armenian. Nonetheless, as in the aforementioned case of the unmarried woman, there was a hierarchy within Armenianness that determined how much wasta one could benefit from, even with the help of a very well-connected person. For poor Armenians, living in Bourj Hammoud meant having consistent access to these networks that were, in no small way, critical to physical and social survival. Through the multiple iterations whereby people negotiate access to various services and flows of favors and resources, people tentatively begin to feel out the boundaries of their belonging in this imagined and materially constructed community (Anderson 1983). It is impossible to map this sense of belonging onto a strictly ethnoreligious definition of community or identity. Those who lobby the social workers at the NGO may have very different ideas about their own place within the community or their sense of identity as Armenian, as non-Armenian, as "Christian," or as something else entirely.

In other words, these channels of services produce a sense of a "public" as people are continually asked to imagine themselves as part of a community, or to prove it, rather, in order to get what they need to survive. Furthermore, these channels also reproduce (in ways similar to the personal status laws in Lebanon, though often with different outcomes) inequalities based on gender and on being well connected that don't always map onto an essentialized "Armenian community" or a particular kind of "Armenian individual"—an Arab woman could potentially mobilize these networks more easily than a Syrian Armenian man, for example. In general, women are better able to mobilize care networks having to do with the provision of medical care or access to schooling. Women can gain access to these networks by claiming Armenianness through gender and gendered division of labor whereby women are regarded as responsible for the "domestic" sphere, including medical care, education, and, when necessary, food assistance.[15] The provision of services is managed by a cadre of professional, middle-class Armenian women who can, potentially, act as mediators to certain channels of services for poor women, provided they can make legitimate claims as described above. Attending the lecture at the beginning, for example, allows women to gain access to circulation of knowledge as well as material resources not only from within Bourj Hammoud and Lebanon but from transnational charities or private companies that disburse free samples or discounts to medications or medical exams. There is no *one* way to make a claim, however, and it is much more complicated than merely having to do with being born into or married into one sectarian "community" or another.

For example, during the course of my fieldwork, I met Rita, a nineteen-year-old Armenian girl who had attended vocational training courses at another Armenian nonprofit in Bourj Hammoud. She was then working part-time at the nonprofit, doing administrative work and running errands for the staff. Because she had dropped out of school at a young age and attended classes at the center for years, she never transitioned completely to the role of an employee, and the staff continued their paternalistic attitude toward her. To most of the staff, Rita had gone from being a teenage "tomboy" to a grown woman dangerously challenging the norms of gendered propriety that they had labored to instill in their female students. Rita had clipped her hair short, wore sneakers and men's clothing, and was uninterested in makeup. One staff member expressed concern that Rita had been "influenced by the wrong people" and continually urged her to "dress like a girl," even going as far as taking her shopping for new clothes and teaching her how to apply makeup. Rita went along with their suggestions at times, not only because she felt compelled to but because she was genuinely hurt and confused by her colleagues' condemnation. Cases like Rita's were quite common, even with women well out of their teenage years, as those who had once been "clients" could never quite transition into being full and equal participants in the management of these organizations. The "clients" always remained subject to paternalistic monitoring, particularly in the realm of policing normative ideas about gender and sexual propriety. Rita eventually started working in a small clothing manufacturing workshop and left her position at the center. While she was likely to face similar pressures from family and neighbors to conform to gendered expectations of dress and comportment, she felt much less scrutiny at her factory job. In Rita's case her position within the network of NGOs as a former client not only put limits on her class mobility within the community and the NGO network but also made her more subject to policing of normative gender roles and notions of propriety.

Lack of access to resources, to certain kinds of formal training or education, affects one's sense of belonging, particularly in the bifurcated world of the professional NGO, where the college-educated social workers are the first point of contact with a largely poor female clientele who often lack a formal education. While occasionally women who start out as "clients" in the world of professionalized NGOs can gain part-time employment with the organization, there is often a clear distinction between them and the professional women that has to do with education as well as their positioning within the network of connections, more so than access to strictly economic resources. In other words, they usually remain "clients" rather than active members of the organizations. Opportunities for gaining employment after completing some kind of vocational training at the NGOs are shrinking even further. Unlike the professionalized NGOs, the channels of services initiated by the nexus of the Tashnag Party and the Armenian Apostolic Church deal more narrowly with Armenians who can claim affiliation with the political party and the church. Nevertheless, the conditions found in the institutions managed by Tashnag and the church mirror the distinctions between the "professional" women like Sevan who work as social workers in NGOs and the "clients" for whom gendered propriety becomes a way for women to access the crucial networks of services.[16]

DEVELOPING "GOOD" WOMEN, PROGRESS THROUGH THE NETWORK

Silvart, an energetic woman in her late fifties, had spent most of her life working in Bourj Hammoud, though she and her family lived in a middle-class suburb nearby. During the long, dark years of the civil war, Silvart had begun her career as a coordinator between various international charities and the prelacy of the Lebanese branch of the Armenian Apostolic Church, which runs several schools and churches in the area. In those days her work was focused on emergency and relief services. Like many of my interlocutors in Bourj Hammoud, Silvart had harrowing tales of the war. A constant barrage of shells falling close enough for her to hear the whizzing sound of their flight through the air, one blowing up her car just in front of her house, militiamen overrunning and claiming her family's shop in a nearby neighborhood—all these were stories she related during our conversations. And yet Silvart also echoed another popular sentiment I'd heard through many of my interviews about Bourj Hammoud during the war—one of nostalgia.

"During the war, people knew who they really were," Silvart said. Ultimately, Silvart thought, "being Armenian" was the only recourse for safety, for stability, for a sense of community and solidarity for an Armenian in Lebanon. There were various ways for women to demonstrate their commitment to being Armenian. One of them was sending one's children to the Armenian schools in Bourj Hammoud or elsewhere. While lower-income families were more likely send their children to Armenian schools, particularly with the assistance of arachnortaran scholarships and subsidies for Armenian students, Silvart suggested that wealthy Armenians seem to have "forgotten their roots" and send their children to exclusive Lebanese Christian academies that do not offer any instruction in Armenian language or history. She noted, sardonically, that the next time Lebanon was enveloped in a violent, cataclysmic war (an inevitability, she thought), these people would be faced with the reality that they are first and foremost Armenians, and only other

Armenians can offer them the protection and security that is so elusive in times of conflict.

Silvart's lifelong work has been to support and maintain the "community," a task that, ironically, has only become more difficult since the civil war in Lebanon ended in 1990. During the war the needs were obvious, and it was easier to attract international assistance. Now, however, despite the economic and political instability that has plagued the country ever since the war ended, it is much harder to attract aid. Silvart enthusiastically listed all the economic development projects for women that she had been involved with since 2000. Two of the projects, a catering business and a job placement service, were illustrative of the types of enterprises that the Tashnag-dominated arachnortaran had embarked on that serve mainly Armenian women. The catering business employed Armenian women who lived in the Bourj Hammoud area. Specializing in Armenian and Lebanese dishes like *manti* (meat dumplings) or *kibbet laqteen* (pumpkin croquettes), the business maintained a food delivery service with a menu that changed daily. While most of the women employed with the business lived in Bourj Hammoud, the food preparation took place on the bottom floor of an Armenian school in a suburb farther away. I was surprised to learn that only a small group of twelve women were responsible for all the food preparation. The entire space, including the kitchen, seemed quite small given the size of the operation.

The manager of the catering business shared her office space with a number of large freezers that contained the food waiting to be shipped out to grocery stores. As she worked at her desk, women used the shrink-wrap machines to pack the aluminum trays of food and stamp them with labels, all in English. She explained that the project started as out as a pitch to a large, transnational charity's development fund. The business model was approved, and the funds went toward procuring the industrial-grade kitchen equipment and hiring the staff. The initiative was a huge success, and the business has expanded its hiring.

When I entered the kitchen, it was buzzing with activity, as tasks were divided into a factory-like system of production. The staff was small but worked quickly and efficiently. One of the women told me about the rigorous audition process they all had to go through to get the job. Each woman had to prepare several dishes that were then tasted by the manager and other staff off-site. It was not enough to simply be willing to be trained; the catering business hired only experienced cooks. For many of these women, however, this job was their first regular work outside of the home. While many had possibly worked small jobs, or perhaps done some light catering work out of their home kitchens, the experience of working fixed hours outside of the home was something new. All of them lived in Bourj Hammoud and met in a prearranged meeting spot early in the morning in order to take a van to the kitchen. They worked until early afternoon, when the same van would take them home.

The job placement service, another arachnortaran initiative, was also designed to help Armenians find employment. Unlike the catering business, however, this was simply a list or a registry that tried to pair unemployed people with different sorts of informal or part-time jobs like housekeeping, childcare, or elder care. While no one stipulated that this list was exclusive to women, I never noticed any men using the service to find work. Most of the jobs listed involved some kind of domestic labor and caregiving—jobs usually assigned to women. Unlike the catering business, the jobs listed did not necessarily offer stability or long-term security.

The Tashnag-dominated arachnorataran development projects, however, gave women access to more than just employment. Initiatives like the catering business and the job placement service are part of the powerful channels of Bourj Hammoud's most dominant political party and religious organization. These channels produce a sense of a particular kind of community and identity that is also very material. The network of organizations is lived and experienced as both a social and symbolic realm and a way in which resources and services are transmitted and obtained (Elyachar 2011). Much like Sevan's office, Silvart's was more than just a place to look at the jobs available on the placement list. Women would often come to Silvart to discuss problems they were having as a way of procuring advice or referrals to other social organizations or individuals that could help. By describing their hardships in these structured visits, whether they be a husband's illness, a lack of income, or an inability to pay for school tuition, they appealed to Silvart as a professional staffer at an important organization as a potential pathway to make the connections necessary to procure assistance. Silvart's various connections to arachnortaran programs, Armenian NGOs, transnational charities, Tashnag initiatives, important local patrons, and even the municipality made her a powerful node within the system, someone who could route people into the proper channels.

However, the ability of professional social workers and managers at various institutions to put networks into motion rested on their ability to position these women as living up to their roles as present or future heads of "Armenian families." Did they attempt to send their children to Armenian schools? Were they married to Armenians? These standards coexist alongside the highly gendered, normative notions of sexual and moral propriety that are a precondition to seeking assistance, particularly from organizations affiliated with the church. An unmarried Armenian mother not only would have difficulty procuring an identity document for her child but could potentially have difficulty procuring other connections within these networks. Even managers in possession of wider fields of connectivity had to appeal to the right people to gain access to the right channels, and reputation of clients was built through lines of gossip and talk.

Similarly, there were blurred boundaries between these individuals' professional roles as social workers or managers and their roles as notable people within the community, though notable in very different networks. Sevan, for example, had access to the world of college-educated, professionalized social workers and psychologists and was a lecturer at several local professional schools. Silvart, on the other hand, had access to the Armenian Apostolic arachnortaran, the Tashnag Party apparatus, and the transnational Christian charities that provided assistance to their initiatives. There were points at which they interfaced and overlapped, but they also reached out into different realms and had different abilities. Both Sevan and Silvart served within their professional capacities as pathways to the dense network of services and institutions that produce the channels glossed as "sectarian community" in Lebanon.

What I have been arguing thus far is not only that gendered morality can enable or disable connection to these channels but also that what constitutes "sectarian community" is by no means monolithic. There are profound differences between the institutions that provide services, in terms of their funding sources, their logics of operation and staffing, and even the networks of clients they serve in terms of class, geography, professionalization, and very different forms of transnational reach. While all are part of the "Armenian community" and there are connections and pathways between these realms, there are quite a number of differences between a professionalized NGO with funding sources from nonreligious Armenian American diasporic organizations and the network of the Armenian prelacy organizations in Lebanon. These organizations have different definitions of what the Armenian community means and how and when to best serve it. Much of this has to do with the distinction between official church organizations and diasporic Armenian organizations that are not necessarily working in close relationship with religious institutions or the Tashnag Party in Lebanon.

Like many arachnortaran projects with a "development" aim, college-educated professionals who usually did not live in Bourj Hammoud organized both the catering initiative and the job placement service. These projects target less affluent women in Bourj Hammoud. The effect was something of a two-tiered system. Professional Armenian women build their careers as go-betweens, working with international charities or the arachnortaran to create new programs and "develop" the Armenian community by focusing on women's empowerment through employment and work. Silvart, for example, had been able to advance through a system of professional ranking. For the women seeking work through the job placement service, there was much less opportunity for movement up through the ranks. In a sense, they always remained *recipients* of these development projects rather than equal partners in any decision-making process. While the women would benefit from greater access to resources, namely, in the way of economic security, that was often the extent of their participation in the project. The division of labor between the professionals and the beneficiaries was clear, and it seemed that the line was difficult to cross.

For many Armenian women in Bourj Hammoud, even those who worked outside the home, the only realm in which they could participate more actively in community organizational work was within the *masnajoughner* (chapters) of the Lipananian Oknoutian Khatch, or Armenian Relief Cross (often referred to as LOKH). Regarded by my interlocutors in Lebanon as the women's charitable auxiliary affiliated with the Tashnag Party, LOKH is part of an international organization with local chapters throughout the world. It has a large medical clinic in Bourj Hammoud, but its member base consists of several small masnajoughs whose jurisdictions map onto the network of agoumps in each neighborhood that also serve as their meeting places. The masnajoughs are completely run and managed by women from the surrounding neighborhoods. Many of the women who worked at the aforementioned catering business or the job placement service are members of masnajoughs, partly because they do provide certain kinds of material resources and services. More important, they provide opportunities for women to manage and run charitable organizations as well as gain seniority and rank within the community—things that are generally absent from their workplace experiences within the framework of the arachnortaran's "development" programs. These chapters have their own development initiatives at a neighborhood level and operate quite differently from both the professional NGOs and the arachnorataran's joint projects with transnational charities. In this instance, gender propriety is a way not only to gain access to a network but also to become an important node within it, to become a new channel or pathway.

POLITICAL ORGANIZING, RELIEF AS WOMEN'S DOMAIN

I attended my first masnajough meeting of a neighborhood chapter of LOKH in Bourj Hammoud. The women gathered on the top floor of the local agoump of the Tashnag Party in the mid-morning. The network of agoumps served as neighborhood meeting places for the party members living in the immediate vicinity. The agoumps differed in terms of their degree of amenities.[17] Some had offices and computer labs, but most had kitchens and some kind of hall for events. Most Bourj Hammoud residents regard the Tashnag Party as holding the most sway over leadership within the municipality. Tashnag has also long dominated the official institutions of the Armenian Apostolic Church in Lebanon (Joseph 1975; Migliorino 2008; Nalbantian 2011). Thus there is an implicit and sometimes explicit relationship between the church, the municipality, and the agoumps and NGOs affiliated with the Tashnag Party. For many of my Armenian interlocutors in Bourj Hammoud, the agoumps served as the basic unit of the party's functions at the neighborhood level. They were also an entry point for people living in the locality of the agoump to become involved with the party as well as to socialize or share information. The atmosphere at the agoumps I visited was social and relaxed; they felt more like community recreation centers than official political party offices. The agoumps are part of an interlocking and hierarchical network of local chapters under the umbrella of a much larger political party led by higher committee members occupying positions of leadership. However, higher-ranking party members did not necessarily take part in or directly manage local events or activities, nor did members of neighborhood agoumps necessarily seek to rise up to higher ranks within the party. The agoumps served as meaningful places to socialize and, during the war, functioned as key sites of security and the provision of much-needed relief and aid. The connection between feelings of loyalty to the Tashnag Party, a sense of security, and a deep-rooted belonging to the vicinity of the agoump and the neighborhood of its jurisdiction was partially fueled by the memory of the role of the agoump (and the people who belonged to it) during those difficult years of war.

Most of the women attending the masnajough meeting did not work outside of the home, and the majority were over fifty. One of the women explained that this was mainly due to the fact that many younger women have some kind of employment or have young children to care for. Unlike the professional NGO workers who were paid a wage to serve as social workers or social assistants, and who mainly commuted to Bourj Hammoud from middle-class Christian suburbs to the northeast of the city, the masnajough members were unpaid volunteers who lived in the immediate vicinity of the agoump where meetings were held. Only the elected representatives of the local masnajough met weekly; all the other regular members just attended special events. One of the members, Vartoug, was eager to explain the gendered division of labor between Tashnag members. While men met at the agoump at night, the women's masnajough met during the day and had different responsibilities. Men were more concerned with "security," while LOKH was wholly concerned with charity work for local Armenian families in the district. She said that the members of LOKH are exclusively women because of the nature of their activities and explained that, unlike the men's activities within the Tashnag, LOKH was outside of politics. She explained: "It's not governmental nor is it political. It is philanthropic. That's why men withdrew from the organization, so it wouldn't appear as a political organization, and it became a philanthropic organization. Just like the

English have Florence Nightingale, we are like that." Vartoug regarded the
activities of the masnajough as expressly nonpolitical because they focused on
relief and charity, which were seemingly out of the realm of "real" politics.[18]

Despite Vartoug's characterization of LOKH's work as nonpolitical, none of
the members took their work lightly. Like everyone I spoke with who worked
at an NGO or some kind of relief organization during the days of the civil
war, the women all had stories about providing meals, clothing, or shelter
to people in dire need during those desperate and violent times. Today the
activities of the *engerouhi*s, which could translate as "friends" or "comrades,"
focused on making sure that every elderly person in their jurisdiction had
enough food to eat and basic amenities, and that every child had enough
money to buy schoolbooks and, preferably, to attend Armenian schools.
The masnajough would also visit people who were ill or in mourning and
generally served as a kind of communication network for the exchange of all
kinds of important information and favors. Each district was very small, as
the jurisdiction of each agoump was only a few blocks in any direction. If you
were Armenian and living in the vicinity of an agoump in Bourj Hammoud,
you would technically be under its jurisdiction, not only in terms of eligibility
for services but also, theoretically, for issues relating to security.[19]

The Tashnag apparatus is hierarchical in its organization. Its various sub-
organizations, starting with elementary-school-aged children, are divided by
gender, and there are separate associations for college students and young
adults who do not attend college. Still, for many low-income women in
Bourj Hammoud without a formal education, membership and volunteering
with a masnajough was a much more effective means of accessing a network
of prestige, as well as services, and in some cases even employment. While
the masnajoughs are open only to Armenian women, membership provided
them with the opportunity to circulate beyond the immediate neighborhood,
into the wider world of the LOKH organization with its many chapters
throughout Lebanon and its connections to transnational Armenian charities.

Since all the other masnajough members lived in the same, small sub-
neighborhood of that agoump's jurisdiction, there was little separation
between the work done with the masnajough and the socialization in one's
neighborhood and network of kin and friends.[20] Generally the women who
take leadership roles in the masnajoughs are better off financially than those
who access services at NGOs, but there is a degree of crossover between
them, as some masnajough members attend classes or lectures at the NGOs.
While many other Armenian women of a particular neighborhood pay dues
to belong to the organization, taking a leadership role was reserved for the
women who were more permanent fixtures in the neighborhood. The ability
to claim a leadership role rested even more so on one's ability to appear as
an "upstanding" woman in the community and abide by normative ideas of
gendered propriety. Reputation was confirmed through kinship relations,

long-standing residence in the neighborhood, or referrals though friends. In the masnajough meetings I attended, I noticed that most of the senior leaders were Armenian women who had lived in the neighborhood for decades.

Despite friendships across sect in Bourj Hammoud's mixed neighborhoods, the masnajoughs take responsibility only for Armenian residents in their neighborhood's jurisdiction.[21] While I never met a non-Armenian at a masnajough meeting, a few of the women whom I met were married to non-Armenians. Through conversation, I began to understand that the concept of belonging to the Armenian community could be extended by virtue of the woman's good standing in the neighborhood as well as the husband's willingness to support her activities. Other members of the masnajough referred to these husbands in a way that highlighted their desire to extend the boundaries of Armenianness to these members of their friends' family. One member said of another's husband: "He is Arabic speaking (*arab-a-khos*), but trust me he is more Armenian than you or me." Here the husband is not essentialized as an odar, a foreigner or other, but rather is made into an "Arabic speaker" in a move that emphasizes his difference as merely linguistic rather than somehow embodied.

What makes the masnajoughs different from the other two "professionalized" NGOs is that the "friends" are not recipients of charitable services. The masnajoughs are themselves responsible for gathering and redistributing resources, goods, and services throughout their neighborhood. In so doing, members become important nodes in the networked system by which people are integrated into the Tashnag Party, and thus into an Armenian "civil society" of the most politicized form. While the masnajoughs may look diminutive in comparison to professionalized NGOs with the backing of large transnational organizations, the masnajoughs were an important organizing force for the Tashnag Party, which is also, as an Armenian diaspora organization, transnational in scale. The masnajough members were also powerful organizers who had greater autonomy over whom they could deem a legitimate member of the "community" because of the entanglement of their work and the neighborhood network. Just like their male counterparts at the agoump, the masnajough women created a similar kind of disciplinary and surveillance network. Members could potentially enact censure and kept accounts of all activities in the area through their structured visits.[22]

Spatial proximity, neighborhood friendships, and even intersectarian marriage did not alter the members' view of the masnajough/LOKH networks as a strictly Armenian organization for an Armenian social world. Still, a single small neighborhood under the jurisdiction of the agoump could have within it several different networks activated simultaneously for different people who accessed them in different ways that were not reducible to ethnoreligious identity alone, including the arachnortaran development initiatives or the professionalizing NGOs. For the women of the LOKH organization, their neighborhood was one node within the worldwide network of Tashnag and LOKH Armenian charitable and political organizations of the diaspora.

LOGICS OF ACCESS, DEFINITIONS OF COMMUNITY

The professionalized NGOs, top-down Tashnag initiatives, and masnajoughs are all access points into the circulation of organizations and institutions that constitute what appears as a monolithic Armenian public sphere. While the NGOs provide much-needed medical care and services, they do not present a pathway to professionalization for most of the clients. While the professionalized class of social workers could effectively serve as nodes along the channels of other kinds of services not offered at the center, there remained a hierarchy that the clients could never truly join, even after undergoing vocational training and accepting paid positions at the NGO. Similarly, the arachnortaran programs like the catering business and the job placement service gave many women access to the powerful network of Armenian Apostolic Church organizations, though again it involved an appeal to more powerful senior administrators. In both the NGOs and the arachnortaran initiatives, access depended not only on finding a way to claim Armenianness through birth or marriage but also on normative ideas about gender propriety. Any woman who is seen to transgress these gender norms, especially those having to do with marriage and children, could have difficulty accessing the network again.

The local chapters of the masnajoughs, though part of the transnational network of the women's auxiliary of the Tashnag Party, operate on a neighborhood level and present the most opportunities for working-class women to rise up through the ranks of this women's auxiliary to the governing body of the larger organization. These women have much more autonomy over the management of their localized chapters. However, while open and accessible to nonprofessionalized women to assume leadership roles, these are narrowly connected to the Tashnag Party apparatus of local chapters and are not translatable to professionalized employment in the ways that the NGOs are. These masnajoughs, unlike the NGOs, have no stated mission to serve non-Armenian populations, though a member could potentially serve as an important gateway into the network on behalf of a non-Armenian family member using the channels provided by the LOKH network.

In all these cases, interlocking logics of gendered propriety, economic privilege, and social class as well as geographies of place and the neighborhood scale complicate the image of access to these networks as narrowly based on ethnoreligious identity. At the same time, these messy, interlocking, and material webs of infrastructure and services are the very channels through which multiple senses of sectarian belonging and community are produced. The institutions create pathways through which people come to imagine themselves as part of an Armenian public that, as it turns out, is far from monolithic. It is not just through the services but also through the habits and practices of how these services and infrastructures are maintained and accessed that a sense of belonging to an Armenian "community" is produced and reinforced. The institutions can provide new interconnections as people and things circulate between them. However, this dense network of institutions, overlapping but not quite subsuming one another, can also create moments of disconnection where sparks can fly. The networks I detail in this chapter, while different, are interrelated in crucial material ways, both enabling and disabling connections between people and feelings of belonging or exclusion.

As in other chapters, I have continued to unsettle the notion that "Armenianness" or sectarian belonging is something one is automatically born with or into, and that it is not narrowly defined as belonging to ethnoreligious sect. The creation of a sectarian "public sphere" is done not only through imaginaries about sectarian belonging or shared historical time but also through the very mundane networks through which people obtain basic amenities. In this instance, demonstrating normative gender propriety is a way to enter into circulation, as gendered discourses of charity and care-work are the processes through which people come to understand themselves as Armenian or mobilize Armenianness. In the following chapter I shift focus from women's networks of formalized social service institutions to the circuits of exchange produced by informal women's rotating credit associations, as well as political actors' attempts to transform these "unruly" networks into official institutions. How might we approach the infrastructures of debt as part of the way in which community is produced? What happens when previously informal but highly structured credit networks are channeled into official, state-licensed banking systems? How do these channels of debt and credit create the conditions of possibility for certain kinds of inclusion and circulation while excluding others? Most important, how are notions of sectarian community, of belonging and exclusion, shaped and transformed through circulations and exchange? I take up these questions in relation to informal rotating credit associations and licensed lending facilities in Bourj Hammoud in the following chapter.

Chapter 4

FROM SHIRKETS TO BANKAS

Credit, Lending, and the Narrowing of Networks

While store loyalty cards are often the first types of credit cards marketed to consumers in countries where these forms of credit are being made available to wider publics, in Lebanon some banks have taken to marketing credit cards using different ideas of loyalty, identity, and belonging. Even banks that adopt the appearance of a strictly rational, economically based system of lending to those who are most capable of paying back the loan still utilize the logics of sectarian community to market their credit cards. Bank Audi, one of the largest Lebanese banks, has created the "Hi Card" (a mixture of Armenian and English that translates to Armenian Card), which is a credit card that, according to a pamphlet, "combines the Armenian heritage with the Lebanese trends." Emblazoned with a tricolor sunburst reflecting the colors of the Armenian flag, Bank Audi offers Hi Card holders discounts to affiliated Armenian businesses like the furniture store Vanlian, upscale restaurant Mayrig, and Bourj Hammoud gift shop Pascanoush. By assuming that Armenians would prefer an Armenian credit card that gives them discounts to Armenian businesses, the card demonstrates the ways in which the bank's advertising campaign tries to capitalize on assumptions about consumption and sectarian identity. The marketing tactic assumes not only that Armenians frequent Armenian-owned businesses and that this is a way to earn discounts to places customers already frequent but also that shopping and consumption are ways to demonstrate one's sectarian identity and belonging to a sectarian "community" by keeping the networks of consumption and circulation of money within one's "own community."

The Hi Card marketing strategy also plays to popular discourses about Armenians' tight-knit network of services and stores that create a "separate" Armenian public sphere in Lebanon. The strategy is largely symbolic, however, as no credit card from a major bank could replace the informal credit networks of many Armenians in Lebanon. Most of my interlocutors in Bourj Hammoud did not use credit cards because their incomes were too low or irregular to be eligible for bank credit (which is much less accessible in Lebanon than in the United States). Across classes and communities in Lebanon, using official bank credit, particularly in large sums for things like mortgages, is a relatively recent innovation. Many of my interlocutors were unaccustomed to or distrustful of bank loans, or any dealings with a bank. In fact, some who worked at a transnational NGO were highly resistant to the idea of their paychecks being directly deposited to the bank. The accountant at the NGO was astounded that anyone would resist obtaining a bank account or directly depositing salary into it. She imagined it as a requisite step to modernity and "advancement" and attributed the employees' resistance to their "ignorance" and "backwardness" that was "typical of Bourj Hammoud."

However, among the employees who were resisting the move to direct deposit, the idea of simply trusting that their check would go into their account without ever seeing it or dealing with a person face to face was appalling. While their distrust is partially attributable to their unfamiliarity with certain technologies, it has much more to do with the additional meanings behind transactions dealing with money. The rules governing the exchange of money, even for goods, and the borrowing and accruing of money were connected to many important facets of life. It was not merely a folksy trust in a handshake and face-to-face contact. It was, for many people in Bourj Hammoud, a question of creating additional value through relationships. Lebanese banks also reflect the value of personalization in their transactions. Much like visiting a municipal office or going to see a local elected official, opening a bank account or doing long-term business in a Lebanese bank involves drinking coffee, taking one's time, and getting to know the people who work there. This stands in stark contrast to transactions at the larger transnational banks in Lebanon that operate more impersonally and rapidly.

Credit and lending, and more specifically the forms of institutional and infrastructural arrangements that support the circulation of credit, help to construct a social world through exchange.[1] In Lebanon, a country where remittances represent 17 percent of the GDP (7.8 billion dollars), the transfer of money from Brazil, the United States, Sierra Leone, or Qatar is a powerful means of circulation, even for those Lebanese who do not move.[2] Access to consumer credit cards in Lebanon, while still unavailable to most, is one of the ways in which remittances, expatriate spending, and even entrepreneurial expertise brought from abroad are remaking the credit landscape. It might be tempting to think about the formalization of credit as a kind of "great equalizer," one in which the banks' rubrics for a "good lender" are regularized and therefore not subject to bias against members of a particular sect, for example. However, while these forces appear to bring about greater impersonalization, they do not necessarily reflect a move away from the logic of sectarian organizations, which tend to use other criteria—gender, class, geographical location, membership in a sectarian political party—as a means of vouching for someone as a member of the "community" and therefore to be trusted. Even at the level of banking and payment infrastructure, we see the extension of the language of sectarian community to market these services.

In this chapter I argue that in Lebanon economic networks of credit and lending can further contribute to the production of sectarianism as well as the narrowing of the definition of who can be an adequate member of the sectarian "community."[3] In Bourj Hammoud the formalization of credit and lending into official institutions can become a way to hard-wire the notion of a coherent sectarian community that can vouch for one another in quite different ways from informal credit. In fact, the formalization of credit can rewire the circuits through which community is experienced and understood and of course produce new forms of exclusion. The actors involved with these projects position their formalizing efforts not only as a way of extending credit to the unbanked but also as a means of "maintaining" community. But what if we looked at these networks of things in exchange as what is driving the materialization at certain moments of sectarian identity? By starting from these material systems as an origin story, we can shift away from the inevitable-seeming trajectory forged by humans planning and "creating" sectarian community. Certainly the actors involved with promoting Armenian schools, nationalist histories, and narratives shaped understandings of the Armenian community and sectarian identity. What I add to this narrative, however, is that sectarianism is inseparable from the human infrastructure that both sustains it and is sustained by it. These institutions exist in a dialogic relationship with the identities they produce, and there is no one, singular history that sets the precedent for all these things.[4]

The history of credit and debt in Bourj Hammoud reveals a story in which the unruliness of money and lending, particularly in transgressing the boundaries of sect and forging new kinds of networks, is constantly being hemmed in by various forces. Institutional histories, however, can provide opportunities for reclaiming potential futures. Here I trace the transition from women's rotating credit associations, or *shirket*s, to formalized credit institutions as part of the increasing sectarianization of all kinds of human and material infrastructure.[5] This is a very historical analysis, but a history of a different kind. Here, to use the language of economics, sectarianism in Lebanon is a kind of path dependency created by *techniques* put out there in time, not necessarily by human agents pulling the strings.[6] Time does not pass, it accumulates, gathering significances that layer on the sociotechnical arrangements that make possible the sectarianized networks of "community" in the sense that it is defined in Bourj Hammoud. These layers of sociotechnical arrangements do not bury or obscure but rather serve as a platform for further action.

I begin with a discussion of shirkets and the rise of a microlending facility that sought to formalize and contain these practices under the more centralized control of an official, Armenian-run organization. The desire to control or replace the shirket practices can be traced back to political actors' long-standing fear of women's informal networks as a potential site of crosscutting relationships that defy narrow sectarian logics of social relations and are therefore threatening to the sectarian social order (Joseph 1983).[7] Unlike the women involved in official sectarian organizations described in chapter 3 (both the masnajoughs and professionalized NGOs), by working outside of official organizations, women involved in shirkets have different possibilities of circulation that transform their experiences of community and create different potentials for belonging.

WOMEN'S ROTATING CREDIT ASSOCIATIONS IN BOURJ HAMMOUD

Shirkets, or Armenian women's rotating credit associations, are part of the history of the formation of Armenian social institutions and infrastructures in Lebanon. In 1974 anthropologist Arpi Hamalian (1974, 2) described shirkets as a "specific visiting pattern . . . organized around a well-defined economic goal: cooperative saving of money for use in time of need" practiced in Lebanon by Armenian women. The term shirket is taken from the Turkish word for "cooperative" or "association."[8] While Hamalian traces the earliest origins of the shirkets to practices in places where Armenians lived in the former Ottoman Empire, she cites the beginnings of the shirkets in Lebanon as a response to the total absence of social and economic organization in the wake of the genocide. After the various waves of deportations and eventual resettlement of Armenians in Lebanon, household incomes and family and extended community networks were destroyed, scattered, and dismantled. During this period Armenians turned to village and town associations in order to pool resources and reestablish familiar networks of patronage (Migliorino 2008).

It is within this context of crisis, not only economic but also social and, according to Hamalian, "moral," that women living in the camps organized the shirkets as a way of pooling resources.[9] While, for the most part, this appeared to literally mean the sharing of food, the "economy" here is an aggregate that is not just the pooling of "things" but also the sharing of "problems" and the constitution of a community, as visiting and discussion of problems and the formation of friendships were part of the wealth accumulated. The shirkets eventually traveled with the women involved, as "the members often actively helped each other to move into the same neighborhood" (Hamalian 1974, 76). Through the shirket, participants formed a kind of human infrastructure that enabled Armenians to build and sustain, neighborhood by neighborhood, the social networks, infrastructures, and services of Bourj Hammoud.[10] In a dialogic process, it is these networks, in turn, that produce for my interlocutors the sense of Bourj Hammoud as an Armenian public sphere.

While the types of shirkets were diversified and their roles in the community multiple, they remained exclusively a women's activity and evidently were shrouded in secrecy. Nonmembers were never privy to the details of the shirkets' finances or membership, nor the frequency or location of meetings. Husbands of members were also kept ignorant of the details of the shirket. Hamalian (1974, 80) writes that this, in a sense, was a way of protecting the women's savings. The extended and structured visiting sessions served not only as "group-therapy gatherings" but also as a powerful source of social and political discipline and community management. Women in the shirket solved problems, including disputes within families, between neighbors, or with other members of the community. The shroud of secrecy was equally essential to this project, as women could not be openly regarded a potent force for constituting social hierarchies in Bourj Hammoud. Perhaps participation in the shirket was a well-known secret, as the number of people involved "directly or indirectly" with the shirket could attest to their collective power. Hamalian estimates it at 100,000. Inexplicably, this is more than half of her estimate of the population of Armenians in Lebanon at the time she wrote this article, 180,000.

While her article focuses exclusively on Armenian participation in the shirkets, Hamalian briefly acknowledges how the benefit of shirket business crosses sectarian lines. Evidently the shirkets involved in collective grocery buying would only do business with "Muslim merchants" as a way of keeping their activities secret from their husbands who might also work "in the same lines of merchandising" (90). The shirkets were an aspect of Armenian assimilation in Lebanon, even as they were a means of Armenian social formation and cohesion. Hamalian writes: "The Armenian community controls closely and successfully almost all aspects of the life of the Armenians in Lebanon. The only and most effective leakage point is in the realm of the economic activities of the Armenians" (90). The "economic" here is regarded as a leak, or a gap, in Armenian social life—a realm in which interconnection with "Lebanese" social realms is unavoidable.

While Hamalian describes the shirket as an attempt at Armenian social cohesion in the aftermath of displacement, how exactly does a shirket bound an Armenian community or insulate it from a perceived "outside" when the very saving and spending of money in a market as intersectarian as Bourj

Hammoud is a means by which the resources of members of sectarian communities are put into circulation with each other? Here the "economy" is not only a gap whereby Armenian social life assimilates to "Lebanese" practices or habits but a way in which the Armenian community becomes a crucial part of the "Lebanese" market. While the shirkets were exclusive and secretive groups, they were also part of a vast financial network, circulating outside of the purview of the Lebanese government but still a substantial portion of the Lebanese economy. Hamalian estimated the total amount in 1974 at 2,500,000 Lebanese pounds (estimated at nearly one million U.S. dollars at that time).

In some ways the shirket might appear as an informal supplement to a formal credit system, as it provided the opportunity to borrow money to residents who might not otherwise have had access to credit from Lebanese banks.[11] Nevertheless, this distinction in the case of the shirket is quite difficult to make. Where does a shirket end and a "real" economy begin? In this instance, the attempt to make the distinction between the "official" and the "underground" or "unofficial" is even more tenuous, as the shirket is not a labor market but a credit pool where resources are gathered in order for members to make individual purchases in a marketplace.

I take the view that a shirket is a rich form of economic relationships that facilitates the transactions of finances a well as the distribution of other kinds of "surplus," including prestige, reputation, and honor as well as sanction and discipline.[12] Thus shirkets did more than help accrue material resources or provide credit to people who would otherwise be denied access to it. Shirkets also provided a form of social cohesion between Armenians whose social and familial networks had been destroyed through violent displacement.

It was after the time of Arpi Hamalian's research that the lending facility I will discuss later in the chapter, Arpa,[13] was first established in Bourj Hammoud in the early 1980s. Arpa was probably an outgrowth of what Hamalian describes as an emergent type of shirket she observed called a *banka* (an Armenianized term for bank). The bankas involved regular meetings, as did the other types of shirkets, but this form charged significant interest to its members, and the sums of money loaned out were usually much larger than the other types of shirkets were capable of lending. The bankas also allowed for a wider debt community, as most of the members would borrow money in order to lend it to family members or friends and charge even higher interest to them. Hamalian noted that these new bankas were increasing in number and kind, alongside other types of banks and credit unions that were slowly becoming more accessible to more of the middle-income populations that would participate in shirkets.

Today there are several banks in Bourj Hammoud, all of which are Lebanese banks with branches all over the country. Nevertheless, borrowing money from a bank is still inaccessible to most people who lack the necessary income to obtain credit. Shirkets today, while they appear narrowly Armenian, contain within them the potential to create pathways of circulation that are not as circumscribed by sectarian logics as other formalized lending facilities that serve as alternatives to large banks.

A SHIRKET TODAY: NEIGHBORS ACROSS THE CITY

Shirkets are still an important part of social and economic life for many in Bourj Hammoud. Despite my suspicion that most of the women who participate in shirkets would be over sixty, shirket participants ranged in age from young adults in their early twenties to women in their seventies and eighties. Part of this can be attributed to the fact that many in Bourj Hammoud, regardless of age or type of employment, did not have regular bank accounts. It was an Armenian woman in her sixties named Zabel who first told me about her weekly shirket group.

Like many shirkets, Zabel's group met in a different member's house each week. While many shirkets are formed between close-knit neighbors, this group was unique in that it was geographically disbursed. The first meeting I attended happened to be in a different suburb several miles away. Zabel arranged for those of us who lived near Bourj Hammoud to meet near the *dawra* roundabout, a major transit hub to the suburbs and cities to the north and east of Beirut. Slowly the other shirket women started to gather until all eight of us were there. The women, ranging in age from their early thirties to late seventies, walked out to the tangle of buses and shared taxis and dodged the traffic crowding the massive roundabout, asking various drivers to point us toward the right bus that would take us to our destination. It was a suburb I was unfamiliar with, so I was unaware of how long the journey would take. Though it was not far, the bus made several stops and took a circuitous route through winding roads up to the suburbs in the mountains that loomed over the eastern Beirut metropolitan area. A trip that would have taken twenty minutes by private car took about fifty minutes by bus. For the women this was an opportunity to talk, catch up, tell stories about what had transpired in the past week, and make observations about the neighborhoods we were passing through. In fact, despite the intense heat, the bus journey seemed to be an enjoyable part of the experience for the women, who used the time to socialize and have fun together.

During the bus ride, Zabel explained that the shirket started in Bourj Hammoud fifteen years ago. She said: "The group always changed, people would come and go, but we continue this together. We like each other very much and are very good friends." While the long bus ride might seem like an inconvenience or an inefficiency to someone like the accountant at the

NGO who was trying to encourage all employees to sign up for bank accounts, it was clear that what the women were doing was about more than just pooling resources. It would also be a mistake to imagine this as merely the evolution of ingenious survival tactics for the unbanked. Rather, the women were redefining and stretching the social space of Bourj Hammoud beyond the geographical area of the neighborhood. While Hamalian's shirket women helped one another move into the same neighborhoods, pooling resources to facilitate geographic proximity, these women used the shirket as a way of extending the network of people and services beyond Bourj Hammoud into outlying suburbs.

Once we arrived at our destination, one of the women placed a "missed call" to the mobile phone of our host for that afternoon's meeting to let her know we had arrived.[14] We made our way down a narrow street filled with fragrant trees and flowers, a striking contrast from the concrete and diesel of Bourj Hammoud. Our host, Leila, an Arabic-speaking woman in her late fifties, welcomed us into her home and onto the balcony where she and her daughter, a woman in her early twenties, served us lunch, followed by dessert and copious amounts of coffee. Most of the women in the shirket spoke Arabic fluently, though some with a heavily accented Armenian inflection. While we had all spoken exclusively in Armenian on the bus, the group adjusted accordingly at Leila's house and spoke Arabic as much as possible, with Zabel serving as interpreter for those moments when people lapsed into Armenian to express something they could not in Arabic.

The women discussed everything from the cost of water, to rising rents, to the cost of blood pressure medications and where to find them at a discount, while constantly repeating the phrase "Ma fi barakat"[15] followed by the occasional "Allah biy'atiki."[16] I was reminded of Hamalian's account of shirkets as a kind of "group therapy" session in the 1970s while the women shared their legitimate grievances with the rising cost of living. This meeting, however, was also full of valuable information about channels they could utilize to obtain prescription medication, seek medical care, or find the most inexpensive source of safe drinking water. Talk is a technology, then, for negotiating these calculations and activating people and things into motion (Latour and Lepinay 2009). The shirket was a means of maintaining a connection with the dense networked space of Bourj Hammoud through these women's lending practices despite geographic dislocation. This virtual Bourj Hammoud "community" also seemed much more fluid and accessible, defying the boundaries and notions of identity promoted by sectarian political organizations.

The shirket group was not formed strictly on the basis of a shared ethnoreligious Armenian identity. Leila's presence as a member of the group has more to do with her having been a neighbor to one of the members in Bourj Hammoud years before than with any particular performance of

Armenianness. In this shirket it was the relationships forged through mutual indebtedness and not only the money that could be pooled and saved through this endeavor that was a source of value. These relationships, however, were about much more than just fondness for each other; they were about being part of a valuable network of things and people that provided not only resources and services but also a sense of meaning and belonging.

Still, collecting and pooling money is an important part of the shirket activity, and the participants take it very seriously. Given the level of informality surrounding the gathering and the feeling of close friendship between the women, I was surprised by the elaborate ritual surrounding bookkeeping. Zabel and another member both keep books documenting the amount of money contributed by each woman, which ranged from 5,000 to 35,000 pounds, along with 3,000 pounds of *dogos* or "interest" added to the principle amount each time. One of the women keeping the books even made a note of the serial numbers on each bill collected. Zabel and the other member read the amounts each participant contributed, checking the totals for even those women who were not present that day and reading them aloud. Absolute transparency is part of the functioning of the shirket; there is no premium placed on confidentiality. For example, during the meeting Leila was unable to contribute anything aside from the 3,000 pound *dogos* ($2). She announced the amount she was contributing as she handed the money over to the women keeping accounts, saying, "This is all I can do this week," while other members nodded their heads and said "Ma fi barakat."

One might argue that it is precisely the transparency and the public accounting that keep the dealings with money running smoothly and the relationships intact. While the shirket's finances are kept confidential to nonmembers, everyone who is directly involved is completely aware of how much each individual has invested in the group. Since everyone in the group gets back exactly what they contributed in the end, it is not exactly a way of earning money but rather a means of saving and pooling other important resources in a manner completely different in function and purpose from a bank. Through shirket practices like this one, women extend the network beyond the aegis of official Armenian sectarian organizations. The neighborhood friendships forged in Bourj Hammoud are extended across the eastern suburbs. These friendships have never been defined strictly by ethnoreligious boundaries (Joseph 1983). Once credit networks are managed by licensed or official organizations, however, these alliances can be foreclosed and limited.

While banks have proliferated throughout Bourj Hammoud, most people do not have access to formal credit through these institutions. Arpa is an alternative to these banks. Unlike the shirkets, Arpa has a staff, an office, and a much wider membership. While a facility like Arpa does not involve any kind of "structured visiting" as the shirkets do, it still has maintained some of the shirkets' other functions, including regular meetings and social events. Arpa, however, has an official license from the Lebanese government to operate as a credit facility. While the official license requires that Arpa be accessible to Lebanese of all sects, in practice mostly Armenians have utilized its services. The history of Arpa and its role in the community sheds further light on the institutionalization of sectarian lending and credit practices. Rather than creating more access, Arpa can actually limit women's access to credit, in effect closing off the towlines into other communities through credit and purchases made by women outside of the purview of patriarchal sectarian institutions and actors.

ARPA: A LICENSED FACILITY

Like many businesses and facilities in Bourj Hammoud, the Arpa office is marked by a sign in three different languages: Arabic, Armenian, and English.[17] Inside is a small office with a staff of two or three secretaries who sit behind a long counter of the type one might find at a doctor's office. When I visited the office for the first time, they notified Hrayr, the director, of my presence and he emerged from a tiny office at the back of the room with some pamphlets in hand, in both Arabic and Armenian. As he showed me into his office, he asked in Armenian: "Hayeren ge gartak?" (Do you read Armenian?). Despite the availability of pamphlets in Arabic, the office appeared to conduct most of its business in Armenian.

Hrayr narrated the story of Arpa's history. A European national who worked with a relief organization in Bourj Hammoud first came up with the idea to found a lending organization in the 1970s. He appealed to the Lebanese government to grant him an official license to start a formalized lending facility.[18] While a number of well-publicized scandals involving theft within the shirkets occurred in the 1960s (Hamalian 1974), it is unclear whether the idea for the formalized facility was in any way connected to those events or a growing distrust of informality. The license was not officially granted until the 1980s, and Hrayr had started working for Arpa soon after.

Because Arpa operates with an official government license, it must print all its materials in Arabic as well as Armenian. This did not mean, however, that non-Armenian populations in Bourj Hammoud frequently accessed Arpa. According to Hrayr, all employees and 99 percent of participants are Armenian. A few years prior an international microlending institution had spoken with him about setting up operations in Bourj Hammoud for a wider public, but this had failed to materialize. Even as Arpa adopts a formalized, official presence, it still produces a very "Armenian" channel of credit.

Perhaps one of the ways in which an Armenian channel of credit and lending is produced is through the elaborate process of becoming an active member through one's own proximity and access to current members. To borrow money, one must become a member, which requires that the individual reside or work in the Metn (the *qada'a*, or district, in which Bourj Hammoud is located), be at least eighteen years of age, and be recommended by two preexisting members who have been active for at least six months. The management of Arpa then decides whether to approve the application of this new member. If approved, the new member must pay a participation fee of 100,000LL, 200,000LL, or 300,000LL (approximately U.S. $67, $133, and $200, respectively), which is refundable if the member ever wants to withdraw from the organization. The member then has access to credit equal to ten times the amount of money paid for the membership fee. In other words, someone who has paid a 100,000LL membership fee can borrow up to 1,000,000LL, provided two guarantors who agree to pay the loan in case of default can be secured. With the maximum deposit, one could borrow up to the maximum amount lent out by Arpa: 3,000,000LL, equivalent to $2,000. The Arpa bylaws state that the guarantor should ideally not be a relative of the borrower and cannot reside in the same home. The guarantor cannot serve as guarantor to any other member and must earn a minimum salary of $500 a month.

Not all members joined Arpa in order to borrow money. Some members deposit money in a low-interest-yielding account as a way of belonging to the organization while at the same time receiving a small financial incentive for it. Becoming a member is a way of gaining access to official meetings and, more important, to prestigious members of the community. Support for Arpa could be rewarded by access to certain kinds of social capital (Bourdieu 1977, 1984). The bank relied on the supplementary money from the sponsors in order to continue its regular lending activities as well as pay for the overhead expenses of running the organization as a permanent office.

Despite the codification of borrowing and payment installments in Arpa's intimidating pamphlets and documents, Hrayr explained that it has a lot of flexibility in terms of how it typically operates. Arpa is inclusive in the sense that it gives people the ability to borrow money who might not otherwise have access to credit from larger, more established banks in Lebanon. Certainly it provides access to small amounts of money for people who would not qualify elsewhere. Implicitly, however, the willingness to be flexible, to make these concessions and make credit more widely available to certain publics, existed alongside an exclusion of a huge part of the population in Bourj Hammoud that might also benefit from access to credit.

Becoming a member and borrowing money requires social connections that are relatively difficult to obtain, and quite different from becoming a member of a shirket. One must pass through the vetting process by providing all the necessary identity documents as well as electricity bills,

rental agreement forms or verification of property ownership, a photograph, and a "family" identification form that lists all members of one's
immediate family. A potential borrower must also secure two guarantors
(who need not be members) if any money is to be borrowed from Arpa.
Through these criteria, the Arpa community of members who are allowed
to take part in indebtedness is constructed through acceptable networks
of patronage and family connections. One's family identification form,
a document that charts the births, deaths, and marriages of everyone
considered a close relative (parents and siblings if one is unmarried;
spouse and children if one is married), is an important way of placing one
within the community. One's photograph links one to these documents,
identifying one's image to family, property, and assets. One's relationship
to two other "members" who serve as guarantors locks one into mutual
indebtedness, in terms not just of money but also of public shame if one
were to default and pull two other members into deeper debt. As in the
shirket, this information remains a public "secret," acknowledged through
talk and gossip that is powerful in making reputations and creating hierarchies of prestige.

At the same time, while allowing a lower-income group access to
funds, Arpa's membership practices tend to replicate hierarchies within
the Armenian community and implicitly exclude non-Armenians from
participating. Arpa may have been established to rein in the "messy" and
unregulated shirket practices of Armenian women in Bourj Hammoud,
and indeed another important distinction between it and the shirkets is
buried in the Arpa bylaws. While looking through the pamphlet outlining
Arpa procedures, I found the following rule, which Hrayr did not mention during our conversation: any female borrower must have, in addition
to the usual guarantors, the agreement of one of her family members in
securing the loan. While not specifying that the family member should be
male, the pamphlet suggested that a father, brother, husband, or son would
be appropriate choices.

The Arpa project implicitly creates boundaries around Armenian credit
systems. These practices create Armenian channels of credit and lending and reroute women's access to credit through the proper patriarchal
channels. The two systems of patriarchy and sectarian political institutions
in Lebanon are, in fact, inextricable.[19] If, as Hamalian (1974, 90) writes, the
economic is a "leakage" point for Armenian social assimilation, what is at
stake is the definition and constitution of what gets to count as normatively
Armenian.[20] In this context, the formalization of lending is a channeling
process that remakes the terms of social bonds in more narrowly defined
patriarchal and sectarian terms and reins in the human infrastructures of
those credit networks. The project of reigning in control over the lending
practices of Armenians in Bourj Hammoud is thus inextricable from the

project of regulating women's access to credit, and this in turn is part of
how networks of lending produce and reproduce sectarian identities and
notions of belonging.

FORMALIZATION, RATIONALIZATION, SECTARIANIZATION

What is microlending in Bourj Hammoud, then? A closer examination of
the landscape of indebtedness shows that the formalized credit institutions
in Bourj Hammoud do not, in fact, act with more uniform calculability or
purely "economic" rationality. Rather, the "regularizing" of debt in Arpa
excludes women from the circulation of credit, or at least forces them to
ask for family members' permission. One effect of limiting women's access
is to close off these towlines that the women have into other communities
through purchasing power, as described by Hamalian, as well as foreclosing
the possibility of intersectarian credit networks. While credit organizations
like Arpa publish their materials in Arabic and Armenian and must make
credit available to members of all sects, in practice they are much more
limited. Shirket membership is based on other kinds of belonging and
feelings of affinity, such as maintaining the relationship between neighbors
across geographic distances and maintaining relationships formed in the
Bourj Hammoud social organizations even when people have to move
farther away.

Despite the presence of officially licensed facilities like Arpa, there is
still space in Bourj Hammoud and elsewhere for the unruly uses of credit.
Perhaps the most valuable aspect of the shirkets are the channels and pathways they produce. The patriarchal fear of the "leakage point" of women's
economic independence is evidenced through the attempts at controlling women's access to credit. Debt and the relationships that it weaves
are part of one and the same social-technical web by which all kinds of
things are negotiated and calculated, not just the accumulation of material
things but exchanges that constitute prestige and honor, affinities, and of
course politics (Mauss 2000). Credit remains a means by which one can
reach beyond the self to a community of others, though increasingly this
is being limited by sect-dominated organizations that contain the network
within narrowly defined sectarian boundaries. Sectarian organizations use
formalized credit systems in an attempt to harness all kinds of social assets
through debt (Elyachar 2005). Like money, these debt relationships are a
series of contracts between citizens, states, and banks from within Bourj
Hammoud and around the world through remittances and immigration
(Peebles 2008). There is no fixed meaning to debt and no way to harness
the entire debt landscape within the bounds of Bourj Hammoud and across

the vast distances that shape it, just as there are no separable local and global spheres of "economic" entanglement.

Just as remittances and the emergence of new forms of debt and credit circulate on scales that trouble the easy distinction between local and global, so do the building, planning, and provision of urban infrastructure that produce the social/technical landscape of Bourj Hammoud. Sectarian political actors across Lebanese municipalities attempt to consolidate their influence over the space of the city through technologies of urban planning, zoning, and permitting laws (Bou Akar 2012). As the next chapter demonstrates, however, these processes cannot be understood solely as manifestations of "local" micropolitics of the city, or even the interplay of national politics on a "local" scale. The maneuvering of sectarian political parties within the scale of the municipality can be understood only as part of the nexus of transnational and national circulations of urban planning expertise, of the distribution and provision of resources like electricity, and of the production of knowledge about who and what sort of person is part of the "community" to be served by the municipality.

Chapter 5

THE EYES OF ODARS

———————————

City-to-City Collaborations and Transnational Reach

In the summer of 2009 Aram, a staff member at an Armenian medical center in Bourj Hammoud, took me to look at the electricity generator on the roof of the modest two-story building that housed the clinic. The generator, an ancient machine encrusted with oil and dirt, had finally broken down after decades of service. This had made operations in the center extremely difficult, as the generator was its main source of power. Like most businesses and residences throughout Lebanon, the center was always suffering from electricity shortages. While larger businesses in Bourj Hammoud could afford to buy a generator of their own, the vast majority of small businesses and residents would buy a subscription to use a privately owned generator. This system is known as ishtirak, which contains within it the Arabic root word for collaboration and cooperation. Everywhere in Lebanon, but particularly in densely populated urban areas, the jumble of wires leading from apartments to formal and informal sources of electricity dangle precipitously over street corners in enormous heaps of cable.

Electricity supply throughout the country is erratic and tends to be more consistent within the municipal boundaries of Beirut. Between 2008 and 2011, when I conducted most of my ethnographic research, Beirut received around twenty-two hours a day, Bourj Hammoud typically received no more than sixteen hours a day, while other towns and villages received even less.[1] As a result, whoever can afford the price subscribes to an ishtirak service. Ishtirak generator owners in Bourj Hammoud, as elsewhere in Lebanon, reap huge profits and are allowed to operate owing to their connections to elite patrons, in this case presumably municipal actors and the Tashnag Party.

It is not only the ishtirak that channels distinct sources of power and electricity, however. As it turns out, the "formal" and "informal" electricity sources in Lebanon operate very similarly. The physical Lebanese national grid is also a patchwork system, partially powered by a Turkish generator boat, the *Fatmagül Sultan*, docked in the port of Beirut. The ship, owned by Turkish energy company Karadeniz, was contracted by Lebanon's state-run Electricité du Liban for $370 million to provide additional electricity for three years in order to supplement the strained Lebanese system. In an interview featured in the *Guardian* in April 2013, Turkey's ambassador to Lebanon at the time said he regards its energy projects as a way to increase Turkey's cooperation with Lebanon on infrastructural projects, which the journalist interpreted as an attempt to revive Turkey's influence in former Ottoman lands.[2] The idea that Turkey uses infrastructure investments to cultivate closer political relationships is nothing new in Lebanon.[3] During the course of my fieldwork, however, the accusation that Turkey might be aiming to revive its influence in former Ottoman lands was a rhetorical device used by detractors of Turkish policies in the Lebanon context, where there is deep antipathy toward the memory of Ottoman rule.[4] For example, Lebanese Armenians protesting Prime Minister Erdogan's official visit in 2010 held a giant banner reading "The new Ottomans in Lebanon" (*Al-Othmaniyoun al-jadid fi Libnan*). The protest was staged in Martyr's Square in downtown Beirut—a monument to those hanged by the Ottomans in 1916 for fomenting revolt against the Sublime Porte. Lebanese Armenians used this space to protest the Turkish government's ongoing denial of the Armenian genocide of 1915.[5] The critiques of Turkey's revived influence in the region have only intensified with speculations about its role in the Syria conflict since 2011. Electricity infrastructure in Bourj Hammoud, in other words, is made up of alternating currents of various kinds: the layered histories and accretions of the former Ottoman Empire, channels of patronage, sectarian formations of power, and electrical currents.

The tangle of ishtirak cables visible everywhere on Bourj Hammoud's streets is one way to visualize how urban planning and the provision of various infrastructures unfold, from the provision of electricity to the planning and building of bridges and roads. Each wire can be activated in moments where the national grid stops providing a current, circulations of power from different sources that take precedence at different moments. These wires overlap, having jurisdiction at different moments in time. The tangle of wires is an embodiment of the messy webs through which sectarianism is produced through the provision of infrastructure in Lebanon. Sectarianism, as I have argued throughout this book, does not emanate solely from particular sectarian political parties, or even from the sectarian governance structure of Lebanon alone, but is a relationship and a process that is produced, in crucial ways, through the materiality of urban infrastructure and services unfolding on multiple scales.

SOVEREIGNTY, DECENTRALIZATION, OR OVERLAPPING JURISDICTIONS?

While journalistic accounts portray Lebanon as possessing an "absent" or "weak" sovereign state, continually pushed out of the way by powerful religious organizations, whatever we can define as the "state" cannot be separated from these very organizations that make up the formal and informal political institutions of governance (Fregonese 2012). Scholars of urban governance in Beirut have long called for an approach that identifies the complex overlapping of actors occupying multiple positions within urban planning negotiations that resist classification as conflicts between local or national scales of governance (Harb 2001). The idea of overlapping jurisdictions, rather than sovereignty, is a helpful way in which to understand and theorize the role of the various actors involved in urban planning initiatives, infrastructure building, and the procurement of services in Lebanon.

By rethinking the dichotomies of national/local as well as centralization/decentralization and recasting the problem in terms of interconnecting, patched together networks operating through or constituting overlapping jurisdictions and scales, we might better understand the intricacies of governance as it unfolds, not only in Lebanon but increasingly around the world. For example, city-to-city or transnational partnerships to share expertise and develop urban planning projects abound in a number of locations, including the United States. More important for the context of Lebanon is the impact that these partnerships have. Sometimes it is the collaboration itself (the ishtirak, one might say) and the ability to make transnational connections that is the most valuable aspect of the project. In the case of Bourj Hammoud, the ability to connect to transnational currents helps the municipal actors more effectively oppose Lebanon's Council for Development and Reconstruction (CDR) plans.[6] Neither the abstract and idealized "decentralization" model of development nor the equally abstract bolstering of the "sovereign state" adequately describes or addresses Lebanon's infrastructural challenges. Rather, I am inspired by Marianne Valverde's (2008) approach to urban municipal governance, in which the generalization of models of governance itself is called into question. She writes: "If one sets out to document how particular networks are negotiated, built, challenged, rebuilt, and taken apart instead of setting out to investigate a concept or institution, one has a better chance of being able to see the amazing contingency underlying the most stable-looking forms of governance" (921).

This perceived tension between "centralization" and "decentralization," then, has to do with the conflict between overlapping jurisdictions of sectarian political organizations and space. Since the first municipal elections held after the fifteen-year civil war ended in 1990, postwar Lebanon is supposed to move toward "decentralization" as outlined by the Taif Agreement (the peace treaty that ended hostilities between factions).[7] This so-called decentralization, whereby municipalities rather than the central authority would be given much greater authority over infrastructure and services, has played out unevenly. While it is true that individual municipalities wield a great deal of authority over local infrastructures, centralized institutions like the CDR also command great authority over large projects like intercity highways and roads.[8] Much of the tension between municipalities and the CDR, however, stems from a central planning approach that has consistently marginalized the suburban periphery of Beirut in terms of urban planning and infrastructure provision (Harb 2003).

It is important to note that the abstract "national" scale is not necessarily larger or more encompassing than the municipal scale. Rather, the national scale, represented in this case by the CDR, has different imagined beneficiaries of its urban planning projects: different bodies and different spaces. The critique of many CDR projects is that the imagined beneficiary of these infrastructures is a Beirut commuter, circulating with his or her own private car, living in the affluent Metn suburbs and needing to quickly bypass the low-income areas like Bourj Hammoud. Of course, romanticizing the "local" as a rooted, earthly place of resistance against a central authority is equally problematic (Appadurai 1996; Elyachar 2002, 2005; Gupta 1997, 1998).[9] Actors working at the municipal scale, in the case of Bourj Hammoud, maintain a priority of a critical mass of Armenian residences and dwellings as well as businesses. Furthermore, the municipality itself, while managing "local" infrastructures, is widely acknowledged to be dominated by members of the Tashnag Party, and indeed a number of other Armenian diasporic social, religious, and political institutions that are key actors in municipality governance. Both the Tashnag Party *and* the other diasporic political, social service, and religious organizations are also transnational. It becomes difficult to cut the boundaries between scales, or to label one as somehow more rooted to a "local" place than another. Understanding the two as overlapping jurisdictions that put materials, people, and ideas into motion in particular places, rather than a tension between center and periphery, helps to tease out what can often look like contradictory stances taken by CDR and municipal actors, as well as identify why the transnational research projects are so valuable.

Urban infrastructures and the processes of sectarianism are produced across scales of governance and geographical spaces and yet are rooted in very ordinary, material ways in the everyday lives of Bourj Hammoud dwellers. Often it is during a moment of breakdown, interruption of circulation, or collapse that the intricate and overlapping currents that power these infrastructures become visible, as various actors call on them to repair, reestablish, or reconnect.[10] Here I introduce two ethnographic examples to illustrate the ways in which these processes unfold through electricity provision at the neighborhood level as well as transnational urban planning projects.

ELECTRICITY: POWERING THE GRID, CASTING THE WIRE

Aram's clinic, while providing services to residents of other sects, serves mainly the Armenian population of Bourj Hammoud and neighboring areas. While there were a few exceptions, it was generally understood that to access non-essential medical services at many Armenian-run clinics, one had to make a claim to *being* Armenian, which calls for a complex set of negotiations that go far beyond a religious or ethnic definition of sect, including performances of normative gender roles and sexual propriety as well as class position, among other factors (see chapters 2 and 3). Aram's center represented one of the ways in which access to services reinforces a sense of sectarian belonging beyond just an identity category of citizenship or even a religious practice. Belonging to an Armenian "sectarian community" in Bourj Hammoud meant belonging to a social world of Armenian-dominated organizations and all the resultant favors and connections that belonging could represent.

After the generator at the center stopped functioning, Aram was forced to subscribe to one of the ishtirak services on the block. He took me downstairs to show me how the subscription service worked and walked me over to a box mounted on a wall on the street. There were dozens of cables running out of it, snaking along the side of the building and hanging low over the intersection of the narrow streets. After months of buying electricity through the costly and inefficient ishtirak system of privately owned generators, and a lack of funds from the Armenian American diasporic charity that usually helped with operational costs, Aram decided to apply for a grant to obtain a new generator. The grant that he was applying for this time was from a foreign embassy that funded small projects and NGOs in Beirut. Aram shook his head and chuckled at the mess of cables. He was anxious to get another generator and photographed the web of cables to prove to the embassy officials who would be reading the grant application that the situation was dire. He thought that the image of the cables would communicate disorder, disarray. Surely it would compel any foreign granting agency to intervene.

While Aram regarded the mess of wires as evidence of disorder and chaos, his actions in powering the clinic in Bourj Hammoud, not just with electricity but with all its operational costs, embody the entangled web he hoped to bypass by procuring a generator. The clinic was partially powered by historical connections to Armenian diaspora charities that were founded to assist genocide survivors in the 1920s; the clinic received much of its operating

Figure 5.1. Electricity cables hanging over the street in Bourj Hammoud. Photo by Rosy Kuftedjian.

funds from Armenian American charities. The clinic was also powered by a subscription to a private generator owned by a local patron whose permission to operate was implicitly granted by the municipality, which was dominated by the Tashnag Party. Eventually the original generator was replaced with funds from the foreign embassy, and the clinic was again powered by the national grid, the Turkish power boat, the foreign embassy-funded generator, and the usual supplementary Armenian-diasporic charity's operating funds.

The construction of sectarian community takes place in an interrelated way as the powering of the clinic, through currents that reach out and enable or disable circulations of services and resources at the neighborhood level, as well as through diasporic and transnational resources. Just as cities are "hotbeds of demand and exchange within international flows of power and energy resources," they are also "overwhelmingly important in articulating the corporeal movements of people and their bodies" (Graham 2001, 8). The processes that enable institutional channels of services also create the conditions of possibility for certain people to circulate within and across these organizations and exclude many others. It is precisely these alternating currents that are the processes we call sectarianism. These conditions are not unique to Armenians—every Lebanese sectarian organization is con-structed of diasporas, migrations, remittances, and transnational connections.

The building and wiring of urban infrastructures like electricity as well as services provided by sectarian organizations and access to them unfold together.

In this instance, a shifting focal point of infrastructure, made visible through the breakdown of the center's generator, created an opportunity for Aram to obtain funds from a foreign embassy. He foregrounded the messiness of the ishtirak web, what is normally invisible or ignored, to create a new channel of funding for the center. The consolidation of an Armenian "community" survives through the negotiations of actors like Aram, who has an advanced degree and received additional training in nonprofit management in the United States. Aram, unlike many of his colleagues and staff in Bourj Hammoud, is experienced in dealing with foreign charities and funders and can intersect with, extend, and serve as an arbitrator to other networks and resources. In many cases it is through the transactions mediated by professionalized actors like Aram that the consolidation of the Bourj Hammoud Armenian community in its most local and enclosed forms is sustained and reproduced through extensionalities to broader domains of transaction.[11] Actors like Aram, in other words, help to actively produce the "local" through intense negotiations and extensions to resources, actors, and knowledge across different registers and spaces.

ALTERNATE CURRENTS, SOCIAL VALUE, NETWORKING CITIES

While Aram makes connections through space and historical ties, Lebanese municipalities use intricate networks to draw in foreign experts and tap into other powerful currents. Shoghig, a municipal employee, had an interest in historic preservation and Bourj Hammoud's local history and regarded the human infrastructure of the city as a source of value. She often mobilized the discourse of Bourj Hammoud as a historically significant neighborhood within greater Beirut to try to convince both foreign experts and local actors to care about the material infrastructure of Bourj Hammoud. She hoped that this could interrupt the powerful Lebanese Council for Development and Reconstruction's push to build a huge sewage treatment plant on the seafront.

Shoghig's office was on the second floor of one of the many nondescript concrete tower blocks ringing the greater metropolitan Beirut area. Like other municipality offices I visited in Lebanon, the waiting room was always full of Bourj Hammoud residents hoping to resolve an issue or problem. Many residents actively sought out Shoghig as she was known as someone who listened to local concerns. She was keen on collaborating with foreign donors, transnational organizations, and experts who seek out Lebanese municipalities for the purpose of mutual exchange of ideas as well as to get technical support and establish cooperation for urban development programs. Another architect in Lebanon once suggested to me that these collaborative initiatives, including things like city-to-city partnerships between European and Lebanese municipalities, became more popular in the aftermath of the civil war when destroyed infrastructure was in dire need of rebuilding and repair. However, many of these European partnerships are not limited to environmental or developmental concerns and are politically informed.[12] Over the past few years, organizations like Euromed and World Bank or even individual European city governments have reached out to Lebanese municipalities in order to launch urban and social development projects or produce research toward the development of such plans.

Shoghig was involved in different collaborative strategies for city development with European transnational organizations as well as foreign municipalities. She aimed to solve the many environmental concerns of the Bourj Hammoud municipal district, particularly the pollution of the seafront by an illegal garbage dump dating from the civil war era. She was also concerned with the long-standing CDR plan to build a giant sewage treatment plant with outdated designs from 1982 that needed to be reviewed and revised according to new strategies for efficiently treating wastewater. These projects are instrumental in attracting foreign partnerships and donors because they are very large and obvious environmental disasters. Furthermore, because they have such a negative impact on the sea and the shore, they are easily tied in with European projects to limit the pollution of the Mediterranean and develop collaborations on all sides of the sea.

In Lebanon, municipalities have a lot of legal autonomy in terms of urban planning and service provision; this relative autonomy does not come solely through foreign influence but is part of how municipal governance functions in Lebanon. However, greater "decentralization," in which municipalities have greater ability to enact urban development and planning projects independently or with the assistance of other municipalities, is also the dominant international urban development theory. One prominent U.S.-based professional organization that links municipal governments worldwide launched a major study in Lebanon. The findings of the study advanced a platform of greater "decentralization" in various contexts, which generally meant enabling municipalities to produce and enact their own urban and even economic development projects without central state involvement.

The tensions between the CDR and municipalities like Bourj Hammoud are perhaps best illustrated through the infrastructural failures that resulted from their joint negotiations around the Yerevan Flyover Bridge, named after the capital of the Republic of Armenia. The bridge, also known as the PN1 Bridge, cuts through Bourj Hammoud above street level, connecting the PN1 expressway from Beirut to outlying suburbs. This bridge, which will be discussed at length later in the chapter, was an instrument of urban planning that divided the neighborhood and transformed the urban-social fabric of Bourj Hammoud, in many ways reducing its potential for collective action. It was also a means for the urban commuter to quickly bypass Bourj Hammoud and avoid contact with its streets entirely, as the new flyover was placed far above ground level and out of sight of the street.

Shoghig expressed her disappointment with the CDR flyover bridge. Not only was it designed and implemented without any environmental impact assessment, she explained, but also the planners failed to take into consideration the social and urban fabric of neighborhood life. Now the bridge was a huge source of air and noise pollution and a nuisance to the residents who live in close proximity to it. She resolved to oppose another CDR project to build a large sewage treatment plant on Bourj Hammoud's waterfront. That plant would filter the water of several nearby municipalities, putting all the pressure on Bourj Hammoud's shoreline (Asmar 2008). These two projects reflect some of the critiques of CDR planning, namely, that it aims to put all industry and wastewater treatment plants on Bourj Hammoud's shore and to add or widen roads through Bourj Hammoud to improve circulation in and out of Beirut and into the more affluent suburbs to the north and east.

At times foreign expertise can enable or advance infrastructural or development projects alongside central agencies and municipalities. Many collaborative projects at the municipality, however, produced "best practices" reports. While municipalities do have a wide breadth of maneuverability, they are also constrained by central agencies purview—at least legally. The ability of municipalities to maneuver is not all coming from foreign influence. Still, foreign collaborations could prove helpful in bringing attention to more disastrous plans put forward by the CDR. "You need international associations to project yourself in development," a Lebanese Armenian architect once told me. You need, in other words, the eyes of odars, or outsiders, particularly Euro-American experts, to effectively challenge big CDR projects.[13] I had not considered that expertise from outside of Lebanon is being used not only to build new material infrastructures but also to draw greater attention to plans for new, potentially flawed infrastructures in order to challenge them. The logic of including foreign actors in urban development planning is that there will be greater pressure for public accountability and transparency. Furthermore, these projects are intended to increase the participation of different local stakeholders—not just municipal actors—and make the process more transparent and, in the words of one municipality employee, "democratic."

Sometimes good development is what *does not* get done rather than what does.[14] In some ways, the proliferation of these plans is a means of slowing down the rush forward to destroy and rebuild without proper debate, as occurred downtown in the postwar rebuilding era.[15] However, perhaps much more often foreign expertise can also help to *advance* a project. During the downtown rebuilding era, private company Solidere also used the influence of foreign experts, in this case "starchitects," to advance its vision for the new downtown Beirut. In some cases the transnational connection itself, even in the absence of adequate funding to realize a project, is what lends importance to the proposal. The ability to link up to a new source of power creates the potential for new materials to circulate, and the ability to block the circulation of others—processes that are entangled with the sectarian-ization of services and the segregation or gentrification of neighborhoods.

Municipal actors I spoke with in Bourj Hammoud as well as another mu-nicipality just outside of Beirut concurred that the national scale is somehow ineffective at identifying the needs of local municipalities. The national scale is not only too vast, they suggested, it is unable to truly invest in and care for the local. However, this is not only in terms of infrastructural upgrade and environmental cleanup. Infrastructure is much more than "technical equipment," Shoghig argued. There are social uses of space that the CDR scale of planning cannot deal with. It is precisely these areas of sociospatial value that are determined by the municipality and enabled and highlighted through transnational collaborations with foreign experts, institutions, and even other cities. Even the municipality is a site of contestation, however, and not every municipal actor agrees on the importance of historic preservation and development projects that assist the most vulnerable populations that are often targets of eviction.

Urban development research projects, initiated by large transnational organizations as well as foreign municipalities as part of "twin-city" proj-ects, focus on things like "local" character and "soft infrastructure/human infrastructure" as well as "hard infrastructure" like bridges and roads. The emphasis on notions of culture and historic preservation allows foreign donors and researchers along with municipal actors to define what gets to count as important and valuable, what local crafts and trades are "authentic." What is taken for granted here is the construction of the "local," which is not a given but a highly contested space that is constructed through vari-ous negotiations that go far beyond even Lebanon. Thus discourses of the "local" produced through transnational urban planning ventures can serve to legitimate boundaries of who gets to count in the equation of the "com-munity," often defined in ways that map onto sectarian categories in Lebanon.

At the same time, the city-to-city partnerships do sometimes assist mu-nicipalities in challenging larger/national-scale infrastructure projects that are legitimately troubling in terms of their adverse environmental impacts. However, the potential exists for the municipality, acting as a legitimate representative of the "local" community, to enact greater autonomy over determining what gets to count as "social value" and excluding or overlooking the populations that don't fit into that. Eviction can take the form of violent displacement and destruction but also other, quieter forms, such as ignoring or neglecting the neighborhoods within the municipality that do not fit into the image of the authentic Armenian "local," like Sanjak or Naba'a.[16]

What drives municipal actors to initiate transnational partnerships are the failures of the two aforementioned CDR-initiated development projects: the PN1 Bridge and a sewage treatment plant to be constructed on Bourj Hammoud's shoreline. The bridge, and its negative environmental impact on Bourj Hammoud, represents a visible warning to some urban activists about the dangers of leaving these negotiations to the municipality and the CDR. The sewage plant project, which has attracted a number of foreign, city-to-city research projects looking for alternatives, is currently in contestation. Both these projects show that while "local" decision making and decentralization may appear to be a solution to the oversights of broad-based "national" planning initiatives, the municipality cannot really be called a "local" institution. Defining the "local" can potentially produce forms of exclusion through identifying, evicting, or preventing the circulation of many kinds of *others* who do not belong. Ironically, consolidation of the local can also serve to impede or deconstruct the very economic and social circulations that enable that local formation to remain viable.

THE BRIDGE: A SCAR THROUGH THE CITY

The Yerevan Flyover, or PN1, Bridge, constructed in the late 1990s, connects the Beirut neighborhood of Ashrafiyeh to outlying northeastern suburbs and passes through Bourj Hammoud, elevated above a residential and commercial street. What is immediately apparent is the proximity between residential dwellings and the bridge. At some points residential balconies are just a few feet away from the bridge. The sound of cars swishing past is deafeningly loud in those apartments. Below the bridge are a number of small shops and cafes and constant foot traffic. The Armenian-run school for the deaf and blind and a retirement home are also located on the street directly beside the bridge. The area under the bridge is full of activity and people crossing underneath the constant thud of cars passing overhead and the smell of gasoline.

According to a study by Tristan Khayat (2001), the construction of the bridge was a result of intense negotiations. Municipal actors wanted to minimize the number of evictions created by the destruction of housing, particularly the Boghos Aris social housing, built in the 1950s to house Armenians who were living in informal settlements. The municipal actors and their Tashnag counterparts ensured the CDR that it could not begin construction unless it came to an agreement about minimizing the residential impact of the road and made it a raised bridge that would enable pedestrian access and traffic to move underneath. A probable explanation was that the Tashnag Party wanted to maintain Armenian residence in Bourj Hammoud as well as the territorial integrity of the district, regardless of the impact of the bridge on those who remained. In return, as scholar Tristan Khayat suggests, the municipality and Tashnag elite gained political capital for their negotiations with the central authorities, a process typical of the clientelism of the Lebanese system (2001).

Eventually the CDR built the PN1 Bridge, and municipal officials were able to minimize evictions at the expense of building the highway just a few feet from living rooms and balconies. Those who were evicted received a resettlement fee. An interlocutor living in the vicinity of the bridge told me that they were the "lucky ones," as those who remained found that their apartments were unbearably close to a busy, loud, filthy concrete highway. This same interlocutor described the bridge as a "scar" (in English) dividing the city in half, something that happened despite the fact that the municipality succeeded in making it raised rather than a road on the ground.[17] For many urban planning professionals and scholars in Lebanon, the entire bridge project serves as a cautionary tale about how not to conduct development projects.

Figure 5.2. Elevated Yerevan Flyover Bridge bypassing the streets of Bourj Hammoud (PN1 Bridge). Photo by Rosy Kuftedjian.

Figure 5.3. View from below the Yerevan Flyover Bridge in Bourj Hammoud. Photo by Rosy Kuftedjian.

Aside from the negative environmental impact, the bridge left another, perhaps unforeseen impression on the perceived sectarian geography of the city. While political actors use highway projects as a means of articulating dominant visions of urban social life, even contestations against such highway projects are deeply implicated in sectarian notions of community and identity in Lebanon, as they sometimes "generate a space in which sectarian religious identities and relative entitlements to the city are negotiated and strengthened" (Deboulet and Fawaz 2011, 119). The bridge had effectively hoisted an unofficial barrier between the neighborhoods regarded as "more Armenian" in composition north of the bridge and others to the south. This particular division is materially constituted by the bridge, despite the fact that there are many Armenian social institutions south of it, including the large LOKH/Armenian Relief Cross clinic that was an essential hub of medical and social services throughout the district. Still, the attitude among many of my Armenian interlocutors is that the bridge represented a new border between what was part of an authentically Armenian Bourj Hammoud and what was now an unfamiliar zone of migrant workers and odars, or "others." In the popular discourse of many of my interlocutors, what used to be confined further south to Naba'a, a non-Armenian, unknown, and "dangerous" zone full of single male migrant workers, had slowly crept forward in the social

Figure 5.4. Another view from below the Yerevan Flyover Bridge in Bourj Hammoud. Photo by Rosy Kuftedjian.

imaginaries of space. One of my interlocutors, a volunteer at an Armenian NGO, described the area south of the bridge in the most dramatic terms. It had "gangrene," she said in French, and was beyond saving and needed to be severed from Bourj Hammoud.[18] Bodily metaphors of rot, decay, and sickness illustrate the desire to contain, to create boundaries and prevent the circulation of those bodies within Armenian-dominated infrastructures and services north of the bridge.

An interview with a Shi'i *mukhtar*, or local elected official, in one of the neighborhoods directly south of the bridge echoed this sentiment about the change in the neighborhood as one of a shift from a space of intimate engagement between neighbors to a more or less anonymous zone. With the influx Syrian and Kurdish migrant workers, men without any rooted-ness in the area, he argued, there had been a marked shift, a growing sense of distrust and insecurity. The bridge was even more of a boundary in the imagination of younger people who grew up having it as a marker in space. Many younger Armenian residents who lived in, worked in, and frequented areas mainly north of the bridge referred to all areas south as Naba'a. Even though the neighborhood of Naba'a is further south, just beyond neigh-borhoods built by Armenian town associations in the 1930s like Sis (built by Armenians from the former town of Sis, now Kozan in Turkey), Naba'a had become a term for otherness, for that part of Bourj Hammoud where Armenians were a minority and Armenian institutions like the agoumps had less of a presence.

Despite the unintended consequence of dividing Bourj Hammoud and moving the borderline of "Armenian" territory further north, part of what shaped the way that the bridge project was negotiated was the task of keeping Armenians in Bourj Hammoud. Some argue that the reason for Tashnag's concern with keeping Bourj Hammoud populated by Armenians is that this is how Tashnag maintains its political bloc (Khayat 2001). This is not done through voting, however, as the Lebanese system requires that people vote in the town or village where their families were initially registered. Even if Armenians move, if they are registered in Bourj Hammoud, that is where they must vote. So the desire to maintain a critical mass of Armenians in Bourj Hammoud is about keeping alive the social networks and the inherent power of concentration. For example, the fact that the municipality could theoretically block construction, regardless of whether the CDR had the permit to proceed, demonstrates the perceived value of the critical mass of party supporters, not only in Bourj Hammoud but in any municipality in Lebanon.

However, the value of the social networks that help sustain Bourj Hammoud are also instrumentalized in other ways. In the next section I will describe how opposition to the sewage treatment plant project is spearheaded by actors like Shoghig who are influenced by the more recent turn in development toward valuing social networks (or the turn toward "social value"). Her attempts to mobilize foreign experts involves the identification of social value in these Armenian networks in order to block what might become the next environmental disaster for Bourj Hammoud.

STALLING A PROJECT, BUYING TIME, DEFINING VALUE

The sewage treatment plant project is a shoreline redevelopment plan for Bourj Hammoud that the CDR devised in the early 1980s. It was never implemented, not only because of the years of war that prevented any serious reconstruction efforts until the 1990s but also because of the Bourj Hammoud municipality's objection to various aspects of the plan. While the project contains plans for a seaside park and other amenities, its main focus is the construction of water treatment and sewage systems and a treatment plant for fifty municipalities outside of Bourj Hammoud, including a large part of Beirut (Asmar 2008; J. Atallah 1997). The Bourj Hammoud shore has been a center for industrial activity since the 1930s, when the Mandate government allowed the Shell Corporation to build oil facilities there (Achkarian 2007). There is currently a large garbage dump there, no longer in use, dating from the civil war years (Albouy 2001).

Detractors of the project note that the sewage treatment plant proposed by the CDR is based on outdated designs and is far too large and overwhelming for the shore (Asmar 2008). Furthermore, the accompanying plan to build a municipal park on top of the now disused garbage dump was a laughable token of exchange for the serious environmental impact of the sewage treatment plant. Aside from degrading an already polluted seafront area, the expanded plant would ruin the livelihoods of fishers who still use the small nearby port to launch their dinghies to sea.

Shoghig, in her attempts to create alternative plans, has entered the Bourj Hammoud municipality into various collaborations with European cities and transnational organizations. Several of these projects ordered their own research and came up with their own suggestions and plans. For Shoghig, however, collaboration with European municipalities is about more than just infrastructure renewal. Her ability to attract the municipalities' interest in the first place, as well as her involvement with the recommendations and alternatives to the CDR's master plan, always include a lauding of Bourj Hammoud's social value and its public image. The notion of the inherent value in the social networks of the poor is nothing new in the world of development (Elyachar 2002). For Shoghig, however, social value is not just about the networks of survival, the skills and resources of the poor; rather, part of Bourj Hammoud's value lies in the skills and industriousness of its Armenian "character."

In her attempts to publicize the craftspeople and workshops in Bourj Hammoud, Shoghig helped to produce a local guide that featured the work and some biographical details about a number of artisans in the area. The guide contained a map of Bourj Hammoud with the addresses and locations of shoemakers, jewelers, sculptors, clothing designers, and others who owned workshops or small ateliers in the district. Through some of the artisans featured were not Armenian, the catalog emphasized the Armenian character of the area as a feature of the neighborhood where the techniques of handmade craftsmanship were preserved over generations. The catalog promoted Armenians as expert craftspeople and Bourj Hammoud as the most authentic location to "preserve" these talents and traditions. Shoghig would often take foreign researchers and development workers, designers searching for craftspeople, or even tourists around Bourj Hammoud to visit the workshops of those she profiled in the guide. She would also sometimes bring visitors to schools and medical clinics to demonstrate the availability of services initiated by Armenian organizations. It was, in a way, her attempt to show that the hardworking resourcefulness of Armenians, transmitted through generational family businesses, was an asset worthy of being developed and assisted, and any assistance to Bourj Hammoud was the best way of doing that.

Of course, Shoghig's use of the concept of social value in the Armenian community is quite a conscious one. For her it means safeguarding any potential development project against the displacement of the most vulnerable populations, for example the fishers on the seafront. Other infrastructure improvement or redevelopment projects in Beirut have displaced residents. Shoghig thought the best way to counter this was to promote the contribution of the *people* to the space, as part of what makes it most valuable: "My objective is to upgrade the place while upgrading the social condition too, for the people that were in that place. I am not intending to upgrade the place without the people that worked for that place for 50 years and which put their imprints, fingerprints into it."

To protect or minimize the impact of urban development projects like the sewage treatment plant, Shoghig uses an Armenian social value discourse that draws on popular notions about the Armenian community's industriousness, which partly stem from French Mandate era discourses about Armenians (Watenpaugh 2004).[19] Like many urban development research projects, some aspect of developing social capacity or "soft infrastructure" is built into the plan. Municipal actors involved in such projects could put forward their vision about the beneficiaries for these projects, and, as is the case for most cities in Lebanon, act in a way as the legitimate representatives of the community they claim to represent. In this instance, presenting the "local" as a bastion of Armenian authenticity presents one particular vision of what the "community" is and could potentially exclude many others.

The twin-city initiatives between Bourj Hammoud and other municipalities involved visiting experts, usually civil engineers and architects, who came to Lebanon to survey the neighborhood and meet with local counterparts who would help produce research about the area. Local counterparts would provide demographic information, surveys of how the land is used, detailed cadastral maps, and other data. Working with the local counterparts, the foreign experts would draft a master plan and a series of recommendations for the municipality. The result of this research was a study, usually a few drawings and maps. If an infrastructure upgrade was recommended, there might be suggestions as to how to seek international funding, usually in the form of a loan. While there were slight variations among these projects, there was a consistency across all of them that indicated that they were essentially posing the same questions and coming up with very similar answers to the problems they hoped to address. The fact that these studies were repeated numerous times demonstrated the value of increasing the presence of foreign "experts" in Bourj Hammoud, particularly in aiding efforts to block and oppose the CDR sewage plant project. In fact, what draws municipal officials to such collaborations is the inherent value of the collaboration itself as a channel of circulation. The ability to widen the network of actors involved with the project creates potentials for action and influence far beyond the specifics of one particular project. These transnational mobilizations are more than just technical knowledge; they are also instrumental in the process of consolidating and defining the "local" community as beneficiaries of these infrastructures.

CIRCULATION AND SCALES

Urban planning and infrastructure provision takes place on multiple scales through overlapping jurisdictions, city-to-city partnerships, and diasporic resources. The spatialized categories through which we understand the provision of urban infrastructures are inadequate—both a romanticized "local" community that represents the development goal of "greater decentralization" and the popular security discourse of a strong sovereign state that manages its territory and all infrastructures. We should instead look at the ways in which infrastructure and the "local" sectarian community are produced through wide-ranging collaborations, even as they are manifested in particular places and materialities of infrastructure and urban development. Negotiations over infrastructure can sometimes amplify notions of sectarian identity and community (Deboulet and Fawaz 2011). However, claims over the local site as a place of authenticity should be reevaluated in

terms of the way in which local material historical accretions have always
been produced through various forms of circulation and patronage. In fact,
it is in service of the local that municipal actors and NGO professionals alike
seek out resources from far-reaching contexts to keep such consolidations
viable. The Armenian "world" produced by actors like Aram and Shoghig
is sustained, in large part, by extensionality to other domains of exchange
and transaction.

Just as infrastructure is inextricable from the social that it produces and
is produced by, claims to sectarian forms of belonging help forge connections and enable access to various infrastructures at certain points in time.
Municipality actors use the sociospatial value and the human infrastructure
of Bourj Hammoud as evidence that it is worthy of infrastructure upgrade
projects. Collaborations with cities and organizations across Europe might
potentially defer state infrastructure projects. In promoting the social value
of one ethnic or sectarian community, however, there exists the potential of
alienating other Bourj Hammoud residents from the dense network that is
also the product of their labor. Contestations over infrastructure building
demonstrate how sectarian community is not a primordial identity that exists
a priori to urban development. In many cases sectarian discourses arise in
response to or in dialogic relation with shifting urban planning projects and
urban visions. These negotiations over ideas about the constitution of the
local produce the built urban environment and its dually material/sectarian
infrastructures like the PN1 Bridge and the social and sectarian divisions
of space that it fosters.

Popular and analytical default perspectives render sectarianism a product
of local conflict, and yet at the same time attached to something "global"
and out of reach. Foreign journalistic accounts as well as many of my
interlocutors blame many of Lebanon's problems on the meddling of various "external forces." This imagining of conflict as always trickling down
from a larger, abstract global has certain impacts on the way things end up
happening on the ground. In instances where political parties in Lebanon
negotiate, the various stakeholders involved are also imagined as tied to regional or global powers—each viewing the other side as merely the client of
a larger, more powerful country, whether it be the United States, Iran, Saudi
Arabia, France, or, today, maybe even Turkey. A focus on the transnational
and diasporic collaborations that build and maintain urban infrastructure
in Lebanon detracts from polarized perspectives of sectarianism as either
something that comes entirely "from above" or "from outside" *or* something
impossibly local, a hardwired, inevitable outcome of Lebanon's "culture"
and its naturalized, immutable religious and ethnic "communities." The
manifestation of infrastructure as something not underlying and solid but
fluid and changeable shows how electricity cables and bridges put bodies
in motion, creating and recalibrating sectarian networks of circulation that
are both far-reaching and every day.

CONCLUSION

Far More Dangerous Times

In the introduction I recalled an incident in Beirut when a seven-year-old child jumped up and said "Ijit al dawleh!" or "The state is here!" when he heard the familiar switch off of the hum of a private generator subscription, which signaled the start of the flow of energy from the national grid. That incident recalls the familiar refrain of "Meen al mas'oul?" or "Who is in charge?" often heard in Lebanon whenever someone wants to locate power and responsibility in circumstances where service provision and infrastructures are maintained by so many different actors and institutions, the state being only one player among many. In this book I have reoriented the question in order to make a different argument: what are the negotiations between various actors and the materiality of the city, its services, and its infrastructures that produce sectarianism as a form of politics, sectarian community as a kind of public, and the urban as a contested sectarian space? The "sect" is not an ancient, timeless category or community existing "out there," as such, and simply institutionalized within a modern political state. Producing the sect as well as the sectarian system is a process of circulation between entangled scales of municipal, national, and transnational institutions and the materiality of the services and infrastructures these negotiations build.

Throughout the preceding chapters I have argued that infrastructures are not just a material representation of how sectarian political parties operate spatially. Rather, in a dialogic process, the channels of service provision are constitutive of a sense of community, while, in turn, a sense of community and belonging reproduces and reiterates the institutional channels and networked connections that created them in the first place. These pathways of infrastructures and services are not hardwired but malleable and, in fact, subject to change in ways that we might never have imagined had we approached them all as the manifestations of natural, almost primordial and immutable sectarian communities. While they are not wholly contingent, the pathways of infrastructures and services can and *do* change at particular times and places owing to shifts in the configurations of actors and stakes that help produce or reproduce them. For example, an informal property regime in Bourj Hammoud, Sanjak camp, was upheld for decades on the basis of a claim to belonging to a sectarian "community," in this case the Armenian community. That same claim is now undermined not only by increased land values and speculation in the greater Beirut area but also by a shift in understanding of who gets to "count" as part of the sectarian community and therefore part of the equation that calculates the "greater good." Changing notions about the persons, places, and things that make up "community" are connected to shifting ideas about class, geographic histories, and the decline of Armenian-initiated social housing projects. While a few decades earlier housing projects were built to accommodate Armenians displaced from camps, no such plans have materialized in recent years. Sanjak's destruction also takes place within the context of what Mona Fawaz (2009a, 828) calls "neoliberal trends" or market-based approaches to the management of urban space that further foreclose the possibilities for informality or squatting.[1]

The example of Sanjak camp demonstrates how notions of "sectarian community" not only change over time but are deeply entangled with shifting property regimes, urban infrastructures, and development projects. Attention to the shifts in provision of infrastructures and services, and specifically the ways in which people interact with them on an everyday basis, can provide a methodological and theoretical framework for understanding the formation of ideas about "community," defined by sect or otherwise, and the formation of publics in a number of different contexts.[2]

Conflicting visions of urban spaces, things like contestations over the placement of bridges and highways or the future plans for a sewage treatment plant, not only radically reconfigure space but can reorient the stakes and positions of sectarian political actors as they negotiate, oppose, or support these projects while mobilizing sectarian notions of space and belonging. Just as sectarian discourses can be utilized to exclude publics from various services or take certain people and things out of circulation in realms like credit and lending, they can also be used to connect and mobilize resources. For example, sectarian identity can be mobilized as a form of social value to support or justify urban development projects to foreign partners in a shifting international development landscape that values notions of "decentralization" and locates municipalities as key sites of intervention. Individuals can also mobilize notions of sectarian belonging to connect to vital networks of resources like credit and lending, social services, or continued access to housing. However, whatever it means to "belong" to sectarian community, in all these cases, is not narrowly mapped onto religious or ethnic identity but rather includes a number of interlocking factors, such as class, geography, gender, and notions of morality and propriety. Even being Armenian in the context of Bourj Hammoud can vary quite widely; a longtime resident of the informal Sanjak camp has a different set of mobilities within Armenian networks of services and systems of patronage than an Armenian professional who commutes from middle-class suburbs to work at a clinic in Bourj Hammoud. Attention to the proliferation of differences in and through the provision of infrastructures helps to challenge the notion that sectarianism is unchanging, immutable, and ancient, or based solely on religious difference, as the networks people *can* navigate are not solely tied to their ethnic or religious identity.

The institutions through which sectarianism is produced in everyday life are experienced through layers of infrastructure produced in time (Larkin 2008). While infrastructures and the contexts that produce and reproduce notions of sectarianism have histories, the process of producing these channels was never without contingency, from European missionaries who founded relief organizations in the aftermath of the Armenian genocide to the transformation of these institutions into Armenian sectarian organizations that operate within the Lebanese political sectarian system of governance. The Lebanese political system itself did not simply arise in response to ancient communal forms (U. Makdisi 1996). Rather, it was a process worked out among French, British, and Ottoman officials as well as Lebanese through many institutions, including urban planning and infrastructure as well as the institution of modern patriarchal legal forms (Hanssen 2005; Thompson 2000). A focus on infrastructures and services is one way to think about the processes through which notions of sectarian community are produced and transform over time.

As I have argued through many institutional examples, like the messy informal property regimes of "permanently temporary" refugee camps or the entanglement of various sources of electricity from transnational, national, or private suppliers, sectarianism is produced in circulation through powerful but very material channels that allow or compel people and things to move or that block movement. In many instances the product of unintended consequences, these channels of infrastructures and services that people must navigate on a daily basis end up appearing as naturalized "communities." In many of these cases, when sectarian community is taken as a naturalized category, institutional responses to "manage" or deal with it as a given can actually *produce* or reproduce sectarianism, its political formations, as well as notions of sectarian publics glossed as "community." In moments where sectarian community appears to be a static, innate form of identity, it is especially critical to think about the relationships among infrastructure, services, and the formation of sectarian publics *over time* as a way of interrupting that narrative of unchanging and entrenched sectarian conflict.

ANOTHER CONFLICT EMERGES

Since 2011 the situation in neighboring Syria has continued to deteriorate. While the various "Arab Spring" uprisings flared in Tunisia, Egypt, Libya, and Bahrain, I was surprised at the popular media suggestion that the revolts were somehow "contiguous" or even that they were necessarily connected in some way, aside from perhaps the inspiration to change entrenched, though quite different, political systems. Early reports of protests in Syria were brushed off by many of my Lebanese interlocutors, who could not imagine anything disturbing the decades-long regime. During the course of my fieldwork and in the years that followed, the situation in Syria slowly evolved into a war with transnational reach that cannot be explained in terms of religious conflict, although that is the way in which it is often portrayed in popular media accounts.[3]

Given the proximity and interconnection between Syria and Lebanon, an impact on Lebanon was inevitable. Lebanese political factions are divided on the issue of Syria, though again these divisions must be understood in the context of the major Lebanese political factions' connections to regional powers and the relatively recent shifts in regional politics, namely, the divide between Iran/Syria, on one hand, and Saudi Arabia and other Gulf states, on the other.[4] In the wake of major regional tumult and over one million displaced Syrians currently in Lebanon, the charges of growing "sectarianism" as the driving force behind various forms of conflict needs to be revisited. It is particularly important to look more closely and carefully at the rapidity with which the notion of sectarian or ethnic conflict is mobilized and the contexts in which it creates meaning (Donham 2011). One way of doing this is to look critically at the emergence of these discourses, to see where and why they are mobilized and what kinds of institutional and infrastructural projects support these ideas, rather than to assume they have always already existed.

Today, in the wake of the Arab Spring uprisings of 2011 and their still unfinished outcomes, it is critical to properly contextualize the present discourse about the Shi'a versus Sunni conflict within the region and *not* fall into the trap of assuming that this is a continuous, ancient feud emerging from differences in religious beliefs or practices. The "new sectarianism," Toby Matthiesen (2013, xiii) writes, is characterized by state actors, particularly in Saudi Arabia and Bahrain, who "make decisions on the basis of a sectarian assessment of politics," whereby Iran is presented as a Shi'a rival. The fact that these same state actors are opposed to Sunni Islamist groups makes it clear that the mobilization of sectarian rhetoric is, at least in some instances, a cynical tactic of scapegoating. State actors may have also mobilized the sectarian discourse of a Sunni/Shi'a divide to prevent the collaboration between Shi'a and Sunni in a potential uprising in some

Gulf states (xiii). However, and most important to the present context, once the discourse of sectarian rhetoric has been established, particularly in the case of Gulf states like Bahrain and Saudi Arabia, it "becomes as much a bottom-up as a top-down process" (x), no longer solely under the control of state media but taking on a life of its own. State actors' utilization of sectarian rhetoric and political maneuvering based on these discourses has had devastating results in the region. In this instance it is even more clear how the dialogic nature of sectarianism, not only as a set of ideas but also, as I have shown, as a set of material, urban and infrastructural circumstances and, today, military action, is produced and reproduced in various contexts.

As a hub for Syrians, including Syrian Kurds and Syrian Armenians, Bourj Hammoud has seen a major influx of displaced Syrians. One cannot help but recall the other waves of refugees in Lebanon: Armenians in the 1920s, Palestinians in 1948, Iraqis in the 2000s, and now Syrians in 2011 and beyond. According to the UNHCR, there are currently over four million registered Syrian refugees, with over one million of them residing in Lebanon.[5] Of course, the numbers of displaced people are much higher, as not everyone can or will register. My interlocutors in Bourj Hammoud wonder, if the past has taught them anything, if Syrians will ever be able to go back. In response to a transnational Armenian organizational campaign to raise money for displaced Syrian Armenians, one clinic in Bourj Hammoud has started organizing workshops for over three thousand Syrian Armenians to officially register with the UNHCR. As transnational Armenian organizations assist Syrian Armenians in making arrangements to stay in Lebanon, or to resettle permanently in the Republic of Armenia or elsewhere, many tacitly acknowledge that the Armenian community in Syria may be scattered forever. After purchasing a stack of Armenian books in Bourj Hammoud in 2013, I was told by the clerk that the store is no longer receiving anything from that particular press, as it was located in Aleppo and is now closed, its owners having left Syria. Nearly one hundred years later, Armenian descendants of genocide survivors who lived in Aleppo's refugee camps have themselves been displaced.

International organizations have also started to use some of the clinics and social service centers in Bourj Hammoud as hubs for the distribution of things like food staples, blankets, and medical supplies. By 2012 an Armenian-affiliated social welfare organization in Bourj Hammoud had become one of these hubs. Because it was accepting aid for Syrian refugees from large international organizations, it needed to ensure that distribution was equitable. However, some of the funding from transnational Armenian organizations was designated only for Syrian Armenians. The distribution of vital services and aid through these sect-affiliated channels is bound to have a profound impact on both displaced Syrians and the Lebanese who find themselves navigating the same channels without a significant increase in resources to these institutions.

It remains to be seen what the experience of navigating the intricate channels of services and infrastructures in Lebanon will mean for the Syrians who have had to leave everything behind. Syrian Armenians are much more able to navigate additional services and activate informal networks as Armenians in Bourj Hammoud. It is much more difficult for other Syrian refugees to do this, despite the fact that labor migration from Syria has created some pathways to finding work and housing, particularly for those whose family members were already working and living in Bourj Hammoud. However, the mass displacement of over one million Syrians to Lebanon along with Lebanese reluctance to upset the demographic sectarian political balance that determines political representation in the country have already embroiled Lebanon in the conflict. Will their fate be like that of the Palestinians, permanent refugees in a country that will not give them citizenship status? New visa restrictions on Syrians entering Lebanon introduced in January 2015 reflect the growing political tension around these questions.

The ramifications of the Syrian conflict are still unfolding as I write these words. In recent years a number of clashes, particularly in Tripoli and towns bordering Syria, as well as the detonation of several car bombs in civilian areas have left many of my interlocutors wondering if Lebanon is on the brink of another major conflict. At the same time that displaced Syrians are forced to navigate the sectarian arrangement of clinics and social service organizations to obtain vital services, the word "sectarian conflict" is increasingly used to describe the situation in Syria. This term is assimilated frighteningly quickly, flattening the nuances of what sect could mean in a given context and how it can change over time. All too often, "sectarian conflict" becomes a shortcut way to insist that a conflict is the inevitable outgrowth of the natural and intrinsic ethnic or religious hatred of a given context. It is my hope that, with more careful scholarship, we can demonstrate that even the most entrenched-seeming identity categories are constructed through more emergent processes that are, in many cases, entangled with the processes that build cities and provide infrastructures and services.

What kind of city is Bourj Hammoud likely to be in the wake of these regional upheavals and population movements? It is likely that notions of sectarian community, specifically an Armenian "community," will shift or change given the influx of displaced Syrians and Syrian Armenians in recent years. With the continued pressure of land speculation and rising land values remaking the urban landscape all over the greater Beirut area, further evictions and demolitions may result. What sorts of claims to community or belonging might be evoked to challenge or oppose these displacements in the future? What kinds of negotiations, contestations, and conflicts will occur as a result of these pressures on residency? What I have shown throughout this book is that notions of sectarian community recalibrate over time in relation to shifting relationships among people, things, and spaces as well as other notions of "community." As cities, both Beirut and Bourj Hammoud have long been modalities through which understandings of the sectarian have been worked out.[6] As the city transforms and shifts, so too will the networks of service provision and infrastructures that power urban life and, possibly, the way in which sectarianism is lived, understood, and experienced in the everyday.

Infrastructure shifts and changes over time, even as it carries within it sediments of various pasts. Lebanese political sectarian actors have long tried to harness the "symbolic logic" of infrastructure in order to do certain kinds of work in constructing the pathways and channels that produce sectarian notions of community and sectarian publics, even as infrastructures elude their initial design or meaning (Larkin 2008). But what happens when the *meaning* of infrastructure, both its failures and its potentials, is reworked, reimagined, or recontextualized? In moments of upheaval, can *existing* social infrastructures that are not narrowly circumscribed within sectarian channels become visible and available again (Elyachar 2014)? As this book goes to press, events in Lebanon give us reason to hope that the malleability of the technical and symbolic meaning of infrastructures can serve as the ground on which emergent forms of belonging and new publics can be imagined.

"YOU STINK"—GARBAGE, POPULAR PROTEST, REIMAGINING A PUBLIC

In July 2015 residents of a town called Naimeh blocked access to the road to a landfill to lend urgency to their demands that it not be expanded. The landfill, which served as a collection point for much of Beirut's garbage, was already filled beyond capacity and had overwhelmed the town. Protestors had blocked the road before but had ceased their protest after the government promised them that it would find alternative facilities. When it became clear that no other alternatives were being pursued, the protesters resumed their blockade and garbage throughout Beirut piled up. For weeks, mountains of garbage piled up on Beirut's streets. Out of desperation, people started burning the garbage on the streets, releasing noxious fumes and odors into the thick, humid summer air. After weeks of inaction, the government made plans to remove the garbage by dumping it in sites around Lebanon that were not suitably prepared as landfills.[7]

Anger and disgust continued to grow in the aftermath of this latest infrastructural failure. In the days and weeks following the removal of the garbage, people took to the streets to protest the state's inability and unwillingness to manage public goods and services, as well as the illegal extension of Parliament, deferral of elections that were supposed to happen in 2014, and the lack of an acting president. By August over fifteen thousand people had gathered in downtown Beirut under a nonpartisan rallying cry that became an often-repeated hashtag on social media sites, *tala'at rihatkom*, or youstink, referring to the politicians and government figures they found responsible for inefficiencies in all utilities and services. The protest went far beyond a demand for better sanitation services into a comment on the state of electricity, water, and public goods in general. When police and military fired on the peaceful protests, social media users began posting photos of police violence. Artist Jana Traboulsi created iconic graphics juxtaposing these photos along with phrases like "Kif ma fi dawleh? Hon al dawleh wa hek shekleha!" (What do you mean there is no state? Here is the state and this is how it looks!).[8] The "here is the state" phrase appearing all over social media sites is an obvious reference to the often-repeated "Wayn al dawleh?" (Where is the state?), used to locate responsibility for the failing infrastructure in Lebanon. The protestors of 2015 insisted that there *is* a state, but it does not provide adequate services, it just uses violence to quell any demands made to improve or manage infrastructures or public goods.

Infrastructure has long been used as a means of producing various publics and notions of community and belonging. In Lebanon this has all too often meant cultivating and reproducing notions of distinctly sectarian publics, even as people can and do continually reach beyond these definitions of community. The "you stink" protests, at least in their early stage, are reconfiguring community in this way by demanding that the state be accountable for providing infrastructures and services in the context of a newly emergent definition of a public. Infrastructure here is a highly visible and odorous way to make a set of demands, even as the contents of those demands can and will necessarily shift. The protesters and networks of activists have cultivated their calls for better services through a critique of state actors, not only in terms of well-worn charges of corruption but also by denouncing their long-standing practices of using sectarian discourses as divisive tactics. While the protests have so far been popular in Beirut, it remains to be seen whether they will be effective in mobilizing participants elsewhere in Lebanon. Class is also emerging as a key component in the protests, and as a factor that both the protesters and the state will need to address. This serves as a reminder of the key lesson of this book: that sectarian community in Lebanon cannot be understood outside of the nexus of class and geography, particularly as it is produced through networks of infrastructures and services. In other words, class is an important aspect of the construction of sectarianism in Lebanon and cannot necessarily be *extracted* from sectarian formations. For many working-class and poor Lebanese, even those who are most affected by the inadequacies of state-provided infrastructures, sectarian community networks have provided important channels and pathways to security, to services, and to a sense of stability and belonging. People do not necessarily view these networks as coercive. Still, the hope remains that infrastructure—which has been used for so long to create pathways and channels to sectarian notions of "belonging" and "community"—may someday form the basis for other kinds of collaborations and solidarities yet unformed and unknown.

NOTES

INTRODUCTION

1. See conclusion for further discussion of the 2015 garbage revolts and the "youstink" movement.

2. Partha Chatterjee (2006, 47) writes of a shift in governance: "from formally organized structures such as political parties with well-ordered internal constitutions . . . to loose and often transient mobilizations, building on communication structures that would not be ordinarily recognized as political (for instance, religious assemblies or cultural festivals, or more curiously, even associations of cinema fans, as in some of the southern Indian states)". In the case of Lebanon, religious organizations are entangled with state institutions in the sense that nearly all political parties are affiliated with religious organizations. Furthermore, fifteen religious courts corresponding to the eighteen legally recognized religious sects have jurisdiction over personal status laws. The popular discourse of "chaos" embedded within the *wayn al dawleh* comment has to do with the perceived lack of formally organized structures. Chatterjee's idea that these organizations and alliances do the work that states fail at does not quite describe the intricate overlap and entanglement between what might be considered "the state," "civil society," and the perceived nontraditionally political "religious organizations" in Lebanon.

3. Scholars like geographer Sara Fregonese (2012) have noted how the discourse of "weak state" can have deleterious effects on Lebanon, even normalizing moments of great violence as somehow inevitable or even cyclical and wholly attributed to the "weak state" hypothesis. Both Fregonese and Mona Harb (2001) argue for an approach that looks at sovereignty as hybrid, activated by numerous state and nonstate actors in the working out of urban planning and other projects.

4. For more on political-sectarian geographies, see Deeb and Harb (2013).

5. See also Abu Rish (2015b).

6. It is important to emphasize that infrastructural arrangements are not merely a representation of the configuration of sectarianism in Lebanon or even a way of illustrating or translating the concept of sectarian identity. Infrastructures work as sieves (Kockelman 2013), or, borrowing from Dilip Parameshwar Gaonkar and Elizabeth Povinelli's notion of transfiguration, "the politics of recognition is never as simple as identity and difference but is always already a politics of transfiguration from one culture of circulation to another" (2003, 396).

7. See also Graham and McFarlane (2015).

8.   For more on the mobilization of sectarian discourses to justify or explain repression or violence in the Gulf states, see Matthiesen (2013, 2014); also see Wehrey (2013). For an important intervention on the discourse of sectarianism as a "cause" for the recent conflict in Syria, see Wedeen (2013). For more on the intersection between class and sect underlying Syrian citizenship in the 1990s, see Salamandra (2004).

9.   A network can be described as an aggregate of individuals connected by lines of differing relationships and "trust"—an assemblage of signs, words, and symbols that don't necessarily represent a deeper form of knowing but rather afford a certain potential for material action (Granovetter 1985).

10.   My study owes much to Joseph's (2008) findings and her ongoing engagement with sectarianism as a concept.

11.   In Bourj Hammoud, the "national council" or Azkayin Khorourt, formed in 1976 by a joint committee consisting of Armenian political party leaders, churches, town associations, and other Armenian organizations, took over "the provision of those services that had been disrupted by the war: the care of the sick and wounded, electricity supply, telephone and postal communication" (Miglorino 2008, 165).

12.   We even saw this during rebuilding and humanitarian aid provision in the aftermath of the 2006 war with Israel (Harb 2008).

13.   I owe this insight to Julia Elyachar.

14.   As Lara Deeb and Mona Harb (2013, 210) argue, "Sect and class in Lebanon cannot be understood in isolation from one another," and both are inextricable from the city's sectarian and class-based geographies.

15.   See, for example, Limbert (2010) for a discussion of the ways in which a new highway in an Omani town profoundly shaped local understandings of inside and outside, safety and danger.

16.   By drawing out the "urban" as a peculiar scale that is neither diminutive of the "national" nor completely contained by it, Mariana Valverde (2009) suggests that the daily working of urban municipal governance and appeals to justice can actually jump between scales. She challenges the normative view of "scales" of governance whereby "small" or "local" is a valorized site for theorization against a supposedly more abstract, "larger" or "national" scale.

17.   Legal scholars have argued against the notion of governance as a binary between state and territorialized society (Dean and Henman 2004), and the linking of legal jurisdiction to territory, preferring instead to imagine territorial jurisdiction as a "governmental technique" rather than a fixed, or a priori fact (Ford 1999). Bradin Cormack adds to these discussions of jurisdiction by emphasizing it as an ongoing project, consisting of negotiations between various actors, that is often worked out in so-called "mundane" processes (2008).

18.   Jens Hanssen (2005, 4) writes: "Beirut was at once the product, the object, and the project of imperial and urban politics of difference. Overlapping European, Ottoman, and local civilizing missions competed in the political fields of administration, infrastructure, urban planning, public health, education, public morality, journalism, and architecture."

19.   For more on the logics of the Mandate system and the League of Nations agreements, see Anghie (2002).

20.   Ironically, the National Pact was never officially written down and was largely an "informal agreement" (Joseph 1996, 112; see also Deeb 2006).

21.   Owing to sectarian political parties' interests in keeping their proportion of parliamentary seats, there has not been a census taken in Lebanon since 1932. Some suggest that the accuracy of the 1932 census was undermined by a desire to present Lebanon as a majority "Christian" nation. See Deeb (2006); Maktabi (1999).

22.   The Taif agreement of 1990 that marked the end of the Lebanese civil war also revised the proportional representation between various Muslim and Christian sects in

Parliament to 50:50 and "increased the power of the Prime Minister (a Sunni position) relative to the President (a Maronite position)" (Joseph 1996, 113).

23.   The eighteen recognized sects are Alawite, Armenian Apostolic (also known as Orthodox), Armenian Catholic, Assyrian, Chaldean, Copts, Druze, Greek Catholic, Greek Orthodox, Isma'ili, Jewish, Roman Catholic, Maronite, Protestant, Sunni, Shi'a, Syriac Catholic, and Syriac Orthodox.

24.   For more on personal status in Lebanon, see Mikdashi (2014).

25.   Thompson (2000, 3) writes: "Gender hierarchy was a pillar of colonial paternalism, wherein the French and indigenous elites bargained to maintain hierarchies of privilege."

26.   This overlapping of jurisdiction is clearly demonstrated by Mona Harb's (2001) study of the negotiations between sectarian political parties, the Council for Development and Reconstruction (CDR) of the Lebanese state, and the various local notables and community leaders that went into the Elyssar urban development project in southern Beirut.

27.   While this is by no means an exhaustive list, for more on the Armenian genocide, see Akçam (2007, 2012); Hovannisian (2003); Kevorkian (2011); Suny (2015).

28.   It is important to note that the Lebanese sectarian confessional system also necessitates Lebanese Armenians to maintain juridico-religious institutions that function within the confessional political sectarian system (Migliorino 2008; Schahgaldian 1979). This lies in sharp contrast to other Armenian diasporic communities, such as those within the United States (Bakalian 1992). For example, many of the organizations operating as political parties in Lebanon are cultural organizations in the United States. See Nalbantian (2011, 2013) for more on the history of Armenian political institutions and their coemergence with and embeddedness in the Lebanese political system, particularly by the 1950s.

29.   For more, see Shahantookht (1997).

30.   It is critical to note that scholars like Taner Akçam (2012, 449) insist that the genocide was not driven by ethnoreligious hatred or a "clash between the empire's Muslim groups . . . and its Christian elements." Rather, the genocide was a matter of Ottoman state policy to eliminate those groups it perceived as a threat through a project of "ethnoreligious homogenization of Anatolia," by deportation and annihilation.

31.   Many of my interlocutors speculate that the French deliberately set a great fire in the Karantina camp to hasten the resettlement process.

32.   Throughout my research I heard mixed stories about the origin of the name Bourj Hammoud, which roughly translates to "Hammoud's Tower." One publication detailing brief descriptions of various Lebanese municipalities traces the name back to a tall building built by Hammoud Arslan of the powerful Arslan family sometime in the late nineteenth or early twentieth century (Banurama lil-Khidmat al- 'Ammah 2008).

33.   Some town associations are transnational in reach, planning social activities and charity events in different cities around the world. In the 1940s and 1950s some town associations published newspapers and town memorial books in various diasporic locations in Lebanon and elsewhere in the world. Town associations and compatriotic unions still exist today to varying degrees of activity. The Marash association is particularly large and active in Lebanon, though one of the smaller compatriotic unions I met with maintained a small space at the top of a large office building in Bourj Hammoud, with computers for teenagers as well as a meeting place for adults to gather and socialize.

34.   Western Armenian is the standard dialect of most Armenians living in the Middle East aside from Iran and the Republic of Armenia, where Eastern Armenian is spoken. They are mutual comprehensible but distinct dialects, and both are increasingly spoken throughout other diasporic locations including the United States. Kerapar, or classical Armenian, is the liturgical language of the Armenian Apostolic Church as well as classical poetry.

35.   In 1915, 95 percent of Armenians were Apostolic (Miller and Miller 1993). The Protestant missionaries were primarily American but also German and Swiss. See also Arpee (1936).

36.   Town associations also produced town and village memorial books, containing stories, photographs, and local histories recounted by genocide survivors. Some even contained glossaries of dialects that have since disappeared. These memorializing efforts are similar to those practiced by displaced Palestinians (Davis 2010; Slyomovics 1998).

37.   An official census has not been conducted in Lebanon since 1932. This population estimate was taken from a report about Bourj Hammoud and Sin El Fil produced by U.S.-based Christian humanitarian organization World Vision in 2006.

38.   Most Armenians "repatriating" to Soviet Armenia from Lebanon were from lands in what had become, at that point, part of Turkey. The term "repatriation" was built upon the notion of Soviet Armenia as another homeland, though one that did not necessarily replace Armenian territorial claims to former Ottoman lands. In subsequent decades, these territorial claims ceased to be at the forefront of mainstream Armenian political parties' agendas in Lebanon. For more on repatriation see Nalbantian 2011 and 2013.

39.   For more on Armenian political parties in Lebanon, see Geukjian (2009); Messerlian (2014); Migliorino (2008); Nalbantian (2011, 2013); Sanjian (2007). For more on Armenian political parties in the late Ottoman era, see Der Matossian (2014). For further reading on the context of Armenian political parties in the diaspora and their connections to the Republic of Armenia, see Bakalian (1992); Libaridian (1991); Panossian (2006); Suny (1993).

40.   In 1958, during the first Lebanese civil war, the conflict between Tashnag and the other main Armenian political party, Hnchag, exploded into violence. The third major party in Lebanon, Ramgavar, has historically been more marginal to the disputes between Tashnag and Hnchag. See Nalbantian (2011).

41.   Later in the 1970s, religious scholars such as Imam Musa al-Sadr and Sayyid Muhammad Hussein Fadlallah, a leading Shi'a cleric or *marja'*, would begin organizing Shi'as in Bourj Hammoud and Naba'a. Their efforts cultivated political mobilization on the grounds of Shi'a religiosity. For more on Imam Musa al-Sadr, see Ajami (1987); Halawi (1992); and Norton (1987). For more on Sayyid Muhammad Hussein Fadlallah in Bourj Hammoud and Naba'a, see Sankari (2005); Tarhini (2011).

42.   To group all the "progressive" or "left"-leaning factions as pan-Arabist is somewhat inaccurate, as the stance on pan-Arabism evolved during the course of the 1975–90 war. The Left, in fact, had a number of goals and ideological commitments and discourses, even if they were, at times, aligned across these divides in opposition to the "Right." Often parties as disparate as the communists and more overtly Islamic political groups are classified as "left" simply because they are regarded as oppositional to right-wing Kataib ideology. In fact, despite the fact that the conflicts of the 1950s and 1960s may have played out along the basis of a split between Nasserist (pan-Arabist) and "Lebanist" aims, during the course of the wars a number of discourses emerged that had little to do with this split. Furthermore, factions made constantly shifting alliances with one another across what might seem to be widely disparate ideological divides.

43.   The Phalange or Kataib Party was founded in 1936 by Pierre Gemayel. The fascist imagery of the party is said to have been inspired by the Nazi Party during the Berlin Olympics (Fisk 2002). The Kataib became a stronger voice in Lebanese politics in the late 1950s and early 1960s, its political stance characterized by a rejection of Palestinian presence in Lebanon and opposition to both pan-Arabist and class-solidarity movements and labor unions in Lebanon. The Kataib was one of the key factions during the civil war of 1975–90 (T. Khalaf 1976)

44.   For more on postwar property restitution and compensation for squatters, see Sawalha (2010).

45. For more on Syrian labor migration to Lebanon, see Chalcraft (2009).

46. *Zawarib*, which means alleyways or small streets, is a pocked-sized Beirut street atlas. I only ever saw foreign tourists or students using it.

47. In her work on Cairo, Julia Elyachar (2011) writes that movement on the street is crucial to the way people experience a sense of identity and belonging. For more on the anthropology of walking, see Ingold and Vergunst (2008).

48. For more on belonging, identity, memory, and urban neighborhoods in Beirut, see Sawalha (2010).

49. For more on the observational genre of ethnographic film, see Grimshaw (2009).

50. Anthropologist and filmmaker Jean Rouch (2003) used a collaborative ethnographic approach to filmmaking with his interlocutors through fictional reenactments, interviews, staged encounters, as well as more observational forms. Anthropologist Elizabeth Povinelli's (2015) "improvisational realism" is another approach to collaboration, as scenarios are improvised without a written script. The process of filming and watching helps participants "discover what we never knew we knew by hearing what we say in moments of improvisation." In both instances, filmmaking becomes an important ethnographic encounter and process in itself.

CHAPTER 1: ALL THAT ENDURES FROM PAST TO PRESENT

1. As anthropologist Sami Hermez (2012, 330) writes, the anticipation of war, specifically war as "metaphor for uncertainty," pervades everyday life in Lebanon. He also argues that the mundane or the quotidian, not only the extraordinary, can also be quite violent in situations of protracted conflict.

2. This line of questioning, of course, can extend beyond Lebanon. Donald Donham (2011, 4) challenges the way in which conflicts worldwide have been labeled as "ethnic conflict." He writes: "Ethnicity seems the natural basis on which social actors compete in times of upset and uncertainty . . . and yet, if we examine specific cases, looking beyond the initial newspaper reports, this clarity invariably begins to blur."

3. I use Bergson's notion of duration even though he refers to individualized, subjective time, which differs from my object of analysis. However, my use of *durée* is not entirely novel. Nancy Munn (1992, 95) writes that Bergson's ideas about qualitative time, while referring to an individualized experience, was influential for both Durkheim and Hubert, particularly in the latter's notion of "qualitative temporal rhythms in objective, social life."

4. Recent ethnographies have focused on various kinds of "memory" at work in Lebanon. Aseel Sawalha (2010) explores Beirut's urban heritage as a site for reclaiming the past. Lucia Volk (2010) looks at the legacy of Lebanese national monuments that memorialize "Lebanese" events that do not erase sectarian identities but rather promote their mutual belonging to a united Lebanese nation.

5. Paul Kockelman, personal communication, December 16, 2015.

6. Walter Benjamin (2007, 255) writes: "To articulate the past historically does not mean to recognize it 'the way it really was' (Ranke). It means to seize hold of a memory as it flashes up at a moment of danger. Historical materialism wishes to retain that image of the past which unexpectedly appears to man singled out by history at a moment of danger." Benjamin's historical materialism is a view of the past from the perspective of the present moment. The object is not to reconstruct a definitive history of the past from a detached perspective. It is key here that a memory that flashes up in a moment of danger is what

is most important to maintain in order to produce, critique, or shape possibilities for the future—in this case, a potentially revolutionary future.

7. For Elizabeth Grosz (2004), the political potential of this mode of thinking about the past allows for radical critiques to imagine as yet unimaginable and contingent futures. Bergson helps to conceptualize a vision of the present that remains connected and cognizant of a shared virtual past that brims over with possibility rather than creates inevitable futures.

8. Almost all political parties in Lebanon are associated with a religious sect owing to the particularities of the confessional system. See introduction.

9. The March 8 and March 14 coalitions are named after the dates of two different demonstrations launched in Beirut in 2005 in the aftermath of the assassination of Prime Minister Rafic Hariri, namely, in support of and against ongoing Syrian involvement in Lebanon, respectively, although there were many other points of contention. The March 14 faction called for the withdrawal of Syria from Lebanon, launching the so-called cedar revolution, and Syria did eventually withdraw. The coalitions have been referred to by the dates of their respective demonstrations during that critical year ever since. For more on the Sunni-Shiʿa split as a contemporary political manifestation in Lebanon and its relationship to regional politics, see Deeb and Harb (2013).

10. The relegation of this violent incident to the "domestic" and thus "nonpolitical" sphere is in keeping with what feminists have long critiqued as part of the private/public dichotomy framework which excludes women and the "domestic" sphere they represent from "real" politics (Rosaldo and Lamphere 1974).

11. For more on the mobilization of sectarian discourses in the Gulf, see Matthiesen (2013).

12. Max Weiss (2010, 229) argues that it is highly problematic to suggest that the "Shiʿi community in Lebanon is only discernible through the lens of contemporary political Shiʿism, global political trends, or the influence of the Iranian Revolution." He calls for historic specificity in understanding Shiʿa political mobilization in Lebanon, rather than generalizing across a number of countries. He is particularly trying to argue against tying Shiʿa mobilization back to Iran in a way that limits and distorts the various developments in Lebanon throughout the twentieth century, not just in the 1970s and 1980s.

13. I owe this insight to historian Linda Sayed.

14. For more about Hadjin, see Dakessian (2013).

15. For example, see the biography of Monte Melkonian, who grew up in California but went to Lebanon in the 1970s and 1980s to fight with the Armenian Secret Army for the Liberation of Armenia (ASALA) during the Lebanese civil war. He ultimately went to fight in Nagorno-Karabakh, where he was killed (Melkonian 2005).

16. There are still two informal "camp" spaces remaining in Bourj Hammoud, in which the residents of the dwellings do not own the land on which their apartments or houses are built. Both were established as a response to the Armenian refugee crisis of the 1920s and 1930s but have remained to the present day. One of these informal spaces, Sanjak, is slowly being torn down. See chapter 2 for more on these informal settlements.

17. I owe this ethnographic insight to anthropologist Jared McCormick.

18. Many scholars have argued that vigilante justice is a result of the lack of state support in arbitrating conflict and is directly connected to increasing violence in the wake of "privatization" and neoliberal state agendas that roll back public services (Caldeira 2001; Low 2001). The involvement of the Lebanese Army, however, in a small-scale fight that might otherwise have been handled by Tashnag calls to mind Daniel Goldstein's ethnography of conflict in urban Bolivia. In *The Spectacular City* (2004, 4) he argues that displays of "vigilante" justice are actually a form of "protest against a perceived failure of the state" that has neglected to provide adequate services and protection to its citizens living in the poor urban fringe of the

city, not a call for greater autonomy. At the same time, the popular display of violence, while part of a call to the state for greater "inclusion," also produces "its own forms of belonging and exclusion" (177). People use the spectacles as another form of boundary making—a display through which others are included or excluded from the "community" through acts of violence. Similarly, the outbreak of violence in Bourj Hammoud seemed to herald a shift in people's attitudes about who could and should be living in their neighborhood.

19.   For example, during Abdul Hamid's reign, Kurds were organized into regiments called the Hamidiye, designed to "repress the Armenians and contain the independent ambitions of the urban Turkish notables" (Suny 1993, 105). Kurdish attacks on Armenians during the genocide are also well documented (Kevorkian 2011). Still, even in 1915, during the systematic deportations and massacres perpetrated by the Ottoman state, Talat Pasha expressed fears that "Armenians might unite in a common cause with the Kurds" (Akçam 2012, 174). Indeed, Taner Akçam notes a number of Armenian and Kurdish leaders making joint declarations of collaboration as well as an instance of Alevi Kurds and Armenian military deserters forming "a bandit gang." Kurds were deported to Western Anatolia as a means of "Turkification" from 1915 through the end of the war, with the additional aim of "demographic dilution" in keeping Kurds at no more than 5 percent of the population in any given territory (Ungor 2011, 298).

20.   I owe this insight to Tsolin Nalbantian.

21.   For more on Turkish-Kurdish relations, see also Sasuni (1969).

22.   For official data from UNHCR, see its Syria regional refugee response portal online at http://data.unhcr.org/syrianrefugees/country.php?id=122.

23.   The precariousness faced by Syrian workers in connection with popular opinions about the Syrian regime was last demonstrated in 2005, in the wake of the assassination of then prime minister Rafic Hariri and the subsequent withdrawal of Syrian military from Lebanon after mass protests. At that time many Syrians were subject to increased hostility, and their presence in Lebanon "eventually became a stick that the campaign to get Syria out of Lebanon used, to tremendous effect" (Chalcraft 2009, 223).

24.   These new restrictions have separate entry requirements and lengths of stay for tourists, students, Syrians seeking medical care, Syrians who own property in Lebanon, or those traveling for business. Syrians seeking tourist visas must show proof of having one thousand U.S. dollars in a bank account as well as a hotel booking for the duration of their stay.

CHAPTER 2: PERMANENTLY TEMPORARY

1.   For more on the role of photography and particularly the relationship between photographic exhibitions and cultural representations, see Kratz (2002).

2.   The Armenian-as-craftsperson was also actively promoted by municipality actors who sought to cultivate interest by foreign or transnational development projects, as I will explain in chapter 5.

3.   The inherent problems of using photography to highlight social inequalities recalls James Agee and Walker Evans's famous collaborative work of documentary photography and journalism during the American Dust Bowl in Let Us Now Praise Famous Men (1941). Agee's explosive narrative repeatedly questions his own positionality as well as the project of journalism and its objectives.

4.   In her ethnography of postwar Beirut, Aseel Sawalha (2010) describes the contestations around the fate of the fishing port in 'Ayn al-Mreisse as one in which artists' and local

residents' nostalgic images of the port were pitted against Solidere's images of modernity and progress through Beirut's rebuilding and redevelopment process. The mobilization of nostalgia was one tactic of making claims to space in the context of Beirut's rampant postwar redevelopment that threatened longtime residents and excluded many from formerly public spaces.

5.   However, the municipality cannot be understood as an isolated form of power that dictates the use of space. The Armenian sectarian political organizations, the Apostolic Church, as well as NGOs and local and transnational philanthropic organizations that operate in the area all produce and reproduce ideas about belonging as well as the material networks that sustain these ways of belonging. The overlapping jurisdictions of the church, the political clubhouses, and the municipal actors create both inclusion and exclusion, stitching people and things into the web of what it means to be a good Armenian or a good neighbor, which includes, but ultimately exceeds, religious identity alone.

6.   Using tools such as maps and title deeds has a much longer history for Armenians making territorial claims during the late Ottoman Empire. Sam Kaplan (2004, 414) has written of Armenians' use of "geo-texts," or "textual representations of territory," to lobby French colonial officials to assist them in carving out the state of Cilicia as an independent Armenian nation apart from the Ottoman Empire during World War I. Kaplan argues that Armenian lobbyists mobilized the proper forms of textual formats to represent and legitimize territorial claims in a way that would appeal to French nationalist sentiments.

7.   Hernando De Soto (1989) has argued that legal ownership will result in greater economic success for those living within informal property regimes. In many instances in Lebanon, formal property ownership has not always protected residents from forced eviction through eminent domain, as in the case of the rebuilding of downtown Beirut or, even earlier, the building of the autostrade highway in the 1960s. Likewise, squatting or informal property regimes have been protected by various political organizations, sometimes leading to more secure outcomes for these residents (M. Fawaz 2009a, 2009b; see also M. Fawaz 2013; Sawalha 2010).

8.   Anthropologists have long argued that property is not a "bundle of rights . . . but rather of powers" (Verdery 1998, 161) as well as "a social relation between persons concerning material or immaterial 'things'" (Mundy and Smith 2007, 2). Looking at property regimes during times of transformation helps to illuminate the ways in which "private property is not natural but profoundly social, it requires a degree of planning and deliberation" (Verdery 2003, 4).

9.   For more on rising costs of real estate and high-end development in Beirut, see Krijnen and Fawaz (2010).

10.   By 2014 some residents reported they were no longer sharing electricity between homes, presumably because the municipality was no longer willing to allow them to continue this practice. These residents resorted to paying for ishtirak subscriptions as the government grid proved even less reliable than it had been in 2010.

11.   As Ananya Roy (2004) argues in the context of Calcutta, uncertainty and opacity are in fact part of the process of urbanization and serve to further consolidate power. She writes: "The indeterminacies of exclusion and inclusion ensures political support, consolidating informalization as a mode of accumulation, and patronage as a mode of legitimation" (154).

12.   Anthropologist Aseel Sawalha (2010) noted a similar sentiment among her interlocutors in postwar Beirut, who also remembered the civil war era as a time of greater access to economic resources as well as greater agency over space.

13.   Julia Elyachar's (2005) interlocutors in Cairo described the new workshop district to which the state had resettled them as "empty." Interviews with my interlocutors

also demonstrated how their sense of the richness or fullness of space has to do with the very density of urban social networks that channel feelings of belonging and gave the space of the neighborhood particular meanings, as well as making life possible in very basic ways.

14.   This sentiment was echoed in many different interviews with Armenian interlocutors in Bourj Hammoud.

15.   For more on the *masaken* municipal housing project in which apartments were ultimately given only to Armenian residents in Bourj Hammoud, see Joseph (1975).

16.   Many of the social service organizations in Lebanon have begun to adopt self-sufficiency discourses typical of "professionalizing" NGOs (Murdock 2008). This relates to the larger context of global economic restructuring, the advocacy of "debt" rather than "aid," and the generalized withdrawal of the state from the provision of services or as an employer (see Elyachar 2002, 2005).

17.   Mona Fawaz (2009a, 2013) notes the impact of neoliberal logics in contemporary Lebanon that no longer simply neglect informality but rather integrate these spaces into real estate markets. Lebanese political actors intentionally and deliberately "force market-type relations" onto residents of informal housing (2013, 24). See also M. Fawaz (2014).

18.   I mean neoliberalism, here, as the retreat of sectarian political parties and state institutions from the provisioning of social welfare services, which are then replaced with individual responsibility for self-care. See also Wendy Brown's (2015) discussion of neoliberalism as a form of governance that imposes economic rationality on all domains of life, building on Michael Foucault's (2008) notion of neoliberal governmentality.

19.   Many Armenians in the diaspora, particularly American Armenians, have photographed and documented Sanjak, as have some local Lebanese Armenian artists and activists. However, no organized institutional mobilization around housing the displaced Sanjak residents has materialized in Lebanon.

20.   While popular discourses might assume that class distinctions are not as powerful as sectarian affiliations, in fact they are quite entangled in the process of producing a very different sense of belonging among Armenians in Bourj Hammoud and those who live in middle-class suburbs like Mezher or Antelias. Even those who commute to Bourj Hammoud to work at Armenian organizations or are very involved in Armenian church activities do not necessarily identify with Bourj Hammoud Armenians but often take a paternalistic view toward them. This will be discussed further in chapter 3.

21.   Doreen Massey (1994) writes of the dualisms through which space is gendered through dichotomies of public/private but also formulations of the larger or regional versus the local mapped normatively to the masculine and feminine, respectively.

22.   For more on the political economy of real estate in Lebanon and the particularities of gentrification processes in Beirut, see Krijnen and De Beukelaer (2015).

23.   The popular Beirut neighborhoods of Hadjin and Karm el Zeitoun on the eastern edge of the city directly across the river from Bourj Hammoud were also built through the joint cooperation of French Mandate authorities and Armenian town associations to house Armenian refugees in the late 1920s. These neighborhoods, while still maintaining a large Armenian population, have not been significantly affected by the eastern sweep of upscale cafes, restaurants, and shops. Because Hadjin is located on the main road linking the gentrified neighborhoods of Mar Mikhael and Gemmayze with Bourj Hammoud, there is some likelihood that it will be subject to the same eastward sweep of change. Karm el Zeitoun is located at the top of a hill in Ashrafiyeh, with narrower, less accessible roads, and is still very much a popular neighborhood with Lebanese Armenians as well as non-Lebanese migrants residing there. Unlike Bourj Hammoud, it is not a popular shopping district and is mainly residential.

CHAPTER 3: BUILDING THE NETWORKS

1. There are also other, smaller Armenian-run organizations that do different kinds of social assistance work but did not generally offer services to non-Armenians. This may shift as international organizations seek more local partners to assist in relief work for Syrian refugees in Lebanon.

2. Cammett also argues that some sectarian political groups in Lebanon provide services to members of other religious or ethnic groups as part of a political strategy of alliance building.

3. Joseph (1994a, 274) describes "relational rights" as part of a system in which rights are gained not by mere membership in a community, nor by the inherent fact of being an individual "bounded self." Rather, "a person's sense of rights flowed out of relationships that she/he had" (273). Likewise, Diane Singerman (1995) writes that women's networks in Cairo must be understood as "political" activity.

4. Other scholars have written of the coexistence or entanglement of what I call normative gender roles with various forms of political activity and engagement. In her ethnography of Palestinian women, Iris Jean-Klein (2000, 103) argues that "political activity could not take the place of other less contingent social thresholds such as reproductive events beginning with marriage; it depended on and complemented them." Julie Peteet (1991, 104) writes that despite the various transformations brought about by increasing women's involvement in Palestinian political work in Lebanon in the early 1980s, the sexual division of labor prevailed, and "women's domestic roles became infused with politics as they were called upon to make available to the national struggle their domestic services."

5. See, for example Zeina Zaatari's (2006) work on Lebanese women's roles as mothers as facilitating civil participation and Donna Murdock's (2008) ethnography of women's organizations in the context of ongoing violence in Colombia.

6. Lara Deeb (2006, 219) writes that among Shi'i activists, women's progress "is understood as both evidence of the Shi'i pious modern and necessary to it." Similarly, Armenian discourses of improvement and modernity promote a preservation of "traditional" and "cultural" Armenian activities with new practices that "improve" and "modernize" how women manage the home, care for children, and participate in Armenian social networks. The gendered division of labor in the production of "Armenianness" and sectarianism in general is part of a discourse of modernity, not antithetical to it. For more on communicative pathways and access to expert knowledge, see Elyachar (2005, 2012).

7. This trend toward greater professionalization has been noted in other contexts (Bayat 2002; Murdock 2008).

8. While there are important differences in the Lebanon context versus the Latin American context, these professionalized NGOs tend to take an approach that favors "individual initiative over collective struggle" within the context of broader neoliberal shifts in development (Murdock 2008, 3).

9. Suad Joseph (1996, 4) writes: "People's locations in these various networks affect their relationship to the state. Femaleness, therefore, is not a uniquely bounded and self-referential category, nor is gender a simple dichotomy." Location within networks also configures people's relationships to transnational networks and circulations.

10. Julia's Elyachar's (2010) notion of "phatic labor" in the context of Egyptian women's microfinance projects is important in conceptualizing the ways in which communicative channels are not only linguistic but a "social infrastructure" that can produce and transmit value.

11. Bourdieu's (1984, 110) ideas about social capital are helpful in understanding how hierarchies are constructed through networks of social infrastructures and, crucially, "the skill in operating 'connections.'" In their reading of Bourdieu in the context of leisure

practices in the suburbs of Beirut, Deeb and Harb (2013, 258) argue that "moral and spatial capital" are part of the way in which these hierarchies are constructed. I maintain that
gendered notions of propriety as well as class position and geography are critical to understanding how social capital operates within and as part of the construction of sectarian community as a hierarchical set of networks.

12.   Similarly, even though a law is on the books, we cannot assume that such laws are
being mobilized or upheld for everyone in the same way. Maya Mikdashi (2010) writes:
"Women often win cases against male plaintiffs who technically have more rights according
to the law. They win by employing other technologies of power, such as their class position,
their personal connections, or by gaining the sympathy of the judges, clerks, and legal secretaries who know the legal price of sex that women pay in Lebanon."

13.   Bowker and Starr (1999) write that while classificatory systems aim for totality and
completion, in fact they are often contradictory.

14.   Jane Collier (1997) writes that discourses about women's propriety and morality
according to notions of tradition are not spontaneous but very calculated and learned. The
construction of tradition, and thus women's roles and behaviors that are supposed to be "traditional," is a critical aspect of modernity and is deeply entangled with the cultivation of the
modern self and the construction of a history and identity.

15.   Julia Elyachar (2005) writes that her informants, workshop masters in Cairo, regarded their client networks and their markets as literally an extension of themselves. Just as
a network is a source of value, it is also a source of meaning, belonging, and identity. Working in the different context of an international NGO, Annelise Riles (2001) writes that the
primary activity of her interlocutors, the employees of this organization, is to perpetuate and
maintain the network and its circulation of information. It is their tasks in maintaining the
network that give her informants a sense of purpose and identity through their work.

16.   Clientelism in Lebanon has multiple overlapping forms. Many patrons inherit their
powerful positions from prominent families who are the heads of political dynasties. These
exist alongside and entangled within the sectarian political system in Lebanon but are not
completely collapsible to ethnoreligious identity, though these families have long been affiliated with sectarian political parties. The patron-client system known as *zu'ama*, through
which a powerful local actor or *za'im* serves as a broker between individuals and more powerful institutions, is produced through favors or, more precisely, a "network of transactional
ties" (Hamzeh 2001). The *zu'ama* system is key to understanding the clientelistic sectarian
political space of Lebanon but does not fully capture the interlocking channels of belonging
and exclusion that are produced in and through Armenian social service institutional networks in Bourj Hammoud.

17.   For more on agoumps, see introduction.

18.   The reluctance to consider this work "political" is not limited to my interlocutors
but rather is part of a larger discourse about women's work and kinship networks as belonging to the "private" realm of the domestic versus "public" realm of politics. The association
of women with the "private" and "domestic" realm has been the topic of much discussion in
feminist anthropology (Rosaldo and Lamphere 1974). Suad Joseph (1983) has also written
extensively of the political power of women's structured visiting and informal networks in
Bourj Hammoud.

19.   On many occasions interlocutors described that Armenians in Bourj Hammoud
could appeal to an agoump to intervene in family or neighborhood disputes.

20.   The Tashnag Party's territorial practices in terms of service provision and security can be compared with Mona Harb's (2010, 135) analysis of Hizbullah's "socio-spatial
'embeddedness'" in neighborhoods within Dahiye, Beirut's southern suburbs. This
embededness "helps to develop trust between service users and Hezbollah's institutions,
enhancing their accountability." Furthermore, the jurisdictional territory of the agoumps

can be likened to Hizbullah's *khaliyyat*, which Harb translates as "cells," that divide the territorial space of Dahiye into smaller units. The *khaliyyat* help to "maintain security" as well as "to identify potential beneficiaries of Hezbollah's services" at the neighborhood level (140). For more on the "spatial dimensions of Hizballah's political actions," see Harb (2007, 17).

21.   This is central to the logic of many sectarian organizations in Lebanon, though others deliberately extend services to other sectarian "communities" with the aim of cultivating better political relationships (Cammett 2014).

22.   Both Suad Joseph (1983) and Arpi Hamalian (1974) write of similar patterns of surveillance and censure in women's informal networks in Bourj Hammoud.

CHAPTER 4: FROM SHIRKETS TO BANKAS

1.   The idea of creating a social world through exchange has a long history in anthropology, with classical examples of social theory like Mauss (2000) and Malinowski (1922), though there are many more. However, attention to the value of social networks of exchange is not limited to anthropologists alone, as international microlending development projects target the exchange practices of the poor as a key site of integration into global capital markets (Elyachar 2005).

2.   See World Bank *Migration and Development Brief* for 2014.

3.   Diane Singerman (1995, 243) has argued that analysis of the informal economy in Egypt has largely focused solely on its economic impact. However, these informal networks are a powerful political force that promotes *sha'bi* (popular) interests. Similarly, Julia Elyachar (2011, 96) has written about the *sha'bi* tacit knoweldge and collective resources that are the "'infrastructure' of social life." In both instances, the networks and collective power of informality are instrumental in identity formation and creating a sense of belonging, as well as the provision of material resources.

4.   This process is similar to what Nancy Munn describes in *Fame of Gawa* (1986, 7) as "the practices by means of which actors construct their social world, and simultaneously their own selves and modes of being in the world." In Gawa communal value is produced through the spatiotemporal extensions of the Kula exchange.

5.   My reading of the entanglement between credit and sectarianism in Lebanon is connected to a longer tradition in anthropology of looking at the embeddedness of "the economy" in particular social and historical contexts, rather than a universal system distinct from what we might call "culture" (Polanyi 1957). In his classic work *Peddlars and Princes* (1968, 145), Clifford Geertz argued for a reading of economics that takes into account all that lies beyond the "narrowly economic" in order to challenge the idea that economic development unfolds as the same process everywhere. By looking at two distinct communities in Indonesia, he argued that economic change that might appear rapid, like a sudden increase in per capita earnings, is in fact the result of a much longer social process that has been operating to produce these "economic" conditions for a long time.

6.   In his discussion of actors and the question of agency, Bruno Latour (1993, 2007) does not posit the individual against some anonymous and static social "structure" but rather as a network of coercions By favoring the word "action," he removes the notion of individual agency as a necessary component of the analysis. At the same time, the notion of who is considered an "actor" is extended to the realm of objects.

7.   As Suad Joseph (1983) writes in her research on working-class women's networks in Bourj Hammoud, the formation of crosscutting sectarian relationships between women at

the neighborhood level was threatening to the dominant sectarian Christian political order, which worked to dismantle them.

8.   The Turkish term comes from the Arabic word *shirika*, which means "company" in modern colloquial usage. The root of the word implies collaboration and connectivity. It is also related to the word *ishtirak*, which is the term for the private generator services to which so many Lebanese subscribe. See the introduction and chapter 5 for more on ishtirak and networks of electricity.

9.   The notion of economic accounting as a moral, "balancing" force in social relations and state relations has a long history. In Albert Hirschman's classic intellectual history *The Passions and the Interests* (1977), he writes of the notion of countervailing passions, going back to Augustinian ideas of human nature, that dangerous passions could potentially be tamed by interests or *doux* passions, which later came to mean purely economic interests.

10.   For more on the topic of everyday practices as urban infrastructure, see Simone (2009).

11.   Keith Hart (1973, 67) defines an "informal" economic structure as one that workers take part in as a result of the failure of the "formal" structure to provide adequate wages. He equates the distinction between what can be called formal and informal economies by mapping them onto "employees" and "self-employed" worker categories.

12.   J. K. Gibson-Graham (2005, 12) counters the hegemonic view of capitalist productivity by proposing the concept of a "diverse economy in which what is usually thought of as the mainstream economy—market transactions, wage labour and capitalist enterprise—is joined by all the economic 'others' that sustain material survival and wellbeing."

13.   Arpa is a pseudonym for the organization.

14.   Telecommunications services are notoriously expensive in Lebanon. Many people will make arrangements via text message or a chat service like Viber and then call a friend and hang up in order to signal them to meet up somewhere, come down from their apartment onto the street, or some other prearranged instruction. For more on intentional missed calls as a form of communication, see Donner (2007).

15.   Literally, "There are no blessings," but in this context it means there is no respite from the pressures of life.

16.   This translates to "God will provide."

17.   Sometimes the third language is French rather than English.

18.   It is not surprising that the shift toward formalizing credit in Bourj Hammoud occurred in the 1970s. Julia Elyachar (2005, 77) describes how modernization theory in the 1960s lays out "traditional" versus "modern" markets, with the informal economy regarded as "a resting place on the way to integration into the modern economy of the city." Clifford Geertz (1962, 261), for example, argued that rotating credit in particular represents a middle ground between "increased segregation of economic activities from non-economic ones, a freeing of them from traditional constraints." As Elyachar points out, however, the concept of informal economy itself as the object of international development and intervention was "invented," so to speak, through the production of both ethnographic knowledge and large-scale surveys conducted by international organizations.

19.   See Thompson (2000), Joseph (1996, 1997).

20.   In *Tulipmania* (2007), Anne Goldgar's historical study of the well-known seventeenth-century Dutch tulip crash, the author notes that despite popular ideas about the crash, the economy was not significantly affected. Rather, she notes, the true crisis was about the nature of society itself, and the place of personal honor, not just the exchange of money, in society and social standing.

CHAPTER 5: THE EYES OF ODARS

1. For more on the history and background of electricity shortages and inequality in provision in Lebanon, see Verdeil (2009).

2. See http://www.theguardian.com/world/2013/apr/11/turkish-power-ship-lights-on-lebanon.

3. It is a common pastime in Lebanon to speculate over the realignment of political actors in the region, and Turkey's contribution of funds to rebuild schools and hospitals after the July 2006 war had some of my interlocutors openly wondering by 2009 if Turkey was attempting to play a mediating role between the U.S./Western European/Saudi Arabian nexus of powers and those represented by Iran and Syria.

4. For more on the memory of Ottoman rule in Lebanon, see Volk (2010).

5. A number of Kurds also joined the demonstration that day and articulated their protest against Turkish state violence and discrimination against Kurds.

6. The CDR was established in 1977 to replace the Ministry of Planning and rebuild the areas of Lebanon destroyed in the early years of the civil war. In fact, the war went on for much longer, stalling any significant plans for rebuilding until after it ended in 1990.

7. For more on this era, see Favier (2001).

8. The Directorate General of Urbanism (DGU) is a planning agency that can provide exceptions and enable building permits and approve master plans, overriding municipalities (Krijnen and Fawaz 2010). The DGU has been instrumental in providing exceptions to high-rise, luxury developments in the context of a highly speculative real estate market.

9. This is in addition to the well-known existing critiques of development as a form of knowledge-power that sorts the world into zones that are properly "modern" and those that are "underdeveloped" and in need of Western assistance to come into "modernity" (Escobar 1995).

10. Still, infrastructures are not necessarily invisible until a moment of breakdown. See Larkin (2013).

11. I owe this insight to an anonymous reviewer.

12. See, for example, Sylvia Bergh's (2012, 422) work on neoliberal governance reforms in Morocco whose "performance indicators (numbering 49) were determined without consulting those responsible for implementing the programmes at the local level, but were negotiated and agreed between the Moroccan government and the various international partners, mainly the World Bank and the European Union." See also Douay and Bakhos (2009) for more on the implications of North/South Mediterranean city-to-city partnerships in terms of governance and the realignment of private/public actors.

13. This process brings to mind what Nancy Munn (1986, 3) describes as "transformative action through which a community seeks to create the value it regards as essential to its communal viability." In this case, involving Euro-American experts in a project lends legitimacy and viability to the Bourj Hammoud municipality, particularly in their aims to renegotiate CDR plans.

14. James Ferguson's (1994, 21) work on the uses of unintended consequences of development is helpful here. He writes that "outcomes that at first appear as mere 'side effects' of an unsuccessful attempt to engineer an economic transformation become legible in another perspective as unintended yet instrumental elements in a resultant constellation that has the effect of expanding the exercise of a particular sort of state power while simultaneously exerting a powerful depoliticizing effect." In Ferguson's example, however, the unintended consequence is deeper involvement of bureaucratic transnational and state institutions in everyday lives of people in Lesotho toward greater incorporation into the capitalist market while masking its "political" impact. The situation in Lebanon is different,

as the municipality actors' participation in transnational development project studies did not necessarily lead to the implementation of new bureaucratic or administrative infrastructures.

15.   The appropriation and eviction of the entire central Beirut district by then prime minister Rafic Hariri's government allowed for his private development company, Solidere, to redesign the center to suit his vision for a downtown that catered to tourists, luxury consumption, and office buildings for financial or other services. For more discussion of the debates around the rebuilding of downtown and its significance to postwar Lebanon, see S. Makdisi (1997).

16.   For more on Naba'a, see chapter 1. For more on Sanjak, see chapter 2.

17.   The description of the bridge as a "scar" resonates with the idea of "urban 'wounding'" described by Jane Schneider and Ida Susser (2003, 1). Though they were ambivalent about the organic metaphors of homeostasis and the "healing" of the city as a singular and contained body, they note: "The image is crucial and compelling. When we take past histories and external pressures into account, it has the power to evoke collective action, imaginative construction in the face of destruction, creative initiatives in the face of decay." My interlocutor's evocation of the language of scarring on a body to describe a concrete bridge cutting through a city serves less to suggest a future "healing" in the collective body than to raise awareness and direct collective action against such future projects.

18.   See Crang and Thrift (2000), who argue for the connection between space and the making of categories of self and other. See Limbert (2010) for a discussion of the ways in which highway infrastructure can reconfigure previous social boundaries in space.

19.   French Mandate officials actively cultivated these discourses about Armenian industriousness as they sought to create a middle-class Armenian presence in Aleppo and Beirut (see Watenpaugh 2004).

CONCLUSION

1.   See also M. Fawaz (2014) for more on neoliberal urban planning in the aftermath of the 2006 war.

2.   See, for example, Elyachar (2014); Simone (2004).

3.   Christa Salamandra (2013) offers a more nuanced reading of sectarian discourses in Syria before the conflict, positing that sectarian affiliations, class, and geography were interrelated forms of distinction. Lisa Wedeen (2013, 842) offers an excellent analysis of the role of "economic liberalization with fears of sectarian disorder" on muting certain populations' opposition to the Asad regime in the early part of the Syrian uprising.

4.   For more on this context, see chapter 1.

5.   http://data.unhcr.org/syrianrefugees/regional.php.

6.   I owe this insight to an anonymous reviewer.

7.   For more on the "garbage crisis," see S. Atallah (2015).

8.   For more on these graphics, see Abu Rish (2015b).

REFERENCES

Abu Rish, Ziad. 2015a. "Lebanon: What Do You Mean There Is No State?" *Jadaliyya*. http://www.jadaliyya.com/pages/index/22506/lebanon_what-do-you-mean-there-is-no-state.

———. 2015b. "Then and Now: Lebanese State Institutions during the Early Years of Independence." Interview by the Lebanese Center for Policy Studies, *Setting the Agenda*.

Achkarian, Vicken. 2007. "Le développement de la Ville de Bourj Hammoud à travers le réaménagement du Camp Sandjak." MA thesis, Université de Balamand.

Agee, James, and Walker Evans. 1941. *Let Us Now Praise Famous Men: Three Tenant Families*. Boston: Houghton Mifflin.

Ajami, Fouad. 1987. *The Vanished Imam: Musa al Sadr and the Shia of Lebanon*. Ithaca: Cornell University Press.

Akçam, Taner. 2007. *A Shameful Act: The Armenian Genocide and the Question of Turkish Responsibility*. New York: Henry Holt.

———. 2012. *The Young Turks Crime against Humanity*. Princeton: Princeton University Press.

Albouy, Delphine. 2001. "Jeuz d'acteurs autour de la gestion des ordure's ménagères dans le grand Beyrouth." MA thesis, Institut d'Urbanism de Lyon.

Amin, Ash, and Nigel Thrift. 2002. *Cities: Reimagining the Urban*. Cambridge, MA: Blackwell.

Anderson, Benedict. 1983. *Imagined Communities: Reflections on the Origin and Spread of Nationalism*. New ed. London: Verso.

Anghie, Antony. 2002. "Colonialism and the Birth of International Institutions: Sovereignty, Economy and the Mandate System of the League of Nations." *New York University Journal of International Law and Politics* 34 (3): 513–633.

Appadurai, Arjun. 1996. *Modernity At Large: Cultural Dimensions of Globalization (Public Worlds)*. Minneapolis: University of Minnesota Press.

Aretxaga, Begoña. 1997. *Shattering Silence: Women, Nationalism, and Political Subjectivity in Northern Ireland*. Princeton: Princeton University Press.

Arpee, Leon. 1936. "A Century of Armenian Protestantism." *Church History* 5 (2): 150–67.

Asmar, Fadi Moussa. 2008. "Revitilizing Waterfronts or Urban Fragmentations: The Northern Shoreline of Beirut and the Isolation of Bourj Hammoud's Waterfront." MA thesis, American University of Beirut.

Atallah, Joumana Ghandour. 1997. "The Northern Sector: Projects and Plans at Sea." In *Projecting Beirut: Episodes in the Construction and Reconstruction of a Modern City*. Edited by Peter Rowe and Hashim Sarkis, 202–16. New York: Prestel.

Atallah, Sami. 2015. "Garbage Crisis: Setting the Record Straight." Lebanese Center for Policy Studies. http://www.lcps-lebanon.org/featuredArticle.php?id=48.

Baibourtian, Vahan. 2013. *The Kurds, the Armenian Question and the History of Armenian-Kurdish Relations.* Translated by Mariam Mesropyan. Ottawa: Vahan Baibourtian.

Bakalian, Anny. 1992. *Armenian-Americans: From Being to Feeling Armenian.* New Brunswick, NJ: Transaction.

Banurama lil-Khidmat al-'Ammah. 2008. *Baladat wa-baladiyat Lubnan: Muhafazata Beirut–Jebel Lubnan* (Towns and municipalities in Lebanon: The governates of Beirut–Mount Lebanon). Beirut: All Prints Distributors and Publishers.

Bayat, Asef. 2002. "Activism and Social Development in the Middle East." *International Journal of Middle East Studies* 31 (1): 1–28.

Benjamin, Walter. 2007. *Illuminations.* New York: Schocken Books. First published 1969.

Bergh, Sylvia I. 2012. "Introduction: Researching the Effects of Neoliberal Reforms on Local Governance in the Southern Mediterranean." *Mediterranean Politics* 17 (3): 303–21.

Bergson, Henri. 1929. *Matter and Memory.* Translated by Nancy Margaret Paul and W. Scott Palmer. London: G. Allen; New York: Macmillan.

———. 1984. *Creative Evolution.* Translated by Arthur Mitchell. Lanham, MD: University Press of America. First published 1911.

Bou Akar, Hiba. 2012. "Contesting Beirut's Frontiers." *City & Society* 24 (2): 150–72.

Bourdieu, Pierre. 1977. *Outline of a Theory of Practice.* Cambridge Studies in Social and Cultural Anthropology. Cambridge: Cambridge University Press.

———. 1984. *Distinction: A Social Critique of the Judgement of Taste.* Cambridge, MA: Harvard University Press.

Bowker, Geoffrey C., and Susan Leigh Star. 1999. *Sorting Things Out: Classification and Its Consequences.* Cambridge, MA: MIT Press.

Brown, Wendy. 2015. *Undoing the Demos: Neoliberalism's Steal Revolution.* New York: Zone Books.

Caldeira, Teresa P. R. 2001. *City of Walls: Crime, Segregation, and Citizenship in São Paulo.* Berkeley: University of California Press.

Cammett, Melanie. 2014. *Compassionate Communalism: Welfare and Sectarianism in Lebanon*. Ithaca: Cornell University Press.

Chalcraft, John. 2009. *The Invisible Cage: Syrian Migrant Workers in Lebanon*. Stanford: Stanford University Press.

Chatterjee, Partha. 2006. *The Politics of the Governed: Reflections on Popular Politics in Most of the World*. Leonard Hastings Schoff Lectures. New York: Columbia University Press.

Collier, Jane. 1997. *From Duty to Desire: Remaking Families in a Spanish Village*. Princeton: Princeton University Press.

Cormack, Bradin. 2008. *A Power to Do Justice: Jurisdiction, English Literature, and the Rise of Common Law*. Chicago: University of Chicago Press.

Crang, Mike, and Nigel Thrift. 2000. "Introduction." In *Thinking Space*. Edited by Mike Crang and Nigel Thrift, 1–30. New York: Routledge.

Dakessian, Antranik, ed. 2013. *Hadjno Herosamardi 90 ameagi kidajhoghovi niuter yev vaverakrer oo lusangarner* (Proceedings of the conference for the 90th anniversary of the Battle of Hadjin). Beirut: Patriotic Union of Hadjin in Lebanon.

Davie, Michael F. 1991. "La gestion des services urbaines en temps de guerre, circuits parallèles à Beyrouth." In *Reconstruire Beyrouth Paris sur possible table ronde tenue à Lyon 27 au 29 Novembre 1990*. Edited by Nabil Beyhum, 157–93. Beirut: Maison de l'Orient.

Davis, Rochelle. 2010. *Palestinian Village Histories: Geographies of the Displaced*. Stanford: Stanford University Press.

Dean, Mitchell, and Paul Henman. 2004. "Governing Society Today: Editors' Introduction." *Alternatives: Global, Local, Political* 29 (5): 483–94.

Deboulet, Agnes, and Mona Fawaz. 2011. "Contesting the Legitimacy of Urban Restructuring and Highways in Beirut's Irregular Settlements." In *Cities and Sovereignty: Identity Politics in Urban Spaces*. Edited by Diane E. Davis and Nora Libertun de Duren, 117–51. Bloomington: Indiana University Press.

Deeb, Lara. 2006. *An Enchanted Modern: Gender and Public Piety in Shi'i Lebanon*. Princeton Studies in Muslim Politics. Princeton: Princeton University Press.

———. 2009. "Emulating and/or Embodying the Ideal: The Gendering of Temporal Frameworks and Islamic Role Models in Shi'i Lebanon." *American Ethnologist* 36 (2): 242–57.

Deeb, Lara, and Mona Harb. 2013. *Leisurely Islam: Negotiating Geography and Morality in Shi'ite South Beirut*. Princeton: Princeton University Press.

Der Matossian, Bedross. 2014. *Shattered Dreams of Revolution: From Liberty to Violence in the Late Ottoman Empire*. Stanford: Stanford University Press.

De Soto, Hernando. 1989. *The Other Path: The Economic Answer to Terrorism*. New York: Basic Books.

Diab, Hassan. 1999. *Beirut: Reviving Lebanon's Past*. Westport, CT: Praeger.

Donham, Donald. 2011. *Violence in a Time of Liberation: Murder and Ethnicity at a South African Gold Mine, 1994*. Durham: Duke University Press.

Donner, Jonathan. 2007. "The Rules of Beeping: Exchanging Messages via Intentional 'Missed Calls' on Mobile Phones." *Computer-Mediated Communication* 13 (1): 1–22.

Douay, Nicolas, and Walid Bakhos. 2009. "Métropolisation méditerranéenne: des enjeux aux défis de la coopération." In *La Méditerranée à l'heure de la métropolisation*. Edited by Nicolas Douay, 79–96. Paris: Observatoire des territoires et de la métropolisation dans l'espace méditerranéen.

Elyachar, Julia. 2002. "Empowerment Money: The World Bank, Non-Governmental Organizations, and the Value of Culture in Egypt." *Public Culture* 14 (3): 493–513.

———. 2003. "Mappings of Power: The State, NGOs, and International Organizations in the Informal Economy of Cairo." *Comparative Studies in Society and History* 45 (3): 571–605.

———. 2005. *Markets of Dispossession: NGOs, Economic Development, and the State in Cairo*. Politics, History, and Culture. Durham: Duke University Press.

———. 2010. "Phatic Labor, Infrastructure, and the Question of Empowerment in Cairo." *American Ethnologist* 37 (3): 452–64.

———. 2011. "The Political Economy of Movement and Gesture in Cairo." *Journal of the Royal Anthropological Institute* 17 (1): 82–99.

———. 2012. "Before (and After) Neoliberalism: Tacit Knowledge, Secrets of the Trade and the Public Sector in Egypt." *Cultural Anthropology* 71 (1): 76–96.

———. 2014. "Upending Infrastructure: Tamarod, Resistance, and Agency after the January 25th Revolution in Egypt." *History and Anthropology* 25 (4): 452–71.

Escobar, Arturo. 1995. *Encountering Development: The Making and Unmaking of the Third World*. Princeton: Princeton University Press.

Favier, Agnès. 2001. *Municipalités et pouvoirs locaux au Liban*. Beirut: Centre d'études et de recherches sur le Moyen-Orient contemporain.

Fawaz, Leila Tarazi. 1995. *An Occasion for War: Civil Conflict in Lebanon and Damascus in 1860*. Berkeley: University of California Press.

Fawaz, Mona. 2009a. "Neoliberal Urbanity and the Right to the City: A View from Beirut's Periphery." *Development and Change* 40 (5): 827–52.

———. 2009b. "The State and the Production of Illegal Housing: Public Practices in Hayy el Sellom." In *Comparing Cities: The Middle East and South Asia*. Edited by Ali Kamran and Martina Rieker, 197–220. Oxford: Oxford University Press.

———. 2013. "Towards the Right to the City in Informal Settlements." In *Routledge Studies in Human Geography: Locating Right to the City in the Global South*. Edited by Tony Roshan, Shenjing He, and Guo Chen, 23–40. Florence, KY: Taylor and Francis.

———. 2014. "The Politics of Property in Planning: Hezbollah's Reconstruction of Haret Hreik (Beirut, Lebanon) as Case Study." *International Journal of Urban and Regional Research* 38 (3): 922–34.

Fawaz, Mona, Mona Harb, and Ahmad Gharbieh. 2012. "Living Beirut's Security Zones: An Investigation of the Modalities and Practice of Urban Security." *City & Society* 24 (2): 173–95.

Fawaz, Mona, and Isabelle Peillen. 2003. "The Case of Beirut, Lebanon." In *Understanding Slums: Case Studies for the Global Report on Human Settlements, UN-Habitat and University College London Reports*. http://www.ucl.ac.uk/dpu-projects/Global_Report/home.htm.

Ferguson, James. 1994. *The Anti-politics Machine: "Development," Depoliticization, and Bureaucratic Power in Lesotho*. Minneapolis: University of Minnesota Press.

Fisk, Robert. 2002. *Pity the Nation: Lebanon at War*. New York: Atheneum. First published 1990.

Ford, Richard. 1999. "Law's Territory (a History of Jurisdiction)." *Michigan Law Review* 97 (4): 843–930.

Foucault, Michel. 2008. *The Birth of Biopolitics Lectures at the Collège de France, 1978–79*. Edited by Michel Senellart, Francoise Ewald, and Alessandro Fontana. New York: Palgrave Macmillan.

Fregonese, Sara. 2012. "Beyond the 'Weak State': Hybrid Sovereignties in Beirut." *Environment and Planning D: Society and Space* 30 (4): 655–74.

Gaonkar, Dilip Parameshwar, and Elizabeth A. Povinelli. 2003. "Technologies of Public Forms: Circulation, Transfiguration, Recognition." *Public Culture* 15 (3): 385–97.

Geertz, Clifford. 1962. "The Rotating Credit Association: A 'Middle Rung' in Development." *Economic Development and Cultural Change* 10:240–63.

———. 1968. *Peddlers and Princes: Social Development and Economic Change in Two Indonesian Towns*. Comparative Studies of New Nations. Chicago: University of Chicago Press.

Geukjian, Ohannes. 2009. "From Positive Neutrality to Partisanship: How and Why the Armenian Political Parties Took Sides in Lebanese Politics in the Post-Taif Period (1989–Present)." *Middle Eastern Studies* 45 (5): 739–67.

Gibson-Graham, J. K. 2005. "Surplus Possibilities: Postdevelopment and Community Economies." *Singapore Journal of Tropical Geography* 26 (1) (March): 4–26.

Gilsenan, Michael. 1996. *Lords of the Lebanese Marches: Violence and Narrative in an Arab Society*. Berkeley: University of California Press.

Goldgar, Anne. 2007. *Tulipmania : Money, Honor, and Knowledge in the Dutch Golden Age*. Chicago: University of Chicago Press.

Goldstein, Daniel M. 2004. *The Spectacular City: Violence and Performance in Urban Bolivia*. Durham: Duke University Press.

Graham, Stephen. 2001. *Splintering Urbanism: Networked Infrastructures, Technological Mobilities and the Urban Condition*. New York: Routledge.

Graham, Stephen, and Colin McFarlane, eds. 2015. *Infrastructural Lives: Urban Infrastructure in Context*. New York: Routledge.

Granovetter, Mark. 1985. "Economic Action and Social Structure: The Problem of Embeddedness." *American Journal of Sociology* 91 (3): 481–510.

Grimshaw, Anna. 2009. *Observational Cinema: Anthropology, Film, and the Exploration of Social Life*. Bloomington: Indiana University Press.

Grosz, Elizabeth. 2004. *The Nick of Time: Politics, Evolution, and the Untimely*. Durham: Duke University Press.

Gupta, Akhil. 1997. *Culture, Power, Place : Explorations in Critical Anthropology*. Durham: Duke University Press.

———. 1998. *Postcolonial Developments: Agriculture in the Making of Modern India*. Durham: Duke University Press.

Halawi, Majed. 1992. *A Lebanon Defied: Musa al Sadr and the Shi'a Community*. Boulder: Westview Press.

Hamalian, Arpi. 1974. "The Shirkets: Visiting Pattern of Armenians in Lebanon." *Anthropological Quarterly* 47 (1): 71–92.

Hamieh, Christine Sylva, and Roger Mac Ginty. 2010. "A Very Political Reconstruction: Governance and Reconstruction in Lebanon after the 2006 War." *Disasters* 34:S103–S123.

Hamzeh, Nizar A. 2001. "Clientalism, Lebanon: Roots and Trends." *Middle Eastern Studies* 37 (3): 167–78.

Hanf, Theodor. 1994. *Co-Existence in Wartime Lebanon: Decline of a State and Rise of a Nation*. London: I. B. Tauris.

Hanssen, Jens. 2005. *Fin de Siècle Beirut: The Making of an Ottoman Provincial Capital* (Oxford Historical Monographs). New York: Oxford University Press.

Harb, Mona. 2001. "'Urban Governance in Post-War Beirut: Resources, Negotiations, and Contestations in the Elyssar Project.'" In *Capital Cities: Ethnographies of Urban Governance in the Middle East*. Edited by Seteney Khalid Shami, 111–33. Toronto: Toronto University Press.

———. 2003. "La Dahiye de Beyrouth." *Geneses* 2 (51): 70–91.

———. 2007. "Deconstructing Hizballah and Its Suburb." *MERIP*, no. 242: 12–17.

———. 2008. "Faith-Based Organizations as Effective Development Partners? Hezbollah and Post-War Reconstruction in Lebanon." In *Development, Civil Society and Faith-Based Organizations: Bridging the Sacred and the Secular*. Edited by Gerard Clark and Michael Jennings, 214–39. New York: Palgrave Macmillan.

———. 2010. "On Religiosity and Spatiality: Lessons from Hezbollah in Beirut." In *The Fundamentalist City*. Edited by Nezar AlSayyad and Mejgan Massoumi, 125–54. London: Routledge.

Harik, Judith P. 1993. "Change and Continuity among the Lebanese Druze Community: The Civil Administration of the Mountains, 1983–90." *Middle Eastern Studies* 29 (3): 377–98.

Hart, Keith. 1973. "Informal Income Opportunities and Urban Employment in Ghana." *Journal of Modern African Studies* 11 (1): 61–89.

Harvey, David. 1985. *Consciousness and the Urban Experience*. Baltimore: Johns Hopkins University Press.

Hermez, Sami. 2012. "'The War Is Going to Ignite': On the Anticipation of Violence in Lebanon." *Political and Legal Anthropology Review* 35 (2): 327–44.

Hirschman, Albert. 1977. *The Passions and the Interests: Political Arguments for Capitalism before Its Triumph*. Princeton: Princeton University Press.

Holston, James. 1989. *The Modernist City: An Anthropological Critique of Brasilia*. Chicago: University of Chicago Press.

Hourani, Albert. 1981. *The Emergence of the Modern Middle East*. Berkeley: University of California Press.

Hovannisian, Richard, ed. 2003. *Looking Backward, Moving Forward: Confronting the Armenian Genocide*. New Brunswick, NJ: Transaction.

Hudson, Michael C. 1977. "The Precarious Republic Revisited: Reflections on the Collapse of Pluralist Politics in Lebanon" (Contemporary Arab Studies Seminar Paper). Institute of Arab Development, Center for Contemporary Arab Studies, Georgetown University.

Ingold, Tim, and Jo Lee Vergunst. 2008. *Ways of Walking: Ethnography and Practice on Foot*. Aldershot, UK: Ashgate.

Jazzini, Ayman. "Dawlat Bourj Hammoud" (The Bourj Hammoud state). November 3, 2011. https://now.mmedia.me/lb/ar/.

Jean-Klein, Iris. 2000. "Mothercraft, Statecraft, and Subjectivity in the Palestinian Intifada." *American Ethnologist* 27 (1): 100–127.

Joseph, Suad. 1975. "'The Politicization of Religious Sects in Borj Hammoud, Lebanon." PhD dissertation, Columbia University.

———. 1983. "Working-Class Women's Networks in a Sectarian State: A Political Paradox." *American Ethnologist* 10 (1): 1–22.

———. 1994a. "Brother Sister Relationships: Connectivity, Love, and Power in the Reproduction of Patriarchy in Lebanon." *American Ethnologist* 21 (1): 50–73.

———. 1994b. "Problematizing Gender and Relational Rights: Experiences from Lebanon." *Social Politics* 1 (3): 271–85.

———. 1996. "Gender and Citizenship in Middle Eastern States/Middle East Research and Information Project." *Middle East Research and Information Project* 198.

———. 1997. "The Public Private: The Imagined Boundary in the Imagined Nation State Community: The Lebanese Case." *Feminist Review* (57): 73–92.

———. 1999. *Intimate Selving in Arab Families: Gender, Self, and Identity*. Syracuse: Syracuse University Press.

———. 2008. "Pensée 2: Sectarianism as Imagined Sociological Concept and as Imagined Social Formation." *International Journal of Middle East Studies* 40:553–54.

Kanaan, Claude Boueiz. 2005. *Lebanon 1860–1960: A Century of Myth & Politics*. London: Saqi Books.

Kaplan, Sam. 2004. "Territorializing Armenians: Geo-texts and Political Imaginaries in French-Occupied Cilicia, 1919–1922." *History and Anthropology* 15 (4): 399–423.

Kevorkian, Raymond. 2011. *The Armenian Genocide: A Complete History*. London: I. B. Taurus.

Khalaf, Samir. "Urban Design and the Recovery of Beirut." *In Recovering Beirut: Urban Design and Post-war Reconstruction*. Edited by Samir Khalaf and Philip S. Khoury, 11–62. New York: E.J. Brill.

Khalaf, Samir, and Philip S. Khoury, eds. 1993. *Recovering Beirut: Urban Design and Post-war Reconstruction*. New York: Brill.

Khalaf, Tewfik. 1976. "'The Phalange and the Maronite Community: From Lebanonism to Maronitism.'" In *Essays on the Crisis in Lebanon*. Edited by Roger Owen, 43–58. London: Ithaca Press.

Khalidi, Walid. 1983. *Conflict and Violence in Lebanon: Confrontation in the Middle East*. Harvard Studies in International Affairs. Cambridge, MA: Center for International Affairs, Harvard University.

Khater, Akram F. 2001. *Inventing Home: Emigration, Gender, and the Middle Class in Lebanon, 1870–1920*. Berkeley: University of California Press.

Khayat, Tristan. 2001. "La Route de la Discorde: Construction du territoire municipal et aménagement métropolitain à Borj Hammoud." Theme issue, "Municipalités et Pouvoirs Locaux Au Liban." *Les Cahiers du CERMOC* 24:207–25.

Kingston, Paul W. T. 2013. *Reproducing Sectarianism: Advocacy Networks and the Politics of Civil Society in Postwar Lebanon*. Albany: State University of New York Press.

Kleinman, Arthur, Veena Das, and Margaret M. Lock, eds. 1997. *Social Suffering*. Berkeley: University of California Press.

Kockelman, Paul. 2010. "Enemies, Parasites, and Noise: How to Take Up Residence in a System without Becoming a Term in It." *Journal of Linguistic Anthropology* 20 (2): 406–21.

———. 2013. "The Anthropology of an Equation: Sieves, Spam Filters, Agentive Algorithms, and Ontologies of Transformation." *HAU: Journal of Ethnographic Theory* 3 (3): 33–61.

Kratz, Corinne A. 2002. *The Ones That Are Wanted: Communication and the Politics of Representation in a Photographic Exhibition*. Berkeley: University of California Press.

Krijnen, Marieke. 2013. "Filling Every Gap: Real Estate Development in Beirut." *Jadaliyya*, Nov. 15. http://www.jadaliyya.com/pages/index/14880/filling-every-gap_real-estate-development-in-beiru.

Krijnen, Marieke, and Christiaan De Beukelaer. 2015. "Capital, State and Conflict: The Various Drivers of Diverse Gentrification Processes in Beirut, Lebanon." In *Global Gentrifications: Uneven Development and Displacement*. Edited by Loretta Lees, Hyun Bang Shin, and Ernesto López-Morales, 285–309. Bristol, UK: Policy Press.

Krijnen, Marieke, and Mona Fawaz. 2010. "Exception as the Rule: High-End Developments in Neoliberal Beirut." *Built Environment* 36 (2): 245–59.

Larkin, Brian. 2008. *Signal and Noise: Media, Infrastructure, and Urban Culture in Nigeria*. Durham: Duke University Press.

———. 2013. "The Politics and Poetics of Infrastructure." *Annual Review of Anthropology* 42:327–43.

Latour, Bruno. 1993. *We Have Never Been Modern*. Cambridge, MA: Harvard University Press.

———. 2007. *Reassembling the Social: An Introduction to Actor-Network-Theory*. Clarendon Lectures in Management Studies. Oxford: Oxford University Press.

Latour, Bruno, and Vincent Antonin Lepinay. 2009. *The Science of Passionate Interests: An Introduction to Gabriel Tarde's Economic Anthropology*. Chicago: Prickly Paradigm Press.

Le Corbusier. 1987. *The City of To-morrow and Its Planning*. New York: Dover.

Lefebvre, Henri. 1991. *The Production of Space*. Cambridge, MA: Blackwell.

Lefort, Bruno. 2011. "Mobilisations et pratiques électorales estudiantines. Le cas des élections à l'Université Saint-Joseph." In *Metamorphose des figures du leadership au Liban*. Edited by Myriam Catusse, Karam Karam, and Olfa Lamloum, 105–34. Beirut: Presses de l'Ifpo.

Le Thomas, Catherine. 2010. "Socialization Agencies and Party Dynamics: Functions and Uses of Hizballah Schools in Lebanon." In *Returning to Political Parties? Partisan Logic and Political Transformations in the Arab World*. Edited by Myriam Catusse and Karam Karam, 217–49. Beirut: Presses de l'Ifpo, The Lebanese Center for Policy Studies.

Libaridian, Gerard. J. 1991. *Armenia at the Crossroads: Democracy and Nationhood in the Post-Soviet Era: Essays, Interviews, and Speeches by the Leaders of the National Democratic Movement in Armenia*. Watertown, MA: Blue Crane Books.

"Lights, Handguns, Action." 2015. *Economist*, Feb. 28. Web. Dec. 13. http://www.economist.com/news/middle-east-and-africa/21645233-lebanons-fractured-society-even-keeping-lights-battle-lights.

Limbert, Mandana. 2010. *In the Time of Oil: Piety, Memory and Social Life in an Omani Town*. Stanford: Stanford University Press.

Longrigg, Stephen Hemsley. 1958. *Syria and Lebanon Under French Mandate*. Oxford: Oxford University Press.

Low, Setha M. 2001. "The Edge and the Center: Gated Communities and the Discourse of Urban Fear." *American Anthropologist* 103 (1): 45–58.

Makdisi, Jean Said. 1990. *Beirut Fragment: A War Memoir*. New York: Persea Books.

Makdisi, Saree. 1997. "Laying Claim to Beirut: Urban Narrative and Spatial Identity in the Age of Solidere." *Critical Inquiry* 23 (3): 661–705.

Makdisi, Ussama. 1996. "Reconstructing the Nation-State: The Modernity of Sectarianism in Lebanon." *MERIP*, no. 200: 23–30. http://www.merip.org/mer/mer200/modernity-sectarianism-lebanon.

———. 2000. *The Culture of Sectarianism: Community, History, and Violence in Nineteenth-Century Ottoman Lebanon*. Berkeley: University of California Press.

Maktabi, Rania. 1999. "The Lebanese Census of 1932 Revisited: Who Are the Lebanese?" *British Journal of Middle Eastern Studies* 26:219–41.

Malinowski, Bronislaw. 1922. *Argonauts of the Western Pacific: an Account of Native Enterprise and Adventure in the Archipelagoes of Melanesian New Guinea*. London: Routledge.

Mandel, Maud. 2003. *In the Aftermath of Genocide: Armenians and Jews in Twentieth Century France*. Durham: Duke University Press.

Massey, Doreen. 1994. *Space, Place and Gender*. Minneapolis: University of Minnesota Press.

Matthiesen, Toby. 2013. *Sectarian Gulf: Bahrain, Saudi Arabia, and the Arab Spring That Wasn't*. Stanford: Stanford University Press.

———. 2014. *The Other Saudis: Shiism, Dissent and Sectarianism*. Cambridge: Cambridge University Press.

Maurer, Bill. 1997. *Recharting the Caribbean: Land, Law, and Citizenship in the British Virgin Islands*. Ann Arbor: University of Michigan Press.

———. 2013. "Transacting Ontologies: Kockelman's Sieves and a Bayesian Anthropology." *HAU: Journal of Ethnographic Theory* 3 (3): 63–75.

Mauss, Marcel. 2000. *The Gift: The Form and Reason for Exchange in Archaic Societies*. New York: Norton. First published 1954.

Mead, George Herbert. 2002. *The Philosophy of the Present*. New York: Prometheus Books. First published 1932.

Melkonian, Markar. 2005. *My Brother's Road: An American's Fateful Journey to Armenia*. London: I. B. Tauris.

Messerlian, Zaven. 2014. *Armenian Participation in the Lebanese Legislative Elections 1934–2009*. Beirut: Haigazian University Press.

Meymarian, Euphronia Halebian, and Gomidas Institute. 2004. *Housher: My Life in the Aftermath of the Armenian Genocide*. London: Taderon Press.

Migliorino, Nicola. 2008. *(Re)constructing Armenia in Lebanon and Syria*. New York: Berghahn Books.

Mikdashi, Maya. 2010. "A Legal Guide to Being a Lebanese Woman (Part 1)." *Jadaliyya*. Last modified Dec. 3. http://www.jadaliyya.com/pages/index/376/a-legal-guide-to-being-a-lebanese-woman-(part-1).

———. 2014. "Sex and Sectarianism: The Legal Architecture of Lebanese Citizenship." *Comparative Studies of South Asia, Africa and the Middle East* 34 (2): 279–93.

Miller, Donald E., and Lorna Touryan Miller. 1993. *Survivors: An Oral History of the Armenian Genocide*. Berkeley: University of California Press.

Milligan, Maren. 2012. Tripoli's Troubles to Come. *MERIP*, no. 274. http://www.merip.org/mero/mero081312.

———. 2014. "Making Sense of Tripoli," parts 1 and 2. *Jadaliyya*. http://www.jadaliyya.com/pages/index/20179/making-sense-of-tripoli-i_the-security-trap-or-con.

Mohsen, Ahmad. 2012. "Lebanon's Electricity Mafia." *Al-Akhbar*. http://english.al-akhbar.com/node/9087.

Mumford, Lewis. 1968. *The City in History: Its Origins, Its Transformations, and Its Prospects*. New York: Harcourt, Brace & World.

Mundy, Martha, and Richard Saumarez Smith. 2007. *Governing Property, Making the Modern State: Law, Administration and Production in Ottoman Syria*. Library of Ottoman Studies. London: I. B. Tauris.

Munn, Nancy. 1986. *The Fame of Gawa: A Symbolic Study of Value Transformation in a Massim (Papua New Guinea) Society*. Cambridge: Cambridge University Press.

———. 1992. "The Cultural Anthropology of Time: A Critical Essay." *Annual Review of Anthropology* 21:93–123.

Murdock, Donna. 2008. *When Women Have Wings: Feminism and Development in Medellín, Colombia*. Ann Arbor: University of Michigan Press.

Nalbantian, Tsolin. 2011. "Fashioning Armenians in Lebanon, 1946–1958." PhD dissertation, Columbia University.

———. 2013. "Going Beyond Overlooked Populations in Lebanese Historiography: The Armenian Case." *History Compass* 11:821–32.

Norton, Augustus R. 1987. *Amal and the Shiʻa: Struggle for the Soul of Lebanon*. Austin: University of Texas Press.

Panossian, Razmik. 2006. *The Armenians: From Kings and Priests to Merchants and Commissars*. New York: Columbia University Press.

Papovka, Irina. 2014. "The Three Religions of Armenians in Lebanon." In *Armenian Christianity Today: Identity Politics and Popular Practice*. Edited by Alexander Agadjanian, 171–95. Surrey, UK: Ashgate.

Park, Robert E., and Ernest Burgess. 1925. *The City*. Chicago: University of Chicago Press.

Peebles, Gustav. 2008. "Inverting the Panopticon: Money and the Nationalization of the Future." *Public Culture* 20 (2): 233–65.

Peirce, Charles S. 1960. *Collected Papers*. Vol 1. Cambridge, MA: Belknap Press of Harvard University Press.

Peteet, Julie. 1991. *Gender in Crisis: Women and the Palestinian Resistance Movement*. New York: Columbia University Press.

Picard, Elizabeth. 2000. "The Political Economy of Civil War in Lebanon." In *War, Institutions, and Social Change in the Middle East*. Edited by Steven Heydemann, 292–322. Berkeley: University of California Press.

———. 2002. *Lebanon: A Shattered Country: Myths and Realities of the Wars in Lebanon*. Teaneck, NJ: Holmes & Meier. First published 1996.

Polanyi, Karl. 1957. *The Great Transformation*. Boston: Beacon Press.

Povinelli, Elizabeth. 2011. "Routes/Worlds." *E-Flux Journal* 27. http://www.e-flux.com/journal/routesworlds.

———. 2015. "Review: Windjammeru, the Stealing C * nts." *Supercommunity: E-Flux Journal, 56th Venic*. http://supercommunity.e-flux.com/texts/windjarrameru-the-stealing-c-nts/.

Rabinow, Paul. 1989. *French Modern: Norms and Forms of the Social Environment*. Cambridge, MA: MIT Press.

Riles, Annelise. 2001. *The Network Inside Out*. Ann Arbor: University of Michigan Press.

Rivoal, Isabelle. 2014. "Intimate Politics: The Art of the Political Relationship in Lebanon." *Anthropology of the Middle East* 9 (1): 1–17.

Rosaldo, Michelle, and Louise Lamphere, eds. 1974. *Woman, Culture, and Society*. Stanford: Stanford University Press.

Rouch, Jean. 2003. *Ciné-ethnography*. Minneapolis: University of Minnesota Press.

Roy, Ananya. 2003. *City Requiem Calcutta: Gender and the Politics of Poverty*. Minneapolis: University of Minnesota Press.

———. 2004. "The Gentlemen's City: Urban Informality in the Calcutta of New Communism." In *Urban Informality: Transnational Perspectives from the Middle East, Latin America and South Asia*. Edited by Ananya Roy and Nezar Al Sayed, 147–70. Oxford: Lexington Books.

Salamandra, Christa. 2004. *A New Old Damascus: Authenticity and Distinction in Urban Syria*. Bloomington: Indiana University Press.

———. 2013. Sectarianism in Syria: Anthropological Reflections. *Middle East Critique* 22 (3): 303–6.

Salibi, Kamal S. 1965. *The Modern History of Lebanon*. Praeger: New York.

———. 1988. *A House of Many Mansions: The History of Lebanon Reconsidered*. London: I. B. Tauris.

Sanjian, Ara. 2001. "The Armenian Minority Experience in the Modern Arab World." *Bulletin of the Royal Institute for Inter-Faith Studies* 2 (1): 149–79.

———. 2007. "Homeland Relations under Khrushchev and Brezhnev: Soviet Embassy Reports from Beirut on the Armenian Community in Lebanon, 1959–1982 (A Preliminary Study)." In *Arméniens et Grecs en diaspora: approaches comparatives*. Edited by Michel Bruneau, Ioannis Hassiotis, Martine Hovanessian, and Claire Mouradian, 272–82. Athens: Actes du colloque européen et international a l'École française d'Athènes [October 4–7, 2001].

Sankari, Jamal. 2005. *Fadlallah: The Making of a Radical Shi'ite Leader*. London: Saqi Books.

Sarkis, Hashim. 1993. "Territorial Claims: Architecture and Post-War Attitudes Toward the Built Environment." In *Recovering Beirut: Urban Design and Post-War Reconstruction*. Vol. 47 of Social, Economic, and Political Studies of the Middle East. Edited by Samir Khalaf and Philip Khoury, 101–127. New York: Brill Academic.

Sasuni, Garo. 1969. *Kurt azgayin sharzhumnere ew hay-kurdakan haraperootiunnere* (Kurdish national movements and Armenian-Kurdish relations). Beirut: Hamazgayin.

Sawalha, Aseel. 2010. *Reconstructing Beirut: Memory and Space in a Postwar Arab City*. Austin: University of Texas Press.

Schahgaldian, Nikola Bagrad. 1979. "The Political Integration of an Immigrant Community into a Composite Society: The Armenians in Lebanon, 1920–1974." PhD dissertation, Columbia University.

Schneider, Jane, and Ida Susser, eds. 2003. *Wounded Cities: Destruction and Reconstruction in a Globalized World*. Oxford: Berg.

Shahantookht. 1997. *Burj Hammud gu kam* (I come to Bourj Hammoud), parts 1 and 2. Beirut: Hamazgayini Vahe Setian Press.

Simone, Abdou Maliq. 2004. *For the City Yet to Come: Changing African Life in Four Cities*. Durham: Duke University Press.

———. 2009. "City Life from Jakarta to Dakar Movements at the Crossroads." Hoboken, NJ: Taylor & Francis.

Singerman, Diane. 1995. *Avenues of Participation: Family, Politics, and Networks in Urban Quarters of Cairo*. Princeton: Princeton University Press.

Slyomovics, Susan. 1998. *The Object of Memory: Arab and Jew Narrate the Palestinian Village*. Philadelphia: University of Pennsylvania Press.

Star, Susan Leigh. 1999. "The Ethnography of Infrastructure." *American Behavioral Scientist* 43 (3): 377–91.

Suny, Ronald. G. 1993. *Looking toward Ararat: Armenia in Modern History*. Bloomington: Indiana University Press.

———. 2015. *"They Can Live in the Desert but Nowhere Else": A History of the Armenian Genocide*. Princeton: Princeton University Press.

Tachjian, Vahé. 2004. *La France en Cilicie et en Haute-Mésopotamie: aux confins de la Turquie, de la Syrie et de l'Irak, 1919–1933*. Paris: Karthala.

Tarhini, Muhammad Husayn. 2011. *Al-'Alāmah al-marji' al-sayyid Muḥammad Ḥusayn Faḍl Allāh: mashrū' nahḍat al-ummah* (The teachings of Marja' al Sayyid Muhammad Husayn Fadlallah: Concerning the revival of the Ummah or Islamic community). Beirut: Dar al Mahajjah al Bayda.

Thompson, Elizabeth. 2000. *Colonial Citizens*. New York: Columbia University Press.

Tölölyan, Khachig. 2000. "Elites and Institutions in the Armenian Transnation." *Diaspora* 9 (1): 107–36.

Traboulsi, Fawwaz. 2007. *A History of Modern Lebanon*. London: Pluto Press.

Ungor, Ugur U. (2011). "'Turkey for the Turks': Demographic Engineering in Eastern Anatolia, 1914–1945." In *A Question of Genocide: Armenians and Turks at the End of the Ottoman Empire*. Edited by Ronald G. Suny, Fatima M. Gocek, and Norman M. Naimark, 287–305. Oxford: Oxford University Press.

Valverde, Mariana. 2008. "The Ethic of Diversity: Local Law and the Negotiation of Urban Norms." *Law Social Inquiry* 33 (4): 895–923.

———. 2009. "Jurisdiction and Scale: Legal Technicalities as Resources for Theory." *Social & Legal Studies* 18 (2): 139.

Verdeil, Eric. 2009. "Electricity et territoire: un regard sur la crise libanaise." In *Revue Tiers Monde*, 421–36. Paris: Presses Universitaires de France.

Verdery, Katherine. 1998. "Property and Power in Translyvania." In *Property Relations: Renewing the Anthropological Tradition*. Edited by C. M. Hann, 160–80. Cambridge: Cambridge University Press.

———. 2003. *The Vanishing Hectare: Property and Value in Postsocialist Transylvania*. Culture and Society after Socialism. Ithaca: Cornell University Press.

Volk, Lucia. 2010. *Memorials and Martyrs in Modern Lebanon*. Public Cultures of the Middle East and North Africa. Bloomington: Indiana University Press.

Watenpaugh, Keith. 2004. "Towards a New Category of Colonial Theory: Colonial Cooperation and the Survivors Bargain—the Case of the Post-Genocide Armenian Community in Syria." In *The British and French Mandates in Comparative Perspective*. Edited by Nadine Méouchy, Peter Sluglett, Gérard Khoury, and Geoffrey Schad. Leiden: Brill.

———. 2015. *Bread from Stones: The Middle East and the Making of Modern Humanitarianism*. Berkeley: University of California Press.

Wedeen, Lisa. 2013. "Ideology and Humor in Dark Times: Notes from Syria." *Critical Inquiry* 39 (4): 841–73.

Wehrey, Frederic. M. 2013. *Sectarian Politics in the Gulf: From the Iraq War to the Arab Uprisings.* New York: Columbia University Press.

Weiss, Max. 2010. *In the Shadow of Sectarianism : Law, Shi'ism, and the Making of Modern Lebanon.* Cambridge, MA: Harvard University Press.

World Bank. 2014. *Migration and Development Brief.* http://siteresources.worldbank.org/INTPROSPECTS/Resources/334934–1288990760745/MigrationandDevelopmentBrief23.pdf.

World Vision International, Lebanon. 2006. *Area Assessment Report, Bourj Hammoud & Sin el Fil.*

Zaatari, Zeina. 2006. "The Culture of Motherhood: An Avenue for Women's Civil Participation in South Lebanon." *Journal of Middle East Women's Studies* 2 (1): 33–64.

INDEX

agency, 4, 53, 96, 112, 143n12, 147n6

agoump. *See* Tashnag Party

Akçam, Taner, 138n30, 142n19

ʿAlawi sect, 41–42

Aleppo, 16, 55–56, 131, 150n19

Arabic language, 17, 45, 65, 91, 101, 103, 106

Arakadz settlement, 28, 52, 54, 65–72

Aretxaga, Begoña, 6

Armenian churches, 15, 16, 21, 23, 57, 64, 78, 84, 89, 92

Armenian community, 1, 9, 14–24, 42–44, 47, 50, 51–53, 70, 73–76, 82, 84–85, 87, 91–94, 132–33; "Armenianness," 53, 65, 70, 72, 79, 91, 93, 112, 145n6; language, 138n34; refugee camps and informal settlements, 28, 43, 51–72, 141n16; school preferences in, 77–78, 84, 90

Armenian genocide, 1, 9, 14–15, 16, 31, 42–43, 46, 48–49, 109, 131, 142n19. *See also* Ottoman Empire

Ashrafiyeh, 19, 118, 144n23

Azkayin Khorhourt, 23, 137n11

banking, 94–96, 99–100

Beirut, 3–4, 7, 19–20, 137n18; gentrification of, 53, 70, 117, 143n4, 144n23, 150n15; historical background, 11–12; resources imbalance, 22, 108, 111

Benjamin, Walter, 140n6

Bergh, Sylvia, 149n12

Bergson, Henri, on duration, 32, 36, 140n3, 141n7

Bourdieu, Pierre, on social capital, 145n11

Bourj Hammoud: development of, 14–21, 52, 138n32; during civil war, 22–24, 48, 84–85, 90; violence in, 33–34. *See also*

Armenian community; credit and lending networks

Cammet, Melanie, 6, 74

channels, defined, 5

Chatterjee, Partha, 136n

citizenship, 13, 78–79, 112, 132

civil war (1975–90), 1, 5, 6, 21–24, 40, 41–43, 61–63; alleged origin of, 38–39; nostalgia for, 63, 84, 143n12; reminders of, 33–36, 63

class, 25, 76, 83, 129, 134–36, 137n14, 144n20

clientelism, 22, 81–84, 119, 146nn14–15; patron-client relationships, 10–11, 13; *zuʿama* system, 146n16

Collier, Jane, 146n14

confessional system, 4, 9, 12–13, 16–17, 138n28

Cormack, Bradin, 137n17

Council for Development and Reconstruction (CDR), 110–11, 114–18, 122–23, 138n26, 149n6

credit and lending networks, 94–107; credit cards, 94–95; *shirket*s, 96–102, 105–6, 148n8

Dahiye, 146n20

decentralization, 29, 110–11, 115, 118, 125, 128

Deeb, Lara, 41, 137n14, 145n6, 146n11

Donham, Donald, 140n2

De Soto, Hernando, 143n7

Directorate General of Urbanism, 149n8

Doueiri, Ziad, 39

Druze, 11, 12